Sources of
Western Society

SINCE 1300

Sources of
Western Society

SINCE 1300

John Beeler
UNIVERSITY OF ALABAMA

Charles Clark
UNIVERSITY OF ALABAMA

BEDFORD/ST. MARTIN'S   BOSTON ◆ NEW YORK

For Bedford/St. Martin's

Publisher for History: Mary Dougherty
Executive Editor for History: Traci Mueller
Director of Development for History: Jane Knetzger
Associate Editor for History: Lynn Sternberger
Assistant Production Manager: Joe Ford
Executive Marketing Manager: Jenna Bookin Barry
Project Management: DeMasi Design and Publishing Service
Text Design: DeMasi Design and Publishing Service
Cover Design: Sara Gates
Cover Art: Juan de Pareja, 1650, by Diego Velázquez (1599–1660). The Metropolitan
    Museum of Art/Bridgeman Art Library.
Composition: Jeff Miller Book Design
Printing and Binding: RR Donnelley & Sons Company

President: Joan E. Feinberg
Editorial Director: Denise B. Wydra
Director of Marketing: Karen R. Soeltz
Director of Editing, Design, and Production: Marcia Cohen
Assistant Director of Editing, Design, and Production: Elise S. Kaiser
Manager, Publishing Services: Emily Berleth

Manufactured in the United States of America.

4 3 2 1 0 9
f e d c b a

For information, write: Bedford/St. Martin's, 75 Arlington Street, Boston, MA 02116 (617-399-4000)

ISBN-10: 0-312-68898-9
ISBN-13: 978-0-312-68898-1

Acknowledgments
Acknowledgments and copyrights are continued on pages xv–xvii, which constitute an extension of the copyright page.

PREFACE

Sources of Western Society is a compilation of primary sources recorded by those who shaped and experienced the development of the Western world — among them rulers and subjects alike, men and women, philosophers, revolutionaries, economists, and laborers, from ancient times to the present. With a parallel chapter structure and documents hand-picked to complement the text, this reader is designed to complement either *A History of Western Society*, ninth edition, or *Western Society: A Brief History*. *Sources of Western Society* aspires to animate the past for students, providing resonant accounts of the people and events that changed the face of Western history, from myths of creation to tallies of the spoils and fatalities of war.

While a good textbook offers a clear framework of major historical figures and movements, *Sources* evokes the experiences of historical times at the moments they were lived and creates a dynamic connection for students, bridging the events of the past with their own understandings of power and its abuses, of the ripple effects of human agency, and of the material conditions of life. For example, John Locke's *Second Treatise of Civil Government* is cited in the textbook for its crucial role in the development of citizens' rights. In *Sources*, Locke himself makes a convincing case for the need for individual empowerment, as well as the study of history: "For he that thinks *absolute Power purifies Mens Bloods*, and corrects the baseness of Humane Nature, need read but the History of this, or any other Age to be convinced of the contrary."

With input from the textbook authors, as well as from current instructors of the Western civilization survey course, we have compiled these documents with one goal foremost in mind: to make history's most classic and compelling voices accessible to students, from the most well-known thinkers of their times to the galvanized or introspective commoner. In Chapter 24, for example, Darwin presents his defense of natural selection and Spencer applies that same "survival of the fittest" theory to human populations with disquieting insight, while home etiquette writer Isabella

Beeton and socialist feminist Clara Zetkin argue for two dramatically different visions of a woman's working life.

We have stepped back from drawing conclusions and instead provide just enough background to enable students' own analyses of the sources at hand. Chapter-opening paragraphs briefly review the major events of the time and place the documents that follow within the framework of the corresponding textbook chapter. A concise headnote for each document provides context about the author and the circumstances surrounding the document's creation, while glossary notes supply information to aid comprehension of unfamiliar terms and references. Each document is followed by Reading and Discussion Questions that spur deep student analysis of the material, while chapter-concluding Comparative Questions encourage students to contemplate the harmony and discord among the sources within and, when called for, between the chapters. The excerpts range widely in length to allow for a range of class assignments.

ACKNOWLEDGMENTS

Instrumental to the creation of this primary source reader were Jay Boggis's contributions to the first volume. For their availability and insight, many thanks to the *History of Western Society* authors John P. McKay, John Buckler, Clare Crowston, and Merry Wiesner-Hanks. Lynn Sternberger at Bedford/St. Martins has been a paragon of editorial ability, efficiency, and tact. Working with her has been an unalloyed pleasure. Kathryn Abbott's editorial guidance and insight was immensely helpful. Emily Berleth of Bedford/St. Martin's and Linda DeMasi of DeMasi Design made production of this reader possible with remarkable finesse.

CONTENTS

29 Dictatorships and the Second World War

30 Cold War Conflicts and Social Transformations 1945–1985

ACKNOWLEDGMENTS

CHAPTER 13

13-3. The Book of the City of Ladies: Advice for a "Wise Princess," Christine de Pizan. Excerpt from *Treasure of the City of Ladies*, by Christine de Pisan, translated with an introduction by Sarah Lawson (Penguin Classics, 1985). This translation copyright © Sarah Lawson, 1985. Reprinted with permission of Penguin Books Ltd.

13-4. Account of an Italian Jew Expelled from Spain, Anonymous. Excerpt from *The Jew in the Medieval World: A Sourcebook, 315–1791* by Jacob Marcus (New York: JPS, 1938), 51–55. Revised edition copyright © 1999 by the Hebrew Union College Press. Reprinted 1990 by the Hebrew Union College Perss, Hebrew Union College Jewish Institute of Religion, by agreement with Jacob Rader Marcus. First published in 1938 by Jacob Marcus. Reprinted by permission of the Hebrew Union College Press.

CHAPTER 15

15-4. Michel de Montaigne, *On the Fallibility of Human Understanding*, from *The Complete Works of Montaigne, Essays, Travel Journal*, Letters by Michel de Montaigne, translated by Donald M. Frame (pp. 817, 818–819). Copyright © 1943 by Donald M. Frame, renewed 1971; © 1948, 1957, 1958 by the Board of Trustees of the Leland Stanford Junior University. Used with the permission of Stanford University Press. www.sup.org. All rights reserved.

CHAPTER 17

17-1. Ludwig Fabritius, The Revolt of Stenka Razin. Excerpt from *Russia Under Western Eyes, 1517–1825*, edited with an introduction by Anthony Glenn Cross (pp. 121–123). Copyright © 1971, Elek Books. Reprinted with permission of Anthony Glenn Cross.

CHAPTER 21

21-5. Francois Dominique Toussaint L'Ouverture, "A Black Revolutionary Leader in Haiti: Toussaint L'Ouverture." Quote from letter in *The Black Jacobins: Toussaint L'Ouverture and the San Domingo Revolution*, 2nd edition, by C. L. R. James. Copyright © Estate of C. L. R. James 1938. Reproduced with permission of Curtis Brown Group Ltd, London on behalf of the Estate of C. L. R. James.

CHAPTER 23

23-2. Karl Marx and Friedrich Engels, *The Communist Manifesto*: "Working Men of All Countries, Unite!" From *The Essential Works of Marxism* by Arthur P. Mendel, 13–17, 19, 23, 40–44. Copyright © 1961 Arthur P. Mendel. Used by permission of Bantam, a division of Random House, Inc.

CHAPTER 27

27-4. Vladimir I. Lenin, "What Is to Be Done?: Russian Autocracy, 1903." Excerpt from "What is to be Done? Burning Question of Our Movement," in *The Lenin Anthology*, by Vladimir Lenin, edited by Robert C. Tucker (pp. 85–89). Copyright © 1975 by W. W. Norton & Company, Inc. Reprinted with permission of W. W. Norton and Company, Inc.

CHAPTER 28

28-1 Friedrich Nietzsche, "The Madman." From *The Portable Nietzsche*, edited by Walther Kaufmann, translated by Walter Kaufmann. Copyright © 1954 by The Viking Press, renewed © 1982 by Viking Penguin, Inc. Used by permission of Viking Penguin, a Division of Penguin Group (USA), Inc.

28-2. Sigmund Freud, *The Interpretation of Dreams*. Excerpt from *The Basic Writings of Sigmund Freud*, translated and edited by A. A. Brill. Copyright © 1938 The Modern Library. Reprinted by permission of The Estate of A. A. Brill.

28-4. Sir Percy Malcolm Stewart, First and Second Reports of the Commissioner for the Special Areas: Parliament Addresses The Great Depression in Britain 1934. Excerpt from First Report of the Commissioner for Special Areas (England and Wales), presented by the Minister of Labour to Parliament by Command of His Majesty, July 1935, Cmd. 4957, His Majesty's Stationery Office, London 1935, pp. 14–15; Second Report of the Commissioner for the Special Areas (England and Wales), presented by the Minister of Labour to Parliament by Command of His Majesty, February 1936, Cmd. 5090, His Majesty's Stationery Office, London, 1936, pp. 4–6, 68–69. Published in *Documents and Readings in the History of Europe Since 1918*, revised and enlarged edition, edited by W. C. Langsam. Copyright © 1951.

CHAPTER 29

29-1. Vladimir Tchernavin, "Second Inquisition" (Chapter XV). Excerpt from *I Speak for the Silent: Stalinist Interrogation Techniques Revealed*. Translated from the Russian by Nicholas M. Oushakoff. Illustrated, Boston/New York. Copyright © 1935 C Hale, Cushman Flint, Incorporated.

29-2. Adolph Hitler, *Mein Kampf: The Art of Propaganda*. Copyright © 1939, 1943 by Houghton Mifflin Company. Reprinted by permission of Houghton Mifflin Harcourt Publishing Company. All rights reserved. Translated by Ralph Mannheim, pp. 42, 179–185. *Mein Kampf*, published by Pimlico. Reprinted by permission of The Random House Group Ltd.

29-4. Winston Churchill, Speech Before the House of Commons, June 18, 1940. From *The Past Speaks, Vol II: Since 1688*, 2nd edition, edited by Walter Arnstein. Copyright © 1981 Wadsworth, a part of Cengage Learning, Inc. Reproduced by permission. www.cengage.com.

29-5. Traian Popovici, The Ghettoization of the Jews: Prelude to the Final Solution. Excerpt from "Mein Bekenntnis" in *Antisemitism in the Modern World*, edited and translated by Richard S. Levy, pp. 243–244. Reprinted by permission of Richard S. Levy.

CHAPTER 30

30-1. George C. Marshall, "An American Plan to Rebuild a Shattered Europe." From *The New York Times*, June 6, 1947 issue. Copyright © 1947 The New York Times. All

—

Sources of
Western Society

SINCE 1300

CHAPTER 12

The Crisis of the Later Middle Ages

1300–1450

B eginning around 1340, a series of disasters devastated much of Western Europe. The Black Death (or Black Plague), beginning in 1347, killed an estimated 30 to 60 percent of Western Europe's population. The Black Death proved so deadly for a number of reasons: some historians have argued that the plague struck a population that in many places was already malnourished and/or suffering the effects of war. Between 1337 and 1453, the Hundred Years' War — in actuality a series of wars and civil wars — wreaked havoc on France. These conflicts helped revolutionize warfare with new technologies, tactics, and strategies. Oddly enough, however, the ideals of chivalry, which were derived from older military practices, remained as popular as ever. New forms of popular piety emerged even as the papacy lost prestige, in part the result of its exile to Avignon, France, between 1309 and 1376, and also because of the conflicts over the papacy during the Great Schism (1378–1417).

DOCUMENT 12-1

GIOVANNI BOCCACCIO

From The Decameron: *The Plague Hits Florence*

ca. 1350

The first wave of the Black Death began in the late 1340s. The disease spread rapidly, and contemporaries understood very little about it, although they did

---

Giovanni Boccaccio, *The Decameron*, ed. Edward Hutton (London: Dent, 1955), 1:13–14.

associate it with rats. The only effective countermeasures were quarantine and isolation. The infection, which spread along trade routes from Central Asia, killed some 75 million people. Even after the first incidence receded, plague returned to Europe in many subsequent outbreaks until the 1700s, with varying mortality rates. In this document, excerpted from his famous collection of novellas, the Italian writer Giovanni Boccaccio detailed the chaos unleashed in Florence as a result of the plague.

"Dear ladies . . . here we tarry, as if, I think, for no other purpose than to bear witness to the number of the corpses that are brought here for intern-ment. . . . And if we quit the church, we see dead or sick folk carried about, or we see those, who for their crimes were of late condemned to exile . . . but who, now . . . well knowing that their magistrates are a prey to death or disease, have returned, and traverse the city in packs, making it hideous with their riotous antics; or else we see the refuse of the people, fostered on our blood, becchini, as they call themselves, who for our tor-ment go prancing about . . . making mock of our miseries in scurrilous songs. . . . Or go we home, what see we there? . . . where once were ser-vants in plenty, I find none left but my maid, and shudder with terror, and feel the very hairs of my head to stand on end; and turn or tarry where I may, I encounter the ghosts of the departed. . . . None . . . having means and place of retirement as we have, stays here . . . or if any such there be, they are of those . . . who make no distinction between things honorable and their opposites, so they but answer the cravings of appetite, and, alone or in company, do daily and nightly what things soever give promise of most gratification. Nor are these secular persons alone, but such as live recluse in monasteries break their rule, and give themselves up to carnal pleasures, persuading themselves that they are permissible to them, and only forbidden to others, and, thereby thinking to escape, are become un-chaste and dissolute.

READING AND DISCUSSION QUESTIONS

1. According to this account, how did civil order broke down during the plague?

2. What responses did people in religious orders have to plague as com-pared with other people?

3. What plan does the writer seem to have for the immediate future?

DOCUMENT 12-2

JEHAN FROISSART

The Sack of Limoges: On Warfare Without Chivalry

ca. 1400

The Hundred Years' War (1337–1453) broke out when Edward III of England claimed to be the legitimate heir to the French throne. Although there were extensive truces, France and England remained at war for most of this period. The war was also a civil war, in that large sections of France, especially Burgundy and Aquitaine, supported the English. Over the course of the conflict, medieval warfare changed radically, as new weapons and tactics were introduced, and both countries supported standing armies, which had not existed in Western Europe since the end of the Roman Empire. One ingeniously designed English attack on the French city of Limoges is described below.

[Having mined the town walls,] the miners set fire into their mine, and so the next morning, as the prince had ordained, there fell down a great piece of the wall and filled the moats, whereof the Englishmen were glad and were ready armed in the field to enter the town. The foot-men might well enter at their ease, and so they did, and ran to the gate and beat down the fortifying and barriers, for there was no defense against them: it was done so suddenly that they of the town were not aware thereof.

Then the prince,[1] the duke of Lancaster, the earl of Cambridge, the earl of Pembroke, Sir Guichard d'Angle, and all the others, with their companies, entered into the city, and all other foot-men ready apparelled to do evil, and to pill and rob the city, and to slay men, women, and children; for so it was commanded them to do. It was a great pity to see the men, women, and children that kneeled down on their knees before the prince for mercy. But he was so inflamed with ire that he took no heed of them,

---

John Froissart, *The Chronicles of England, France and Spain*, in James Harvey Robinson, ed., *Readings in European History* (Boston: Ginn, 1904), 1:472–473.

[1] **the prince**: Edward, Prince of Wales, Edward III's oldest son and the leader of the English armies, also known as the Black Prince.

so that none was heard, but all put to death as they were met withal, and such as were nothing culpable.

There was no pity taken of the poor people who wrought never no manner of treason, yet they bought it dearer than the great personages, such as had done the evil and trespass. There was not so hard a heart within the city of Limoges and if he had any remembrance of God, but that wept piteously for the great mischief that they saw before their eyen, for more than three thousand men, women, and children were slain that day. God have mercy on their souls, for I trow they were martyrs.

And thus entering into the city, a certain company of Englishmen entered into the bishop's palace, and there they found the bishop; and so they brought him to the prince's presence, who beheld him right fiercely and felly, and the best word that he could have of him was how he would have his head stricken off, and so he was had out of his sight. . . .

Thus the city of Limoges was pilled, robbed, and clean brent and brought to destruction.

READING AND DISCUSSION QUESTIONS

1. According to this document, how and why did the English troops destroy the town's fortifications?

2. Why is the scene with the bishop significant?

3. What does this passage reveal about the ideals of chivalry?

DOCUMENT 12-3

The Trial of Joan of Arc
1431

Joan of Arc (ca. 1412–1431), a peasant woman from eastern France, helped the French win important victories against the English in the Hundred Years' War. She claimed to have heard the voices of Saint Michael, Saint

Regine Pernoud, *Joan of Arc, By Herself and Her Witnesses* (New York: 1966), 30, 90–92.

Catherine, and Saint Margaret commanding her to drive out the English and to take the crown prince to Reims for coronation. Some historians argue that Joan was important symbolically for inspiring French morale while others argue that she was a skillful military strategist. After her capture by Burgundian trrops, the English put her on trial for heresy, and she was burned at the stake.

JOAN [*to her inquisitors*]: When I was thirteen years old, I had a voice from God to help me govern my conduct. And the first time I was very fearful. And came this voice, about the hour of noon, in the summertime, in my father's garden. . . . I heard the voice on the right-hand side . . . and rarely do I hear it without a brightness. . . . It has taught me to conduct myself well, to go habitually to church. . . . The voice told me that I should raise the siege laid to the city of Orleans . . . and me, I answered it that I was a poor girl who knew not how to ride nor lead in war.

JEAN PASQUEREL [*priest, Joan's confessor*]: "On the morrow, Saturday, I rose early and celebrated mass. And Joan went out against the fortress of the bridge where was the Englishman Classidas. And the assault lasted there from morning until sunset. In this assault . . . Joan . . . was struck by an arrow above the breast, and when she felt herself wounded she was afraid and wept. . . . And some soldiers, seeing her so wounded, wanted to apply a charm to her wound, but she would not have it, saying: "I would rather die than do a thing which I know to be a sin or against the will of God." . . . But if to her could be applied a remedy without sin, she was very willing to be cured. And they put on to her wound olive oil and lard. And after that had been applied, Joan made her confession to me, weeping and lamenting."

COUNT DUNOIS: "The assault lasted from the morning until eight . . . so that there was hardly hope of victory that day. So that I was going to break off and . . . withdraw. . . . Then the Maid [Joan] came to me and required me to wait yet a while. She . . . mounted her horse and retired alone into a vineyard. . . . And in this vineyard she remained at prayer. . . . Then she came back . . . at once seized her standard in hand and placed herself on the parapet of the trench, and the moment she was there the English trembled and were terrified. The king's soldiers regained courage and began to go up, charging against the boulevard without meeting the least resistance."

JEAN PASQUEREL: "Joan returned to the charge, crying and saying: 'Classidas, Classidas, yield thee, yield thee to the King of Heaven; thou hast called me 'whore'; I take great pity on thy soul and thy people's! Then Classidas, armed from head to foot, fell into the river of Loire and was drowned. And Joan, moved by pity, began to weep much for the soul of Classidas and the others who were drowned in great numbers." . . .

READING AND DISCUSSION QUESTIONS

1. Why is it important that at first the voice Joan heard seems principally to have been concerned with her good conduct?

2. Why would the claim that Joan was a "poor girl who knew not how to ride nor lead in war" have been an important issue at her trial?

3. What does the testimony of the two witnesses establish?

DOCUMENT 12-4

THOMAS À KEMPIS

From The Following of Christ:
On True Charity

1418

Thomas à Kempis (ca. 1379–1471) was the author of The Following of Christ, *one of the most influential spiritual tracts in Christian literature. He belonged to the Brothers and Sisters of the Common Life, a group that tried to imitate the simplicity of the earliest Christians. They were forbidden to beg; many of them earned a living by teaching or by copying manuscripts, as Thomas did. Thomas wrote as a time when many ordinary people throughout Western Europe were forming groups dedicated to Christian devotion and charitable activities.*

Thomas à Kempis, *The Following of Christ* (London: Burns and Oates, 1881), 30–32.

CHAPTER XV

Of works done out of charity.

Evil ought not to be done for anything in the world, nor for the love of any human being; but yet for the benefit of one that is in need, a good work is sometimes freely to be left undone, or rather to be changed for what is better.

For by this means a good work is not lost, but changed into a better. Without charity, the outward work provideth nothing; but whatever is done out of charity, be it ever so little and contemptible, it is all made fruitful, inasmuch as God regardeth more out of how much love a man doth a work, than how much he doth.

2. He doth much who loveth much.

He doth much who doth well what he hath to do.

He doth well, who regardeth rather the common good than his own will.

Oftentimes that seemeth to be charity which is rather carnality; for natural inclination, self-will, hope of reward, study of our own interests, will seldom be absent.

3. He that hath true and perfect charity, seeketh himself in nothing, but only desireth God to be glorified in all things.

And he envieth no man, for he loveth no joy for himself alone.

Neither doth he desire to rejoice in himself, but wisheth to find his blessedness above all good things in God.

He attributeth nothing of good to any man, but referreth it all to God, from whom, as from their fountain, all things proceed, and in whom, as in their end, all the Saints repose in fruition.

Oh, if one had but a spark of real charity, truly would he feel that all earthly things are full of vanity!

READING AND DISCUSSION QUESTIONS

1. Consider all the places where Thomas discusses charity. Explain what he means by this word.

2. According to this document, what is the relationship between "good works" and Christian devotion?

3. Explain why charity frees people from envy.

COMPARATIVE QUESTIONS

1. In what ways do the miracles of Joan of Arc resemble or differ from the miracles detailed in the stories of Saint Boniface (Document 8-2) and Vladimir the Great (Document 8-4)?

2. Compare the religious piety of Joan of Arc with the ideals espoused by Thomas à Kempis. Why do you think that *The Following of Christ* was such a popular spiritual guide?

3. Compare and contrast the ideas of honor and chivalry in the documents in this chapter. What common themes or actions can you identify?

4. Tragedy and warfare served as a breeding ground for Christian idealism and religious martyrdom, but also spurred less admiral behavior. Provide examples from both the description of the plague in Florence and the recounting of the sack of Limoges. Could one be both righteous and violent?

CHAPTER 13

European Society in the Age of the Renaissance

1350–1550

The Renaissance began as a revival and flourishing of learning and art in the Italian cities of the fourteenth century and spread throughout Europe. Many, though not all, of the Renaissance thinkers wrote in Latin, and successful authors such as the Dutchman Erasmus and the Englishman Thomas More acquired international reputations. Although the Italian peninsula was a center of learning and commerce, it was not a unified country. City-states such as Venice, Milan, and Florence often conflicted with one another. In 1494, Charles VIII of France invaded Italy, beginning a series of wars in which Italian states and outside powers were often at war. Although nationalism was still in its earliest stages, modern nation-states were beginning to take shape in France, England and Spain. Spanish rulers even attempted to impose uniformity of religion by expelling Jews and Muslims who resisted conversion to Christianity. In the context of these changes, many writers considered the role of the state and its leaders in creating a stable society.

DOCUMENT 13-1

NICCOLÒ MACHIAVELLI

From The Prince: *Power Politics During the Italian Renaissance*

1513

Niccolò Machiavelli (1469–1527) was a political philosopher and diplomat who had represented the Italian republic of Florence on numerous diplomatic missions. In 1512, when the powerful Medici family regained control of Florence, the anti-Medici Machiavelli was arrested and tortured. In 1513, he wrote The Prince, *a guide to gaining political power, and dedicated to Lorenzo di Medici, perhaps as a way to curry favor with the new rulers. Machiavelli claimed that he was simply drawing conclusions from his reading of history and from the example of successful contemporary rulers. The book circulated privately until after Machiavelli's death.*

Every one understands how praiseworthy it is in a prince to keep faith, and to live uprightly and not craftily. Nevertheless we see, from what has taken place in our own days, that princes who have set little store by their word, but have known how to overreach men by their cunning, have accomplished great things, and in the end got the better of those who trusted to honest dealing.

Be it known, then, that there are two ways of contending, — one in accordance with the laws, the other by force; the first of which is proper to men, the second to beasts. But since the first method is often ineffectual, it becomes necessary to resort to the second. A prince should, therefore, understand how to use well both the man and the beast. . . . But inasmuch as a prince should know how to use the beast's nature wisely, he ought of beasts to choose both the lion and the fox; for the lion cannot guard himself from the toils, nor the fox from wolves. He must therefore be a fox to discern toils, and a lion to drive off wolves.

To rely wholly on the lion is unwise; and for this reason a prudent prince neither can nor ought to keep his word when to keep it is hurtful to him and the causes which led him to pledge it are removed. If all men were good, this would not be good advice, but since they are dishonest and do not keep faith with you, you in return need not keep faith with them; and no prince was ever at a loss for plausible reasons to cloak a breach of faith. Of this numberless recent instances could be given, and it might be shown how many solemn treaties and engagements have been rendered inoperative and idle through want of faith among princes, and that he who has best known how to play the fox has had the best success.

It is necessary, indeed, to put a good color on this nature, and to be skilled in simulating and dissembling. But men are so simple, and governed so absolutely by their present needs, that he who wishes to deceive

---

Niccolò Machiavelli, *The Prince*, trans. N. H. Thomson, in James Harvey Robinson, ed., *Readings in European History* (Boston: Ginn, 1904), 2:10–13.

will never fail in finding willing dupes. One recent example I will not omit. Pope Alexander VI had no care or thought but how to deceive, and always found material to work on. No man ever had a more effective manner or asseverating, or made promises with more solemn protestations, or observed them less. And yet, because he understood this side of human nature, his frauds always succeeded. . . .

In his efforts to aggrandize his son the duke [Caesar Borgia], Alexander VI had to face many difficulties, both immediate and remote. In the first place, he saw no way to make him ruler of any state which did not belong to the Church. Yet, if he sought to take for him a state of the Church, he knew that the duke of Milan and the Venetians would withhold their consent, Faenza and Rimini [towns in the province of Romagna] being already under the protection of the latter. Further, he saw that the forces of Italy, and those more especially of which he might have availed himself, were in the hands of men who had reason to fear his aggrandizement, — that is, of the Orsini, the Colonnesi [Roman noble families] and their followers. These, therefore, he could not trust. . . .

And since this part of his [Caesar Borgia's] conduct merits both attention and imitation, I shall not pass it over in silence. After the duke had taken Romagna, finding that it had been ruled by feeble lords, who thought more of plundering than of governing their subjects, — which gave them more cause for division than for union, so that the country was overrun with robbery, tumult, and every kind of outrage, — he judged it necessary, with a view to rendering it peaceful, and obedient to his authority, to provide it with a good government. Accordingly he set over it Messer Remiro d'Orco, a stern and prompt ruler, who, being intrusted with the fullest powers, in a very short time, and with much credit to himself, restored it to tranquillity and order. But afterwards the duke, apprehending that such unlimited authority might become odious, decided that it was no longer needed, and established [at] the center of the province a civil tribunal, with an excellent president, in which every town was represented by its advocate. And knowing that past severities had generated ill feeling against himself, in order to purge the minds of the people and gain their good will, he sought to show them that any cruelty which had been done had not originated with him, but in the harsh disposition of this minister. Availing himself of the pretext which this afforded, he one morning caused Remiro to be beheaded, and exposed in the market place of Cesena with a block and bloody ax by his side. The barbarity of this spectacle at once astounded and satisfied the populace.

READING AND DISCUSSION QUESTIONS

1. Why must a prince be both a lion and a fox? What qualities do these animals represent?

2. Why does Machiavelli believe that sometimes a prince must break his word?

3. Explain why Machiavelli approves, or disapproves, of the execution of Remiro d'Orco.

4. Is there anything shocking about the examples Machiavelli uses to prove his point?

DOCUMENT 13-2

THOMAS MORE

From Utopia: *On Diplomatic Advice*

1516

Thomas More (1478–1535), a friend and collaborator of the prolific Erasmus (see Document 14-1), was one of the greatest English humanists. The son of a judge, More had a prominent career in the law and served the government in many capacities, eventually becoming the lord chancellor of England. In 1535, during the Protestant Reformation, he was executed when he refused to sign the Act of Supremacy that made Henry VIII head of the church in England. Utopia, *which was written in Latin, was intended for a European audience. A social satire, it is similar in some respects to Erasmus's* Praise of Folly *and other works of the time.*

"Do not you think that if I were about any king, proposing good laws to him, and endeavoring to root out all the cursed seeds of evil that I found in him, I should either be turned out of his court or at least be laughed at for my pains? For instance, what could it signify if I were about the King of France, and were called into his Cabinet Council, where several wise

Thomas More, "Dialogue of Counsel" in *Utopia* (New York: Colonial Press, 1901), 22–24.

men, in his hearing, were proposing many expedients, as by what arts and practices Milan may be kept, and Naples, that had so oft slipped out of their hands, recovered; how the Venetians, and after them the rest of Italy, may be subdued; and then how Flanders, Brabant, and all Burgundy, and some other kingdoms which he has swallowed already in his designs, may be added to his empire. One proposes a league with the Venetians, to be kept as long as he finds his account in it, and that he ought to communicate councils with them, and give them some share of the spoil, till his success makes him need or fear them less, and then it will be easily taken out of their hands. Another proposes the hiring [of] the Germans, and the securing [of] the Switzers by pensions. Another proposes the gaining [of] the Emperor by money, which is omnipotent with him. Another proposes a peace with the King of Aragon, and, in order to cement it, the yielding up [of] the King of Navarre's pretensions. Another thinks the Prince of Castile is to be wrought on, by the hope of an alliance; and that some of his courtiers are to be gained to the French faction by pensions. The hardest point of all is what to do with England: a treaty of peace is to be set on foot, and if their alliance is not to be depended on, yet it is to be made as firm as possible; and they are to be called friends, but suspected as enemies: therefore the Scots are to be kept in readiness, to be let loose upon England on every occasion: and some banished nobleman is to be supported underhand (for by the league it cannot be done avowedly) who had a pretension to the crown, by which means that suspected prince may be kept in awe.

"Now when things are in so great a fermentation, and so many gallant men are joining councils, how to carry on the war, if so mean a man as I should stand up, and wish them to change all their councils, to let Italy alone, and stay at home, since the Kingdom of France was indeed greater than could be well governed by one man; that therefore he ought not to think of adding others to it: and if after this, I should propose to them the resolutions of the Achorians, a people that lie on the southeast of Utopia, who long ago engaged in war, in order to add to the dominions of their prince another kingdom, to which he had some pretensions by an ancient alliance. This they conquered, but found that the trouble of keeping it was equal to that by which it was gained; that the conquered people were always either in rebellion or exposed to foreign invasions, while they were obliged to be incessantly at war, either for or against them, and consequently could never disband their army; that in the meantime they were oppressed with taxes, their money went out of the kingdom, their blood was spilt for the glory of their King, without procuring the least advantage to the people, who received not the smallest benefit from it even in time of peace; and that their manners being corrupted by a long war, robbery and murders everywhere abounded, and their laws fell into contempt; while their King, distracted with the care of two kingdoms, was the less able to apply his mind to the interests of either.

"When they saw this, and that there would be no end to these evils, they by joint councils made an humble address to their King, desiring him to choose which of the two kingdoms he had the greatest mind to keep, since he could not hold both; for they were too great a people to be governed by a divided king, since no man would willingly have a groom that should be in common between him and another. Upon which the good prince was forced to quit his new kingdom to one of his friends (who was not long after dethroned), and to be contented with his old one. To this I would add that after all those warlike attempts, the vast confusions, and the consumption both of treasure and of people that must follow them; perhaps upon some misfortune, they might be forced to throw up all at last; therefore it seemed much more eligible that the King should improve his ancient kingdom all he could, and make it flourish as much as possible; that he should love his people, and be beloved of them; that he should live among them, govern them gently, and let other kingdoms alone, since that which had fallen to his share was big enough, if not too big for him. Pray how do you think would such a speech as this be heard?"

"I confess," said I, "I think not very well."

READING AND DISCUSSION QUESTIONS

1. In what ways do the fictional discussions in the French royal council reflect what you know about the European history of the time?

2. What form of argument does More use, and where else have you seen it employed?

3. To whom does More seem to be addressing his advice? How effective does he expect his advice to be?

DOCUMENT 13-3

CHRISTINE DE PIZAN

From The Book of the City of Ladies:
Advice for a Wise Princess

1404

Christine de Pizan (ca. 1363–1434) may have been the first European woman to earn her living as a writer. After de Pizan's birth in Venice, her father became a physician and astrologer at the French court, where Christine studied languages and the classics. In 1390, when her husband died in an epidemic and left her with three children, Christine began her literary career. She wrote a vast number of poems, often on romantic themes, and took part in an important literary debate over the merits of the great thirteenth-century allegorical poem, The Romance of the Rose, *which some claimed used vulgar language and slandered women.*

17. The Sixth Teaching: How the Wise Princess Will Keep the Women of Her Court in Good Order.

Just as the good shepherd takes care that his lambs are maintained in health, and if any of them becomes mangy, separates it from the flock for fear that it may infect the others, so the princess will take upon herself the responsibility for the care of her women servants and companions, who she will ensure are all good and chaste, for she will not want to have any other sort of person around her. Since it is the established custom that knights and squires and all men (especially certain men) who associate with women have a habit of pleading for love tokens from them and trying to seduce them, the wise princess will so enforce her regulations that there will be no visitor to her court so foolhardy as to dare to whisper privately with any of her women or give the appearance of seduction. If he does it or if he is noticed giving any sign of it, immediately she should take such an attitude towards him that he will not dare to importune them any more. The lady who is chaste will want all her women to be so too, on pain of being banished from her company.

Christine de Pizan, *The Book of the City of Ladies,* in Sarah Lawson, trans., *The Treasure of the City of Ladies* (New York: Penguin, 1985), 74–76.

She will want them to amuse themselves with decent games, such that men cannot mock, as they do the games of some women, though at the time the men laugh and join in. The women should restrain themselves with seemly conduct among knights and squires and all men. They should speak demurely and sweetly and, whether in dances or other amusements, divert and enjoy themselves decorously and without wantonness. They must not be frolicsome, forward, or boisterous in speech, expression, bearing or laughter. They must not go about with their heads raised like wild deer. This kind of behavior would be very unseemly and greatly derisory in a woman of the court, in whom there should be more modesty, good manners and courteous behavior than in any others, for where there is most honor there ought to be the most perfect manners and behavior. Women of the court in any country would be deceiving themselves very much if they imagined that it was more appropriate for them to be frolicsome and saucy than for other women. For this reason we hope that in time to come our doctrine in this book may be carried into many kingdoms, so that it may be valuable in all places where there might be any shortcoming.

We say generally to all women of all countries that it is the duty of every lady and maiden of the court, whether she be young or old, to be more prudent, more decorous, and better schooled in all things than other women. The ladies of the court ought to be models of all good things and all honor to other women, and if they do otherwise they will do no honor to their mistress nor to themselves. In addition, so that everything may be consistent in modesty, the wise princess will wish that the clothing and the ornaments of her women, though they be appropriately beautiful and rich, be of a modest fashion, well fitting and seemly, neat and properly cared for. There should be no deviation from this modesty nor any immodesty in the matter of plunging necklines or other excesses.

In all things the wise princess will keep her women in order just as the good and prudent abbess does her convent, so that bad reports about it may not circulate in the town, in distant regions or anywhere else. This princess will be so feared and respected because of the wise management that she will be seen to practice that no man or woman will be so foolhardy as to disobey her commands in any respect or to question her will, for there is no doubt that a lady is more feared and respected and held in greater reverence when she is seen to be wise and chaste and of firm behavior. But there is nothing wrong or inconsistent in her being kind and gentle, for the mere look of the wise lady and her subdued reception is enough of a sign to correct those men and women who err and to inspire them with fear.

READING AND DISCUSSION QUESTIONS

1. This passage is addressed "the wise princess." What other women, in addition to princesses, might find its advice useful?

2. Discuss the ways in which the princess must watch over the women of her court, especially in their relations with men. What does this reveal more generally about relations between men and women?

3. Why is reputation so important to the princess?

DOCUMENT 13-4

Account of an Italian Jew Expelled from Spain
1492

In 1492, the same year in which the last Islamic stronghold in Spain was overcome, Jews were given the choice of forcible conversion or expulsion. Even those who did convert endured persecution, because the authorities often believed that these conversos *continued to practice their old religion in secret. One of the principal tasks of the Inquisition in Spain was to root out secret Jews. The Jews who were expelled scattered over vast areas of the Muslim and Christian world. Muhammad had ordained that Muslims allow Jews to practice their religion, but there was no similar instruction for Christians.*

And in the year 1492, in the days of King Ferdinand [of Spain], the Lord visited the remnant of his people a second time and exiled them. After the King had captured the city of Granada from the Moors, . . . he ordered the expulsion of all the Jews in all parts of his kingdom — in the kingdoms of Castile, Catalonia, Aragon, Galicia, Majorca, Minorca, the Basque provinces, the islands of Sardinia and Sicily, and the kingdom of Valencia.

The King gave them three months' time in which to leave. . . .

About their number there is no agreement, but, after many inquiries, I found that the most generally accepted estimate is 50,000 families. . . .

Jacob Marcus, *The Jew in the Medieval World: A Sourcebook, 315–1791* (New York: JPS, 1938), 51–55.

They had houses, fields, vineyards, and cattle, and most of them were artisans. At that time there existed many academies in Spain, and at the head of the greatest of them were Rabbi Isaac Aboab in Guadalajara, Rabbi Isaac Veçudó in Leon, and Rabbi Jacob Habib in Salamanca. . . .

In the course of the three months' respite granted them they endeavored to effect an arrangement permitting them to stay on in the country, and they felt confident of success. Their representatives were the rabbi, Don Abraham Seneor, the leader of the Spanish congregations, who was attended by a retinue on thirty mules, and Rabbi Meïr Melamed, who was secretary to the King, and Don Isaac Abravanel, who had fled to Castile from the King of Portugal, and then occupied an equally prominent position at the Spanish royal court. He, too, was later expelled, went to Naples, and was highly esteemed by the King of Naples. . . .

The agreement permitting them to remain in the country on the payment of a large sum of money was almost completed when it was frustrated by the interference of a prior who was called the Prior of Santa Cruz. Then the Queen gave an answer to the representatives of the Jews, similar to the saying of King Solomon: "The king's heart is in the hand of the Lord, as the rivers of water. God turneth it withersoever He will." She said furthermore: "Do you believe that this comes upon you from us? The Lord hath put this thing into the heart of the king."

Then they saw that there was evil determined against them by the King, and they gave up the hope of remaining. But the time had become short, and they had to hasten their exodus from Spain. They sold their houses, their landed estates, and their cattle for very small prices, to save themselves. The King did not allow them to carry silver and gold out of his country, so that they were compelled to exchange their silver and gold for merchandise of cloths and skins and other things.

One hundred and twenty thousand of them went to Portugal, according to a compact which a prominent man, Don Vidal bar Benveniste del Cavalleria, had made with the King of Portugal, and they paid one ducat for every soul, and the fourth part of all the merchandise they had carried thither; and he allowed them to stay in his country six months. This King acted much worse toward them than the King of Spain, and after the six months had elapsed he made slaves of all those that remained in his country, and banished seven hundred children to a remote island to settle it, and all of them died. . . .

Many of the exiled Spaniards went to Mohammedan countries, to Fez, Tlemçen, and the Berber provinces, under the King of Tunis. On account of their large numbers the Moors did not allow them into their cities, and many of them died in the fields from hunger, thirst, and lack of everything. The lions and bears, which are numerous in this country, killed some of them while they lay starving outside of the cities. . . .

When the edict of expulsion became known in the other countries, vessels came from Genoa to the Spanish harbors to carry away the Jews. The crews of these vessels, too, acted maliciously and meanly toward the Jews, robbed them, and delivered some of them to the famous pirate of that time who was called the Corsair of Genoa. To those who escaped and arrived at Genoa the people of the city showed themselves merciless, and oppressed and robbed them, and the cruelty of their wicked hearts went so far that they took the infants from the mothers' breasts.

Many ships with Jews, especially from Sicily, went to the city of Naples on the coast. The King of this country was friendly to the Jews, received them all, and was merciful towards them, and he helped them with money. The Jews that were at Naples supplied them with food as much as they could, and sent around to the other parts of Italy to collect money to sustain them. The Marranos[1] in this city lent them money on pledges without interest; even the Dominican Brotherhood acted mercifully toward them. On account of their very large number, all this was not enough. Some of them died by famine, others sold their children to Christians to sustain their life. Finally, a plague broke out among them, spread to Naples, and very many of them died, so that the living wearied of burying the dead. . . .

He who said unto His world, Enough, may He also say Enough unto our sufferings, and may He look down upon our impotence. May He turn again, and have compassion upon us, and hasten out salvation. Thus may it be Thy will!

READING AND DISCUSSION QUESTIONS

1. Why did the negotiations that might have allowed Jews to remain in Spain fail?

2. Which countries treated Jewish refugees best? Worst? Explain your answer.

---

[1] **Marranos**: Secret Jews, living under the guise of Christianity.

3. Jews suffered greatly even in countries where the rulers tried to act with some decency. What does this reveal about Europe's social and economic infrastructure?

4. How do you think contemporaries reacted to the outbreak of plague that accompanied the arrival of Jews and spread to Naples?

COMPARATIVE QUESTIONS

1. To what extent do Machiavelli and More agree or disagree about the ways that international politics are conducted?

2. Compare and contrast Christine de Pizan to Machiavelli and More. In what ways are they similar or different in their perceived audiences or in the advice they give?

3. "Rulers must be good examples to their subjects." To what extent would Machiavelli, More, and Pizan have agreed with this statement?

4. Ferdinand of Aragon, who ordered the expulsion of Jews described in Document 13-4, was one of the contemporary princes that Machiavelli most admired. What would Machiavelli have found to admire in a prince like Ferdinand?

5. The exodus of Jews from Spain was not the first Jewish exodus. Revisit Document 2-2. How had the plight of the Jewish people changed in the interim?

CHAPTER 14

Reformations and Religious Wars

1500–1600

Even before Martin Luther posted his "Ninety-five Theses on the Power and Efficacy of Indulgences," numerous Catholic practices had come under widespread criticism. Erasmus, one of the most prestigious literary and scholarly figures of his time, had criticized many aspects of popular religion in *The Praise of Folly*. His scholarly work on the New Testament was important for those who believed that the Church had strayed from the teachings of the gospels. Reformers such as Luther and John Calvin believed that Christians should have a more immediate spiritual relationship with God. They argued that the Catholic sacrament of penance, as it was then practiced, could actually hinder spiritual growth. Some reformers, including Michael Servetus, adopted beliefs that were far more radical than the ideas of either Luther or Calvin, and were condemned by Protestants and Catholics alike.

DOCUMENT 14-1

DESIDERIUS ERASMUS

From The Praise of Folly: *On Popular Religious Practice*

1509

Desiderius Erasmus of Rotterdam (1466/1469–1536) was one of the leading scholars and writers of the Northern Renaissance, and produced important Greek and Latin translations of the New Testament. Erasmus wrote The Praise of Folly *in a single week while visiting Thomas More (*Utopia,

Erasmus, *The Praise of Folly*, in James Harvey Robinson, ed., *Readings in European History* (Boston: Ginn, 1904), 2:41–43.

Document 13-2) in England. The book quickly became popular throughout Europe, and, despite its criticism of religious beliefs, Pope Leo X was reported to have been amused by it. Although some expected that Erasmus would embrace the Protestant Reformation, he remained loyal to the Catholic Church.

To this same class of fools belong those who beguile themselves with the silly but pleasing notion that if they look upon a picture or image of St. Christopher, — that huge Polyphemus,[1] — they will not die that day; or that he who salutes an image of St. Barbara with the proper form of address will come back from battle safe; or that one who approaches St. Erasmus on certain days with wax candles and prayers will soon be rich. They have found a new Hercules in St. George, — a sort of second Hippolytus.[2] They seem to adore even his horse, which is scrupulously decked out with gorgeous trappings, and additional offerings are constantly being made in the hope of gaining new favors. His bronze helmet one would think half divine, the way people swear by it.

And what shall I say of those who comfortably delude themselves with imaginary pardons for their sins, and who measure the time in purgatory with an hourglass into years, months, days, and hours, with all the precision of a mathematical table? There are plenty, too, who, relying upon certain magical little certificates and prayers, — which some pious impostor devised either in fun or for the benefit of his pocket, — believe that they may procure riches, honor, future happiness, health, perpetual prosperity, long life, a lusty old age, — nay, in the end, a seat at the right hand of Christ in heaven; but as for this last, it matters not how long it be deferred: they will content themselves with the joys of heaven only when they must finally surrender the pleasures of this world, to which they lovingly cling.

The trader, the soldier, and the judge think that they can clean up the Augean stable[3] of a lifetime, once for all, by sacrificing a single coin from their ill-gotten gains. They flatter themselves that all sorts of perjury, debauchery, drunkenness, quarrels, bloodshed, imposture, perfidy, and treason can be compounded for by contract and so adjusted that, having paid off their arrears, they can begin a new score.

---

[1] **Polyphemus:** A Greek cyclops who appears in Homer's *Odyssey.*

[2] **Hippolytus:** A Greek horseman, praised for his chastity.

[3] **Augean stable:** An epically unclean cattle house. One of Hercules' twelve labors, performed as penance for murdering his family, was to clean the stables in a day.

How foolish, or rather how happy, are those who promise themselves more than supernal happiness if they repeat the verses of the seven holy psalms! Those magical lines are supposed to have been taught to St. Bernard by a demon, who seems to have been a wag; but he was not very clever, and, poor fellow, was frustrated in his attempt to deceive the saint. These silly things which even I, Folly, am almost ashamed of, are approved not only by the common herd but even by the teachers of religion.

How foolish, too, for religious bodies each to give preference to its particular guardian saint! Nay, each saint has his particular office allotted to him, and is addressed each in his special way: this one is called upon to alleviate toothache; that, to aid in childbirth; others, to restore a stolen article, bring rescue to the shipwrecked, or protect cattle, — and so on with the rest, who are much too numerous to mention. A few indeed among the saints are good in more than one emergency, especially the Holy Virgin, to whom the common man now attributes almost more than to her Son.

And for what, after all, do men petition the saints except for foolish things? Look at the votive offerings which cover the walls of certain churches and with which you see even the ceiling filled; do you find any one who expresses his gratitude that he has escaped Folly or because he has become a whit wiser? One perhaps was saved from drowning, another recovered when he had been run through by his enemy; another, while his fellows were fighting, ran away with expedition and success; another, on the point of being hanged, escaped, through the aid of some saintly friend of thieves, and lived to relieve a few more of those whom he believed to be overburdened with their wealth. . . .

These various forms of foolishness so pervade the whole life of Christians that even the priests themselves find no objection to admitting, not to say fostering, them, since they do not fail to perceive how many tidy little sums accrue to them from such sources. But what if some odious philosopher should chime in and say, as is quite true: "You will not die badly if you live well. You are redeeming your sins when you add to the sum that you contribute a hearty detestation of evil doers: then you may spare yourself tears, vigils, invocations, fasts, and all that kind of life. You may rely upon any saint to aid you when once you begin to imitate his life."

As for the theologians, perhaps the less said the better on this gloomy and dangerous theme, since they are a style of man who show themselves exceeding supercilious and irritable unless they can heap up six hundred conclusions about you and force you to recant; and if you refuse, they promptly brand you as a heretic, — for it is their custom to terrify by their thunderings those whom they dislike. It must be confessed that no other group of fools are so reluctant to acknowledge Folly's benefits toward them, although I have many titles to their gratitude, for I make them so in love with themselves that they seem to be happily exalted to the third heaven, whence they look down with something like pity upon all other mortals, wandering about on the earth like mere cattle. . . .

READING AND DISCUSSION QUESTIONS

1. In what ways does Erasmus criticize the veneration of saints?

2. According to this document, why and how do so many priests contribute to the follies of the world?

3. Describe Erasmus's attitude toward theologians.

DOCUMENT 14-2

MARTIN LUTHER

Ninety-five Theses on the Power and Efficacy of Indulgences

1517

Martin Luther (1483–1546), the acknowledged initiator of the Protestant Reformation, was a theologian, preacher, and pamphleteer. His German translation of the Bible was a shaping force in the development of the modern German language. Some historians argue that Luther had no intention of breaking with the Catholic Church when he developed the Ninety-five Theses — he had enclosed a copy in a letter to the archbishop of Mainz and Magdeburg, and the form in which he cast his ideas (the theses) was a common way for scholars to invite others to debate.

1. Our Lord and Master Jesus Christ in saying "Repent ye" etc., intended that the whole life of believers should be penitence.

Martin Luther, "Ninety-five Theses," in *Translations and Reprints from the Original Sources of European History* (Philadelphia: University of Pennsylvania Press, 1898), 2/6:12–18.

2. This word cannot be understood as sacramental penance, that is, of the confession and satisfaction which are performed under the ministry of priests.

3. It does not, however, refer solely to inward penitence; nay such inward penitence is naught, unless it outwardly produces various mortifications of the flesh.

4. The penalty thus continues as long as the hatred of self (that is, true inward penitence); namely, till our entrance into the kingdom of heaven.

5. The Pope has neither the will nor the power to remit any penalties except those which he has imposed by his own authority, or by that of the canons.

6. The Pope has no power to remit any guilt, except by declaring and warranting it to have been remitted by God; or at most by remitting cases reserved for himself; in which cases, if his power were despised, guilt would certainly remain.

7. Certainly God remits no man's guilt without at the same time subjecting him, humbled in all things, to the authority of his representative the priest. . . .

20. Therefore the Pope, when he speaks of the plenary remission of all penalties, does not mean really of all, but only of those imposed by himself.

21. Thus those preachers of indulgences are in error who say that by the indulgences of the Pope a man is freed and saved from all punishment.

22. For in fact he remits to souls in purgatory no penalty which they would have had to pay in this life according to the canons.

23. If any entire remission of all penalties can be granted to any one it is certain that it is granted to none but the most perfect, that is to very few.

24. Hence, the greater part of the people must needs be deceived by this indiscriminate and high-sounding promise of release from penalties. . . .

26. The Pope acts most rightly in granting remission to souls not by the power of the keys (which is of no avail in this case) but by the way of intercession.[4]

27. They preach man who say that the soul flies out of Purgatory as soon as the money thrown into the chest rattles.[5]

---

[4] **intercession**: A prayer to God on another's behalf.

[5] **They preach . . . rattles**: This was the claim being made by the indulgence seller Tetzel in Luther's Saxony.

28. It is certain that, when the money rattles in the chest, avarice and gain may be increased, but the effect of the intercession of the Church depends on the will of God alone.

29. Who knows whether all the souls in purgatory desire to be redeemed from it — witness the story told of Saints Severinus and Paschal?

30. No man is sure of the reality of his own contrition, much less of the attainment of plenary remission. . . .

35. They preach no Christian doctrine who teach that contrition is not necessary for those who buy souls [out of purgatory] or buy confessional licenses.

36. Every Christian who feels true compunction has of right plenary remission of punishment and guilt even without letters of pardon.

37. Every true Christian, whether living or dead, has a share in all the benefits of Christ and of the Church, given him by God, even without letters of pardon.

38. The remission, however, imparted by the Pope is by no means to be despised, since it is, as I have said, a declaration of the divine remission.

39. It is a most difficult thing, even for the most learned theologians, to exalt at the same time in the eyes of the people the ample effect of pardons and the necessity of true contrition.

40. True contrition seeks and loves punishment; while the ampleness of pardons relaxes it, and causes men to hate it, or at least gives occasion for them to do so. . . .

43. Christians should be taught that he who gives to a poor man, or lends to a needy man, does better than if he bought pardons.

44. Because by works of charity, charity increases, and the man becomes better; while by means of pardons, he does not become better, but only freer from punishment. . . .

49. Christians should be taught that the Pope's pardons are useful if they do not put their trust in them, but most hurtful if through them they lose the fear of God. . . .

54. Wrong is done to the Word of God when, in the same sermon, an equal or longer time is spent on pardons than on it.

55. The mind of the Pope necessarily is that, if pardons, which are a very small matter, are celebrated with single bells, single processions, and single ceremonies, the Gospel, which is a very great matter, should be preached with a hundred bells, a hundred processions, and a hundred ceremonies.

56. The treasures of the Church, whence the Pope grants indulgences, are neither sufficiently named nor known among the people of Christ.

57. It is clear that they are at least not temporal treasures, for these are not so readily lavished, but only accumulated, by many of the preachers. . . .

67. Those indulgences, which the preachers loudly proclaim to be the greatest graces, are seen to be truly such as regards the promotion of gain.

68. Yet they are in reality most insignificant when compared to the grace of God and the piety of the cross. . . .

75. To think that the Papal pardons have such power that they could absolve a man even if — by an impossibility — he had violated the Mother of God, is madness.

76. We affirm on the contrary that Papal pardons cannot take away even the least of venial sins, as regards its guilt. . . .

79. To say that the cross set up among the insignia of the Papal arms is of equal power with the cross of Christ, is blasphemy.

80. Those bishops, priests, and theologians who allow such discourses to have currency among the people will have to render an account. . . .

82. As for instance: Why does not the Pope empty purgatory for the sake of most holy charity and of the supreme necessity of souls — this being the most just of all reasons — if he redeems an infinite number of souls for the sake of that most fatal thing, money, to be spent on building a basilica — this being a very slight reason?

83. Again; why do funeral masses and anniversary masses for the deceased continue, and why does not the Pope return, or permit the withdrawal of, the funds bequeathed for this purpose, since it is a wrong to pray for those who are already redeemed?

84. Again; what is this new kindness of God and the Pope, in that, for money's sake, they permit an impious man and an enemy of God to redeem a pious soul which loves God, and yet do not redeem that same pious and beloved soul out of free charity on account of its own need?

85. Again; why is it that the penitential canons, long since abrogated and dead in themselves, in very fact and not only by usage, are yet still redeemed with money, through the granting of indulgences, as if they were full of life?

86. Again; why does not the Pope, whose riches are at this day more ample than those of the wealthiest of the wealthy, build the single Basilica of St. Peter with his own money rather than with that of poor believers? . . .

89. Since it is the salvation of souls, rather than money, that the Pope seeks by his pardons, why does he suspend the letters and pardons granted long ago, since they are equally efficacious? . . .

91. If all these pardons were preached according to the spirit and mind of the Pope, all these questions would be resolved with ease; nay, would not exist. . . .

READING AND DISCUSSION QUESTIONS

1. In Thesis 36, Luther writes, "Every Christian who feels true compunction has of right plenary remission of punishment and guilt even without letters of pardon." Why would many interpret this as an attack on the papacy?

2. Luther claims that in some cases, people who buy indulgences are actually purchasing the anger of God (see Thesis 35). What does this suggest about his notions of charity?

3. According to the theses, in what ways have the leaders of the church failed to teach true Christian doctrine?

4. Based on your reading of Theses 82–91, how would you classify the sorts of reform that Luther would like to see within the church?

DOCUMENT 14-3

IMPERIAL DIET OF AUGSBURG
On the Religious Peace of Augsburg
1555

The Peace of Augsburg, a treaty between the Holy Roman emperor, Ferdinand I, and Protestant rulers who were nominally his subjects, was an attempt to end a series of religious wars. The treaty established the principle that each ruler could decide which religion — Catholicism or Lutheranism — would be practiced within his domain. It was a partial solution at best, particularly because it did not adequately deal with Protestant sects other than the Lutherans or divisions between Catholics and Protestants within individual political regions.

"The Religious Peace of Augsburg," in James Harvey Robinson, ed., *Readings in European History* (Boston: Ginn, 1904), 2:114–116.

In order that . . . peace, which is especially necessary in view of the divided religions, as is seen from the causes before mentioned, and is demanded by the sad necessity of the Holy Roman Empire of the German nation, may be the better established and made secure and enduring between his Roman Imperial Majesty and us, on the one hand, and the electors, princes, and estates of the Holy Empire of the German nation on the other, therefore his Imperial Majesty, and we, and the electors, princes, and estates of the Holy Empire will not make war upon any estate of the empire on account of the Augsburg Confession[6] and the doctrine, religion, and faith of the same, nor injure nor do violence to those estates that hold it, nor force them, against their conscience, knowledge, and will, to abandon the religion, faith, church usages, ordinances, and ceremonies of the Augsburg Confession, where these have been established, or may hereafter be established, in their principalities, lands, and dominions. Nor shall we, through mandate or in any other way, trouble or disparage them, but shall let them quietly and peacefully enjoy their religion, faith, church usages, ordinances, and ceremonies, as well as their possessions, real and personal property, lands, people, dominions, governments, honors, and rights. . . .

On the other hand, the estates that have accepted the Augsburg Confession shall suffer his Imperial Majesty, us, and the electors, princes, and other estates of the Holy Empire, adhering to the old religion, to abide in like manner by their religion, faith, church usages, ordinances, and ceremonies. They shall also leave undisturbed their possessions, real and personal property, lands, people, dominions, government, honors, and rights, rents, interest, and tithes. . . .

But all others who are not adherents of either of the above-mentioned religions are not included in this peace, but shall be altogether excluded. . . .

No estate shall urge another estate, or the subjects of the same, to embrace its religion.

But when our subjects and those of the electors, princes, and estates, adhering to the old religion or to the Augsburg Confession, wish, for the sake of their religion, to go with wife and children to another place in the lands, principalities, and cities of the electors, princes, and estates of the Holy Empire, and settle there, such going and coming, and the sale of property and goods, in return for reasonable compensation for serfdom and arrears of taxes, . . . shall be everywhere unhindered, permitted, and granted. . . .

---

[6] **Augsburg Confession**: The statement of faith in Lutheran churches.

READING AND DISCUSSION QUESTIONS

1. What does this decree pledge to do? Why?

2. To what extent does this decree support religious toleration? What are the limits of that toleration?

3. What provisions are made for people who remain true to the old religion?

4. What provisions are made for people who want to leave their homes because of their religion, and why were such measures necessary?

DOCUMENT 14-4

NICHOLAS DE LA FONTAINE

The Trial of Michael Servetus in Calvin's Geneva

1553

Michael Servetus (1511–1553) was a Spanish scientist, humanist, and theologian. Both Catholics and Protestants condemned his teachings, especially his rejection of both the doctrine of the Trinity and the practice of infant baptism. While fleeing from Catholic authorities in France, he passed through Geneva, which was then under the leadership of the Protestant reformer John Calvin. The author of this document, Nicholas de la Fontaine, took the most active role in the prosecution of Michael Servetus and drew up the list of charges. After being found guilty of heresy, Servetus was burned at the stake.

Nicholas de la Fontaine asserts that he has instituted proceedings against Michael Servetus, and on this account he has allowed himself to be held prisoner in criminal process.

1. In the first place that about twenty-four years ago the defendant commenced to annoy the churches of Germany with his errors and heresies, and was condemned and took to flight in order to escape the punishment prepared for him.

Nicholas de la Fontaine, in *Translations and Reprints from the Original Sources of European History* (Philadelphia: University of Pennsylvania Press, 1898), 3/2:12–15.

2. Item, that on or about this time he printed a wretched book, which has infected many people.
3. Item, that since that time he has not ceased by all means in his power to scatter his poison, as much by his construction of biblical text, as by certain annotations which he has made upon Ptolemy.[7]
4. Item, that since that time he has printed in secrecy another book containing endless blasphemies.
5. Item, that while detained in prison in the city of Vienne [in France], when he saw that they were willing to pardon him on condition of his recanting, he found means to escape from prison.

Said Nicholas demands that said Servetus be examined upon all these points.

And since he is able to evade the question by pretending that his blasphemies and heresies are nought else than good doctrine, said Nicholas proposes certain articles upon which he demands said heretic be examined.

6. To wit, whether he has not written and falsely taught and published that to believe that in a single essence of God there are three distinct persons, the Father, the Son, and the Holy Ghost, is to create four phantoms, which cannot and ought not to be imagined.
7. Item, that to put such distinction into the essence of God is to cause God to be divided into three parts, and that this is a threeheaded devil, like to Cerberus, whom the ancient poets have called the dog of hell, a monster, and things equally injurious. . . .
9. Item, whether he does not say that our Lord Jesus Christ is not the Son of God, except in so much as he was conceived of the Holy Ghost in the womb of the virgin Mary.
10. Item, that those who believe Jesus Christ to have been the word of God the Father, engendered through all eternity, have a scheme of redemption which is fanciful and of the nature of sorcery.
11. Item, that Jesus Christ is God, insomuch as God has caused him to be such. . . .
27. Item, that the soul of man is mortal, and that the only thing which is immortal is an elementary breath, which is the substance that Jesus Christ now possesses in heaven and which is also the elementary and divine and incorruptible substance of the Holy Ghost. . . .

---

[7] **certain annotations . . . Ptolemy**: Servetus wrote about the Roman-Egyptian's treatise *Geography*.

32. Item, that the baptism of little children is an invention of the Devil, an infernal falsehood tending to the destruction of all Christianity. . . .

37. Item, that in the person of M. Calvin, minister of the word of God in the Church of Geneva, he has defamed with printed book the doctrine which he preached, uttering all the injurious and blasphemous things which it is possible to invent. . . .

READING AND DISCUSSION QUESTIONS

1. When had Michael Servetus come into conflict with religious authorities on earlier occasions? Why are these earlier occasions mentioned in the present indictment?

2. Why is the charge that Michael Servetus argued that the human soul is mortal such an important part of the indictment? To what extent, if any, is this charge justified?

3. What are the major points on which Michael Servetus disagreed with orthodox Christian teachings?

COMPARATIVE QUESTIONS

1. Compare and contrast the views of Erasmus and Luther.

2. Which thinker, Luther or Servetus, posed the most serious threat to traditional Christianity? Why?

3. Compare and contrast the issues addressed in the Peace of Augsburg with those confronted during the investiture controversy (Document 9-3). Which posed a more serious threat to established authority and why?

4. In each of these documents, identify which doctrines or points seem to be most important to the author(s) of the document. How might their emphasis on these doctrines have influences other Christians?

CHAPTER 15

European Exploration and Conquest

1450–1650

I n the mid-1400s, Western Europe faced a rapidly expanding Muslim power in the east. The Ottoman Empire captured Constantinople in 1453 and over time came to rule, directly or indirectly, much of Eastern Europe. In the west, the Portuguese began exploring the west coast of Africa, eventually rounding the tip of Africa and reaching India. After the voyages of Columbus, the Spaniards and the Portuguese began to explore and conquer the Americas. The establishment of colonial empires in the Americas led to a new era of worldwide trade in African slaves. Europeans came into increasing contact with peoples of whom they had previously had little or no knowledge. In the context of threats from the Ottomans in the East and European competition in the West, a series of religious wars affecting all of Europe tore apart western Christendom.

DOCUMENT 15-1

DUCAS

From Historia Turcobyzantia: *The Fall of Constantinople to the Ottomans*

ca. 1465

On May 29, 1453, Constantinople, the city that had been "the second Rome" — the capital of the eastern half of the Roman Empire — and a center

Ducas, *Historia Turcobyzantia, 1341–1462*, in Deno John Geanokoplos, ed., *Byzantium: Church, Society, and Civilization Seen Through Contemporary Eyes* (Chicago: University of Chicago Press, 1984), 389.

of Christian learning throughout the Middle Ages, fell to the Ottoman Turks. In the years that followed Constantinople's fall, the Ottomans continued to advance into Central Europe, seizing control of the Balkan Peninsula and even besieging Vienna, once in the sixteenth century and again in the seventeenth century. The account excerpted here is from a member of a prominent Byzantine family.

And the entire City [its inhabitants and wealth] was to be seen in the tents of the [Turkish] camp, the city deserted, lying lifeless, naked, soundless, without either form or beauty. O City, City, head of all cities! O City, City, center of the four corners of the world! O City, City, pride of the Romans, civilizer of the barbarians! O City, second paradise planted toward the west, possessing all kinds of vegetation, laden with spiritual fruits! Where is your beauty, O paradise, where the beneficent strength of the charms of your spirit, soul, and body? Where are the bodies of the Apostles of my Lord, which were implanted long ago in the always-green paradise, having in their midst the purple cloak, the lance, the sponge, the reed, which, when we kissed them, made us believe that we were seeing him who was raised on the Cross? Where are the relics of the saints, those of the martyrs? Where the remains of Constantine the Great and the other emperors? Roads, courtyards, crossroads, fields, and vineyard enclosures, all teem with the relics of saints, with the bodies of nobles, of the chaste, and of male and female ascetics. Oh what a loss! "The dead bodies of thy servants, O Lord, have they given to be meat unto the fowls of the heaven, the flesh of thy saints unto the beasts of the earth round about New Sion and there was none to bury them." [Psalm 78:2–3]

O temple [Hagia Sophia]! O earthly heaven! O heavenly altar! O sacred and divine places! O magnificence of the churches! O holy books and words of God! O ancient and modern laws! O tablets inscribed by the finger of God! O Scriptures spoken by his mouth! O divine discourses of angels who bore flesh! O doctrines of men filled with the Holy Spirit! O teachings of semi-divine heroes! O commonwealth! O citizens! O army, formerly beyond number, now removed from sight like a ship sunk into the sea! O houses and palaces of every type! O sacred walls! Today I invoke you all, and as if incarnate beings I mourn with you, having Jeremiah[1] as [choral] leader of this lamentable tragedy!

---

[1] **Jeremiah**: The famously "broken-hearted prophet."

READING AND DISCUSSION QUESTIONS

1. This account was written more than ten years after the fall of Constantinople. How does this affect its value as an eyewitness account?

2. What does the reference to Psalm 78 at the end of the first paragraph tell you about both the siege and the author of this account?

3. How does Ducas describe the destruction of Constantinople, both physical and spiritual?

4. What does Ducas's account reveal about the place of Constantinople in the Christian world?

DOCUMENT 15-2

HERNANDO CORTÉS

*Two Letters to Charles V: On the Conquest
of the Aztecs*

1521

*In a number of letters to his sovereign, the Holy Roman emperor Charles V,
who was also king of Spain, Hernando Cortés described his conquest of the
Aztec Empire of Mexico. While Cortés was surprised, even impressed by
the advanced culture he encountered, his conquests were not without considerable violence. In one incident, one of his men ordered the massacre of
thousands of unarmed members of the Aztec nobility who had assembled
peaceably. Under examination, Cortés claimed that this act was done to instill fear and prevent future treachery. Some contemporaries speculated that
Cortés embellished his accounts in order to retain the favor of the king.*

This great city of Tenochtitlan is built on the salt lake. . . . It has four approaches by means of artificial causeways. . . . The city is as large as Seville or Cordoba. Its streets . . . are very broad and straight, some of these, and all the others, are one half land, and the other half water on which they go about in canoes. . . .There are bridges, very large, strong, and well constructed,

---

Letters of Cortés, trans. Francis A. MacNutt (New York: 1908), 1:256–257, 2:244.

so that, over many, ten horsemen can ride abreast. . . . The city has many squares where markets are held. . . . There is one square, twice as large as that of Salamanca, all surrounded by arcades, where there are daily more than sixty thousand souls, buying and selling . . . in the service and manners of its people, their fashion of living was almost the same as in Spain, with just as much harmony and order; and considering that these people were barbarous, so cut off from the knowledge of God and other civilized peoples, it is admirable to see to what they attained in every respect. [Second letter]

It happened . . . that a Spaniard saw an Indian . . . eating a piece of flesh taken from the body of an Indian who had been killed. . . . I had the culprit burned, explaining that the cause was his having killed that Indian and eaten him which was prohibited by Your Majesty, and by me in Your Royal name. I further made the chief understand that all the people . . . must abstain from this custom. . . . I came . . . to protect their lives as well as their property, and to teach them that they were to adore but one God . . . that they must turn from their idols, and the rites they had practiced until then, for these were lies and deceptions which the devil . . . had invented. . . . I, likewise, had come to teach them that Your Majesty, by the will of Divine Providence, rules the universe, and that they also must submit themselves to the imperial yoke, and do all that we who are Your Majesty's ministers here might order them. . . . [Fifth letter]

READING AND DISCUSSION QUESTIONS

1. Although Cortés describes the people of Tenochtitlan as "barbarous" and laments that they are "cut off from the knowledge of God and other civilized peoples," what positive qualities does he attribute to the city and its people?

2. Why do you think Cortés chooses to describe an act of cannibalism? What does his commentary on this incident reveal about his conception of his mission?

3. What different images of Mexico was Cortés trying to impress upon Charles?

ALVISE DA CA' DA MOSTO

Description of Capo Bianco and the Islands Nearest to It: Fifteenth-Century Slave Trade in West Africa

1455–1456

Alvise da Ca' da Mosto (ca. 1428–1483) was an Italian trader and explorer. After Alvise's father was banished from Venice, Alvise took up service with Prince Henry of Portugal, who was promoting exploration of the West African coast. In 1455, he traveled to the Canary and Madeira Islands and sailed past Cape Verde to the Gambia River. During another voyage in 1456, Alvise discovered islands off Cape Verde and sailed sixty miles up the Gambia River. In the excerpt that follows, Alvise describes trade with African Muslim middlemen that included the traffic in humans for the Atlantic slave trade.

You should also know that behind this Cauo Bianco on the land, is a place called Hoden,[2] which is about six days inland by camel. This place is not walled, but is frequented by Arabs, and is a market where the caravans arrive from Tanbutu [Timbuktu], and from other places in the land of the Blacks, on their way to our nearer Barbary. The food of the peoples of this place is dates, and barley, of which there is sufficient, for they grow in some of these places, but not abundantly. They drink the milk of camels and other animals, for they have no wine. They also have cows and goats, but not many, for the land is dry. Their oxen and cows, compared with ours, are small.

Alvise da Ca' da Mosto, "Description of Capo Bianco and the Islands Nearest to It," in J. H. Parry, *European Reconnaissance: Selected Documents* (New York: Walker, 1968), 59–61.

[2] **Hoden**: Wadan, an important desert market about 350 miles east of Arguim. Later, in 1487, when the Portuguese were endeavoring to penetrate the interior they attempted to establish a trading factory at Wadan which acted as a feeder to Arguim, tapping the northbound caravan traffic and diverting some of it to the west coast.

They are Muhammadans, and very hostile to Christians. They never remain settled, but are always wandering over these deserts. These are the men who go to the land of the Blacks, and also to our nearer Barbary. They are very numerous, and have many camels on which they carry brass and silver from Barbary and other things to Tanbuto and to the land of the Blacks. Thence they carry away gold and pepper, which they bring hither. They are brown complexioned, and wear white cloaks edged with a red stripe: their women also dress thus, without shifts. On their heads the men wear turbans in the Moorish fashion, and they always go barefooted. In these sandy districts there are many lions, leopards, and ostriches, the eggs of which I have often eaten and found good.

You should know that the said Lord Infante of Portugal [the crown prince, Henry the Navigator] has leased this island of Argin to Christians [for ten years], so that no one can enter the bay to trade with the Arabs save those who hold the license. These have dwellings on the island and factories where they buy and sell with the said Arabs who come to the coast to trade for merchandise of various kinds, such as woollen cloths, cotton, silver, and "alchezeli," that is, cloaks, carpets, and similar articles and above all, corn, for they are always short of food. They give in exchange slaves whom the Arabs bring from the land of the Blacks, and gold tiber. The Lord Infante therefore caused a castle to be built on the island to protect this trade for ever. For this reason, Portuguese caravels are coming and going all the year to this island.

These Arabs also have many Berber horses, which they trade, and take to the Land of the Blacks, exchanging them with the rulers for slaves. Ten or fifteen slaves are given for one of these horses, according to their quality. The Arabs likewise take articles of Moorish silk, made in Granata and in Tunis of Barbary, silver, and other goods, obtaining in exchange any number of these slaves, and some gold. These slaves are brought to the market and town of Hoden; there they are divided: some go to the mountains of Barcha, and thence to Sicily, [others to the said town of Tunis and to all the coasts of Barbary], and others again are taken to this place, Argin, and sold to the Portuguese leaseholders. As a result every year the Portuguese carry away from Argin a thousand slaves. Note that before this traffic was organized, the Portuguese caravels, sometimes four, sometimes more, were wont to come armed to the Golfo d'Argin, and descending on the land by night, would assail the fisher villages, and so ravage the land. Thus they took of these Arabs both men and women, and carried them to Portugal for sale: behaving in a like manner along all the rest of the coast, which stretches from Cauo Bianco to the Rio di Senega and even beyond. . . .

READING AND DISCUSSION QUESTIONS

1. What evidence can you discern from this document as to why Alvise wrote it?

2. Describe the principal patterns of commerce in northern Africa.

3. Describe the groups that were involved in the various facets of the slave trade.

4. In what ways did the Portuguese change slavery and the slave trade?

DOCUMENT 15-4

MICHEL DE MONTAIGNE

From Essays: *On the Fallibility of Human Understanding*

1580

The essayist Michel de Montaigne lived in the midst of the religious civil wars that tore France apart. Although a Catholic, Montaigne supported the Protestant prince Henry of Navarre, who later became King Henry IV of France. As a statesman, Montaigne was respected by Protestants and Catholics alike. Montaigne's writings focus on skepticism, secularism (nonreligious thinking), and toleration, thus foreshadowing the Enlightenment of the eighteenth century. In the excerpt that follows, Montaigne takes on a variety of ideas and writers, from the Greek philosophers to Martin Luther.

I do not know what to say about it, but it is evident from experience that so many interpretations disperse the truth and shatter it. Aristotle wrote to be understood; if he did not succeed, still less will another man, less able, and not treating his own ideas. By diluting the substance we allow it to escape and spill it all over the place; of one subject we make a thousand, and, multiplying and subdividing, fall back into Epicurus' infinity of atoms. Never did two men judge alike about the same thing, and it is impossible to find

Michel de Montaigne, *Essays*, trans. Donald Frame (Stanford, Cal.: Stanford University Press, 1957), 817, 818–819.

two opinions exactly alike, not only in different men, but in the same man at different times. Ordinarily I find subject for doubt in what the commentary has not deigned to touch on. I am more apt to trip on flat ground, like certain horses I know which stumble more often on a smooth road.

Who would not say that glosses [interpretations, translations, annotations] increase doubts and ignorance, since there is no book to be found, whether human or divine, with which the world busies itself, whose difficulties are cleared up by interpretation? The hundredth commentator hands it on to his successor thornier and rougher than the first one had found it. When do we agree and say, "There has been enough about this book; henceforth there is nothing more to say about it"?

This is best seen in law practice. We give legal authority to numberless doctors, numberless decisions, and as many interpretations. Do we therefore find any end to the need of interpreting? Do we see any progress and advance toward tranquillity? Do we need fewer lawyers and judges than when this mass of law was still in its infancy? On the contrary, we obscure and bury the meaning; we no longer find it except hidden by so many enclosures and barriers.

Men do not know the natural infirmity of their mind: it does nothing but ferret and quest, and keeps incessantly whirling around, building up and becoming entangled in its own work, like our silkworms, and is suffocated in it. *A mouse in a pitch barrel* [Erasmus's allegory]. It thinks it notices from a distance some sort of glimmer of imaginary light and truth; but while running toward it, it is crossed by so many difficulties and obstacles, and diverted by so many new quests, that it strays from the road, bewildered. . . .

It is more of a job to interpret the interpretations than to interpret the things, and there are more books about books than about any other subject: we do nothing but write glosses about each other. The world is swarming with commentaries; of authors there is a great scarcity.

Is it not the chief and most reputed learning of our times to learn to understand the learned? Is that not the common and ultimate end of all studies?

Our opinions are grafted upon one another. The first serves as a stock for the second, the second for the third. Thus we scale the ladder, step by step. And thence it happens that he who has mounted highest has often more honor than merit; for he has only mounted one speck higher on the shoulders of the next last.

How often and perhaps how stupidly have I extended my book to make it speak for itself! Stupidly, if only for this reason, that I should have remembered what I say of others who do the same: that these frequent sheep's eyes at their own work testify that their heart thrills with love for it, and that even the rough, disdainful blows with which they beat it are only the love taps and affectations of maternal fondness; in keeping with Aristotle, to whom self-appreciation and self-depreciation often spring from the same sort of arrogance. For as for my excuse, that I ought to have more liberty in this than others, precisely because I write of myself and my writings as of my other actions, because my theme turns in upon itself — I do not know whether everyone will accept it.

I have observed in Germany that Luther has left as many divisions and altercations over the uncertainty of his opinions, and more, as he raised about the Holy Scriptures.

Our disputes are purely verbal. I ask what is "nature," "pleasure," "circle," "substitution." The question is one of words, and is answered in the same way. "A stone is a body." But if you pressed on: "And what is a body?" — "Substance." — "And what is substance?" and so on, you would finally drive the respondent to the end of his lexicon. We exchange one word for another word, often more unknown. I know better what is man than I know what is animal, or mortal, or rational. To satisfy one doubt, they give me three; it is the Hydra's head.[3]

Socrates asked Meno what virtue was. "There is," said Meno, "the virtue of a man and a woman, of a magistrate and of a private individual, of a child and of an old man." "That's fine," exclaimed Socrates; "we were in search of one virtue, and here is a whole swarm of them."

READING AND DISCUSSION QUESTIONS

1. What does Montaigne see as being inherently flawed in commentaries on difficult texts or laws?

2. How does Montaigne assess Martin Luther's writings on the Scriptures?

3. Why do you think Montaigne wrote this essay? What larger point is he trying to make?

---

[3] **Hydra's head**: In Greek mythology, a hydra was a many-headed water monster. Heracles (Hercules) killed the Lerneaen Hydra as the second of his twelve labors.

COMPARATIVE QUESTIONS

1. Compare and contrast the fall of Constantinople as portrayed by Ducas and Cortés's capture of Tenochtitlan, taking into consideration the different perspective of each account.

2. Compare and contrast the descriptions of non-European peoples by the conqueror Cortés and the explorer Alvise.

3. Based on your reading of these documents, which distinctions among peoples seem most important for Europeans of the fifteenth and sixteenth centuries?

4. Compare and contrast the account of an Italian Jew expelled from Spain (Document 13-4) to the letters by Cortés. What differences between European Christians and "others" do these two documents highlight?

CHAPTER 16

Absolutism and Constitutionalism in Western Europe

ca. 1589–1715

The fundamental political struggle in early modern Europe in the 1500–1600s was the battle for power between absolutist rulers and the institutions put in place as representative forms of government. Many factors influenced the course of these struggles, and the outcomes varied from country to country. In France, Kings Henry IV, Louis XIII, and Louis XIV gradually managed to suppress much of the opposition to their royal power. Although these absolutist monarchs lacked the power and authority to exert their will over all of their subjects — the great nobles in particular — they achieved far greater success in consolidating and extending royal authority than did their counterparts in the Netherlands or England.

DOCUMENT 16-1

HENRY IV

From Edict of Nantes: *Limited Toleration for the Huguenots*

1598

Prince Henry of Navarre (1553–1610) was a Huguenot, or Protestant, in an overwhelmingly Roman Catholic country. He ascended to the French throne as Henry IV in 1589 in the midst of the French wars of religion. A pragmatist,

---

King Henry of Navarre, "Edict of Nantes," excerpted in James Harvey Robinson, ed., *Readings in European History* (Boston: Ginn, 1904), 2:183–185.

Henry realized that the country's Catholic majority would never accept a Protestant as their legitimate ruler, so he converted to Catholicism. However, in order to protect the Huguenots against religiously motivated attacks, as well as to establish peace among the people he was determined to rule, he issued the Edict of Nantes. In so doing, Henry legally sanctioned a degree of religious tolerance in a Europe previously characterized by the formula "one king, one people, one faith."

Among the infinite benefits which it has pleased God to heap upon us, the most signal and precious is his granting us the strength and ability to withstand the fearful disorders and troubles which prevailed on our advent in this kingdom. The realm was so torn by innumerable factions and sects that the most legitimate of all the parties was fewest in numbers. God has given us strength to stand out against this storm; we have finally surmounted the waves and made our port of safety, — peace for our state. For which his be the glory all in all, and ours a free recognition of his grace in making use of our instrumentality in the good work. . . . We implore and await from the Divine Goodness the same protection and favor which he has ever granted to this kingdom from the beginning. . . .

We have, by this perpetual and irrevocable edict, established and proclaimed and do establish and proclaim:

I. First, that the recollection of everything done by one party[1] or the other between March, 1585, and our accession to the crown, and during all the preceding period of troubles, remain obliterated and forgotten, as if no such things had ever happened. . . .

III. We ordain that the Catholic Apostolic and Roman religion shall be restored and reestablished in all places and localities of this our kingdom and countries subject to our sway, where the exercise of the same has been interrupted, in order that it may be peaceably and freely exercised, without any trouble or hindrance; forbidding very expressly all persons, of whatsoever estate, quality, or condition, from troubling, molesting, or disturbing ecclesiastics in the celebration of divine service, in the enjoyment or

---

[1] **one party:** Henry's reference to "party" refers to the three factions, two of them Catholic, one of them Protestant, struggling for control of the French throne in the French Wars of Religion (1561–1598).

collection of tithes, fruits, or revenues of their benefices, and all other rights and dues belonging to them; and that all those who during the troubles have taken possession of churches, houses, goods or revenues, belonging to the said ecclesiastics, shall surrender to them entire possession and peaceable enjoyment of such rights, liberties, and sureties as they had before they were deprived of them. . . .

VI. And in order to leave no occasion for troubles or differences between our subjects, we have permitted, and herewith permit, those of the said religion called Reformed [Protestant] to live and abide in all the cities and places of this our kingdom and countries of our sway, without being annoyed, molested, or compelled to do anything in the matter of religion contrary to their consciences, . . . upon conditions that they comport themselves in other respects according to that which is contained in this our present edict.

VII. It is permitted to all lords, gentlemen, and other persons making profession of the said religion called Reformed, holding the right of high justice [or a certain feudal tenure], to exercise the said religion in their houses. . . .

IX. We also permit those of the said religion to make and continue the exercise of the same in all villages and places of our dominion where it was established by them and publicly enjoyed several and divers times in the year 1597, up to the end of the month of August, notwithstanding all decrees and judgments to the contrary. . . .

XIII. We very expressly forbid to all those of the said religion its exercise, either in respect to ministry, regulation, discipline, or the public instruction of children, or otherwise, in this our kingdom and lands of our dominion, otherwise than in the places permitted and granted by the present edict.

XIV. It is forbidden as well to perform any function of the said religion on our court or retinue, or in our lands and territories beyond the mountains, or in our city of Paris, or within five leagues of the said city. . . .

XVIII. We also forbid all our subjects, of whatever quality and condition, from carrying off by force or persuasion, against the will of their parents, the children of the said religion, in order to cause them to be baptized or confirmed in the Catholic Apostolic and Roman Church; and the same is forbidden to those of the said religion called Reformed, upon penalty of being punished with special severity. . . .

XXI. Books concerning the said religion called Reformed may not be printed and publicly sold, except in cities and places where the public exercise of the said religion is permitted.

XXII. We ordain that there shall be no difference or distinction made in respect to the said religion, in receiving pupils to be instructed in universities, colleges, and schools; or in receiving the sick and poor into hospitals, retreats and public charities.

XXIII. Those of the said religion called Reformed shall be obliged to respect the laws of the Catholic Apostolic and Roman Church, recognized in this our kingdom, for the consummation of marriages contracted, or to be contracted, as regards to the degrees of consanguinity and kinship.

READING AND DISCUSSION QUESTIONS

1. Why was Henry so intent on "obliterating" memory of "everything done by one party or the other" in the years immediately prior to his coronation as king of France?

2. Was the Edict of Nantes consistent with Henry's aim of increasing the monarchy's and the state's power? Why or why not?

3. Why might Henry's son, Louis XIII, have regarded the Huguenots as "a state within a state"?

4. Based on the details of the edict regarding ceremonies, property, literature, and education, what sorts of practices defined a religion before and during Henry's reign? What, if any practices did he consider irreligious, or purely civil?

DOCUMENT 16-2

JEAN-BAPTISTE COLBERT
The Advantages of Colonial Trade
1664

Jean-Baptiste Colbert (1619–1683) came from a family of wealthy French merchants. He first achieved political prominence during the early years of Louis XIV's reign, in the service of Cardinal Jules Mazarin, Louis's political mentor and advisor. Following Mazarin's death in 1661 until his own in 1683, Colbert served Louis XIV as both minister of finance and minister of marine and colonies. He was a staunch proponent of mercantilism, in which the government regulates economic activities in order to increase the wealth of the state. To this end, he commissioned a pamphlet from which the following excerpt is drawn, in which he tried to encourage French merchants to invest in the state's East India Company.

Now of all commerces whatsoever throughout the whole world, that of the East Indies[2] is one of the most rich and considerable. From thence it is (the sun being kinder to them, than to us) that we have our merchandise of greatest value and that which contributes the most not only to the pleasure of life but also to glory, and magnificence. From thence it is that we fetch our gold and precious stones and a thousand other commodities (both of a general esteem and a certain return) to which we are so accustomed that it is impossible for us to be without them, as silk, cinnamon, pepper, ginger, nutmegs, cotton cloth, ouate [cotton wadding], porcelain, woods for dyeing, ivory, frankincense, bezoar [poison antidote], etc. So that having an absolute necessity upon us, to make use of all these things, why we should not rather furnish ourselves, than take them from others, and apply that profit hereafter to our own countrymen, which we have hitherto allowed to strangers, I cannot understand.

Jean-Baptiste Colbert, "A Discourse . . . ," trans. R. L'Estrange (London: 1664), in Geoffrey Symcox, ed., *War, Diplomacy, and Imperialism, 1618–1763* (New York: Walker, 1974), 257–260.

[2] **East Indies**: That is to say, modern-day Malaysia and Indonesia. In Colbert's time, and for more than two centuries afterward, they were known as the Dutch East Indies and included the islands of Java, Sumatra, Borneo, and the Celebes.

Why should the Portuguese, the Hollanders [Dutch], the English, the Danes, trade daily to the East Indies possessing there, their magazines, and their forts, and the French neither the one nor the other? . . . To what end is it *in fine* that we pride ourselves to be subjects of the prime monarch of the universe, if being so, we dare not so much as show our heads in those places where our neighbors have established themselves with power? . . .

What has it been, but this very navigation and traffic that has enabled the Hollanders to bear up against the power of Spain,[3] with forces so unequal, nay, and to become terrible to them and to bring them down at last to an advantageous peace? Since that time it is that this people, who had not only the Spaniards abroad, but the very sea and earth at home to struggle with, have in spite of all opposition made themselves so considerable, that they begin now to dispute power and plenty with the greatest part of their neighbors. This observation is no more than truth, their East India Company being known to be the principal support of their state and the most sensible cause of their greatness.

READING AND DISCUSSION QUESTIONS

1. Why do you think Colbert found it so objectionable that the French depended on middlemen ("the Portuguese, the Hollanders, the English, the Danes") to provide France with the riches of India, rather than obtaining them themselves?

2. Why do you think Colbert stressed "the pleasure of life *but also to glory, and magnificence*" that Indian goods provided to France? What does his emphasis tell us about the culture of French absolutism?

3. Based on the language of his treatise, whom does Colbert seem to blame for the absence of direct French trade with the West Indies?

---

[3] **Hollanders to bear up against . . . Spain**: Owing to their financial and naval strength, part of which derived from their lucrative East India trade, the Dutch prevailed in their long struggle (1568–1648) to gain independence from Spain.

DOCUMENT 16-3

MOLIÈRE

From Le Bourgeois Gentilhomme

1671

Molière (1622–1673) was an outstanding playwright at the court of Louis XIV, and among the very greatest in French history. Unlike his contemporary Jean Racine, who wrote tragedies, Molière excelled at satirical comedies such as Tartuffe, *which played on the prejudices of his employer and mocked the foibles of humankind. In this excerpt from* Le Bourgeois Gentilhomme (The Middleclass Gentleman), *Molière ridicules the aspirations Monsieur Jourdain entertains for his daughter, at the same time depicting Madame Jourdain as a mouthpiece for a social order in which everyone "knows their place."*

M. JOURDAIN: Shut up, saucebox. You're always sticking your oar in the conversation. I have enough property for my daughter; all I need is honor; and I want to make her a marquise.[4]

MME. JOURDAIN: Marquise?

M. JOURDAIN: Yes, marquise.

MME. JOURDAIN: Alas, God forbid!

M. JOURDAIN: It's something I've made up my mind to.

MME. JOURDAIN: As for me, it's something I'll never consent to. Alliances with people above our own rank are always likely to have very unpleasant results. I don't want to have my son-in-law able to reproach my daughter for her parents, and I don't want her children to be ashamed to call me their grandma. If she should happen to come and visit me in her grand lady's carriage, and if by mistake she should fail to salute some one of the neighbors, you can imagine how they'd talk. "Take a look at that fine Madame la Marquise showing off," they'd say. "She's the daughter of Monsieur Jourdain, and when she was little, she was only too glad to play at being a fine lady. She wasn't always so high and mighty as she is now, and both her grandfathers sold dry goods besides

Molière, *Le Bourgeois Gentilhomme*, in Morris Bishop, trans., *Eight Plays by Molière* (New York: Modern Library, 1957), 372.

[4]**make her a marquise**: In other words, to marry her to a nobleman.

the Porte Saint Innocent. They both piled up money for their children, and now perhaps they're paying dear for it in the next world; you don't get so rich by being honest." Well, I don't want that kind of talk to go on; and in short, I want a man who will feel under obligation to my daughter, and I want to be able to say to him: "Sit down there, my boy, and eat dinner with us."

M. JOURDAIN: Those views reveal a mean and petty mind, that wants to remain forever in its base condition. Don't answer back to me again. My daughter will be a marquise in spite of everyone; and if you get me angry, I'll make her a duchess.

READING AND DISCUSSION QUESTIONS

1. Monsieur Jourdain states that he has property enough for his daughter's dowry. Why is he so eager to secure "honor" for her as well?

2. Why does Madame Jourdain object to her daughter marrying "above her own rank"?

3. What does Molière's satire suggest about the relative importance of wealth and social origins in determining one's status in Louis XIV's France? Does Molière seem to prefer Monsieur or Madame Jourdain's opinion?

DOCUMENT 16-4

JOHN LOCKE

From Second Treatise of Civil Government: Vindication for the Glorious Revolution

1690

John Locke (1632–1704) was, along with Thomas Hobbes, one of the two greatest English political theorists of the seventeenth century. Unlike Hobbes, however, whose Leviathan *(1651) provided a justification for monarchical absolutism, Locke's* Second Treatise of Government, *published anonymously*

John Locke, *Two Treatises of Government* (London: Awnsham Churchill, 1690).

in 1690, argued that government is an agreement between the governed, who submitted to governmental authority in return for protection of their life, liberty, and property, and the governors, whose fundamental task is provide those essential protections. According to Locke, a government that failed to do so or became tyrannical lost its claim to legitimacy, and could therefore be cast off by the governed.

87. Man being born, as has been proved, with a Title to perfect Freedom, and an uncontroled enjoyment of all the Rights and Privileges of the Law of Nature, equally with any other Man, or Number of Men in the World, hath by Nature a Power, not only to preserve his Property, that is, his Life, Liberty and Estate, against the Injuries and Attempts of other Men; but to judge of, and punish the breaches of that Law in others, as he is perswaded the Offense deserves, even with Death it self, in Crimes where the heinousness of the Fact, in his Opinion, requires it. But because no *Political Society* can be, nor subsist without having in it self the Power to preserve the Property, and in order thereunto punish the Offenses of all those of that Society; there, and there only is *Political Society*, where every one of the Members hath quitted this natural Power, resign'd it up into the hands of the Community in all cases that exclude him not from appealing for Protection to the Law established by it. And thus all private judgment of every particular Member being excluded, the Community comes to be Umpire, by settled standing Rules, indifferent, and the same to all Parties; and by Men having Authority from the Community, for the execution of those Rules, decides all the differences that may happen between any Members of that Society, concerning any matter of right; and punishes those Offences, which any Member hath committed against the Society, with such Penalties as the Law has established: Whereby it is easie to discern who are, and who are not, in *Political Society* together. Those who are united into one Body, and have a common establish'd Law and Judicature to appeal to, with Authority to decide Controversies between them, and punish Offenders, *are in Civil Society* one with another: but those who have no such common Appeal, I mean on Earth, are still in the state of Nature, each being, where there is no other, Judge for himself, and Executioner; which is, as I have before shew'd it, the perfect *state of Nature*.

88. And thus the Commonwealth comes by a Power to set down, what punishment shall belong to the several transgressions which they think worthy of it, committed amongst the Members of that Society, (which is the *power of making Laws*) as well as it has the power to punish any Injury done unto any of its Members, by any one that is not of it, (which is the

power of War and Peace;) and all this for the preservation of the property of all the Members of that Society, as far as is possible. But though every Man who has enter'd into civil Society, and is become a member of any Commonwealth, has thereby quitted his power to punish Offenses against the Law of Nature, in prosecution of his own private Judgment; yet with the Judgment of Offenses which he has given up to the Legislative in all Cases, where he can Appeal to the Magistrate, he has given a right to the Commonwealth to imploy his force, for the Execution of the Judgments of the Commonwealth, whenever he shall be called to it; which indeed are his own Judgments, they being made by himself, or his Representative. And herein we have the original of the *Legislative* and *Executive Power* of Civil Society, which is to judge by standing Laws how far Offenses are to be punished, when committed within the Commonwealth; and also to determin, by occasional Judgments founded on the present Circumstances of the Fact, how far Injuries from without are to be vindicated, and in both these to imploy all the force of all the Members when there shall be need.

89. Where-ever therefore any number of Men are so united into one Society, as to quit every one his Executive Power of the Law of Nature, and to resign it to the publick, there and there only is a *Political, or Civil Society*. And this is done where-ever any number of Men, in the state of Nature, enter into Society to make one People, one Body Politick under one Supreme Government, or else when any one joyns himself to, and incorporates with any Government already made. For hereby he authorizes the Society, or which is all one, the Legislative thereof to make Laws for him as the publick good of the Society shall require; to the Execution whereof, his own assistance (as to his own Decrees) is due. And this *puts Men* out of a State of Nature *into* that of a *Commonwealth*, by setting up a Judge on Earth, with Authority to determine all the Controversies, and redress the Injuries, that may happen to any Member of the Commonwealth; which Judge is the Legislative, or Magistrates appointed by it. And where-ever there are any number of Men, however associated, that have no such decisive power to appeal to, there they are still *in the state of Nature*.

90. Hence it is evident, that *Absolute Monarchy*, which by some Men is counted the only Government in the World, is indeed *inconsistent with Civil Society*, and so can be no Form of Civil Government at all. For the *end of Civil Society*, being to avoid, and remedy those inconveniencies of the State of Nature, which necessarily follow from every Man's being Judge in his own Case, by setting up a known Authority, to which every one of that Society may Appeal upon any injury received, or Controversie that may arise, and which every one of the Society ought to obey; where-ever

any persons are, who have not such an Authority to Appeal to, for the decision of any difference between them, there those persons are still *in the state of Nature*. And so is every *Absolute Prince* in respect of those who are under his *Dominion*.

91. For he being suppos'd to have all, both Legislative and Executive Power in himself alone, there is no Judge to be found, no Appeal lies open to any one, who may fairly, and indifferently, and with Authority decide, and from whose decision relief and redress may be expected of any Injury or Inconveniency, that may be suffered from the Prince or by his Order: So that such a Man, however intitled, *Czar*, or *Grand Signior*, or how you please, is as much *in the state of Nature* with all under his Dominion, as he is with the rest of Mankind. For where-ever any two Men are, who have no standing Rule, and common Judge to Appeal to on Earth for the determination of Controversies of Right betwixt them, there they are still *in the state of Nature*, and under all the inconveniencies of it, with only this woeful difference to the Subject, or rather Slave of an Absolute Prince: That whereas, in the ordinary State of Nature, he has a liberty to judge of his Right, and according to the best of his Power, to maintain it; now whenever his Property is invaded by the Will and Order of his Monarch, he has not only no Appeal, as those in Society ought to have, but as if he were degraded from the common state of Rational Creatures, is denied a liberty to judge of, or to defend his Right, and so is exposed to all the Misery and Inconveniencies that a Man can fear from one, who being in the unrestrained state of Nature, is yet corrupted with Flattery, and armed with Power.

92. For he that thinks *absolute Power purifies Mens Bloods*, and corrects the baseness of Humane Nature, need read but the History of this, or any other Age to be convinced of the contrary. He that would have been insolent and injurious in the Woods of *America*, would not probably be much better in a Throne; where perhaps Learning and Religion shall be found out to justifie all, that he shall do to his Subjects, and the Sword presently silence all those that dare question it. For what the *Protection of Absolute Monarchy* is, what kind of Fathers of their Countries it makes Princes to be, and to what a degree of Happiness and Security it carries Civil Society where this sort of Government is grown to perfection, he that will look into the late Relation of *Ceylon*,[5] may easily see.

---

[5] **Relation of *Ceylon***: Locke was referring to Robert Knox's *An Historical Relation of the Island Ceylon in the East Indies Together with an Account of the Detaining in Captivity the Author and Divers other Englishmen Now Living There, and of the Author's Miraculous Escape* (1681).

READING AND DISCUSSION QUESTIONS

1. What, according to Locke, distinguishes *"Political, or Civil Society"* from "a state of nature"?

2. What, in Locke's opinion, led to the creation of *"Political, or Civil Society"*?

3. Why does he argue that *"Absolute Monarchy*, which by some Men is counted the only Government in the World, is indeed *inconsistent with Civil Society*, and so can be no Form of Civil Government at all"?

4. Why do you think Locke published this work anonymously, rather than publicly claiming credit for what is now generally regarded as one of the classics of Western political theory?

COMPARATIVE QUESTIONS

1. What do you think Madame Jourdain would say to Locke's argument in the *Second Treatise of Civil Government* that all men are born "with a Title to perfect Freedom, and an uncontroled enjoyment of all the Rights and Privileges of the Law of Nature, equally with any other Man"?

2. What do the *Le Bourgeois Gentilhomme* and Colbert's argument for direct French trade with India tell us about the structure of early modern European society and the economy?

3. Given the four documents in this chapter, list a few of the techniques that writers, politicians, and citizens used to call for change in a monarchy.

CHAPTER 17

Absolutism in Central and Eastern Europe

to 1740

Although historians use the term *absolutist* to describe the governments of Prussia, Austria, Russia, and the Ottoman Empire, there were important social and political differences between the absolutism of these states and that of France. Whereas serfdom — a status closer to slavery than to freedom — had largely vanished from northwest Europe by 1600, it expanded and grew more oppressive in central and eastern Europe. Similarly, while towns grew in size and economic importance in western Europe, they declined east of the Elbe River in central Germany, due in part to the devastating wars that wracked the region. While Louis XIV could turn to the educated urban middle class to staff his bureaucracy, his Prussian, Austrian, and Russian counterparts could not; in return for uncontested power at the national level, monarchs left local power entirely in the hands of the aristocrats, who also staffed the state's bureaucracy — a "service nobility." The losers in this bargain were the voiceless serfs, who made up more than 95 percent of the population.

DOCUMENT 17-1

LUDWIG FABRITIUS

The Revolt of Stenka Razin

1670

With the rise of the Romanov family to the Russian monarchy in 1613, Russian autocracy expanded rapidly. In 1649, Tsar Alexei (r. 1645–1676)

From Anthony Glenn Cross, ed., *Russia under Western Eyes, 1517–1825* (London: Elek Books, 1971), 120–123.

enacted the Code of 1649, making millions of formerly free peasants and urban workers into serfs bound to the land and their aristocratic owners. In 1667, Stenka Razin (ca. 1630–1671), from southern Russia, led a revolt of urban laborers, peasants, and soldiers who resisted becoming serfs. Ludwig Fabritius (1648–1729), a Dutch soldier employed in the Russian army at the time, wrote an account of the revolt.

Then Stenka with his company started off upstream, rowing as far as Tsaritsyn, whence it took him only one day's journey to Panshin, a small town situated on the Don [River]. Here he began straightaway quietly collecting the common people around him, giving them money, and promises of riches if they would be loyal to him and help to exterminate the treacherous boyars.

This lasted the whole winter, until by about spring he had assembled 4,000 to 5,000 men. With these he came to Tsaritsyn and demanded the immediate surrender of the fortress; the rabble soon achieved their purpose, and although the governor tried to take refuge in a tower, he soon had to give himself up as he was deserted by one and all. Stenka immediately had the wretched governor hanged; and all the goods they found belonging to the Tsar and his officers as well as to the merchants were confiscated and distributed among the rabble.

Stenka now began once more to make preparations. Since the plains are not cultivated, the people have to bring their corn [grain] from Nizhniy-Novgorod and Kazan down the Volga in big boats known as *nasady*, and everything destined for Astrakhan has first to pass Tsaritsyn. Stenka Razin duly noted this, and occupied the whole of the Volga, so that nothing could get through to Astrahkan. Here he captured a few hundred merchants with their valuable goods, taking possession of all kinds of fine linen, silks, striped silk material, sables, soft leather, ducats, talers, and many thousands of rubles in Russian money and merchandise of every description. . . .

In the meantime four regiments of *streltsy* [sharpshooters] were dispatched from Moscow to subdue these brigands. They arrived with their big boats and as they were not used to the water, were easily beaten. Here Stenka Razin gained possession of a large amount of ammunition and artillery-pieces and everything else he required. While the above-mentioned [sharpshooters] were sent from Moscow, about 5,000 men were ordered up from Astrakhan by water and land to capture Stenka Razin. As soon as he finished with the former, he took up a good position, and being in possession of reliable information regarding our forces, he left Tsaritsyn and came to meet us half way at Chernyy Yar, confronting us before we had suspected his presence or received any information about him. We stopped at Chernyy Yar for a few days and sent out scouts by water and by land, but were unable to obtain any definite information. On 10 July [*sic*: June] a council of war was held at which it was decided to advance and seek out Stenka. The next morning, at 8 o'clock, our look-outs on the water came hurriedly and raised the alarm as the Cossacks were following at their heels. We got out of our boats and took up battle positions, General Knyaz Semen Ivanovich Lvov went through our ranks and reminded all the men to do their duty and to remember the oath they had taken to His Majesty the Tsar, to fight like honest soldiers against these irresponsible rebels, whereupon they all unanimously shouted: "Yes, we will give our lives for His Majesty the Tsar, and will fight to the last drop of our blood."

In the meantime Stenka prepared for battle and deployed on a wide front; to all those who had no rifle he gave a long pole, burnt a little at one end, and with a rag or small hook attached. They presented a strange sight on the plain from afar, and the common soldiers imagined that, since there were so many flags and standards, there must be a host of people. They [the common soldiers] held a consultation and at once decided that this was the chance for which they had been waiting so long, and with all their flags and drums they ran over to the enemy. They began kissing and embracing one another and swore with life and limb to stand together and to exterminate the treacherous boyars, to throw off the yoke of slavery, and to become free men.

The general looked at the officers and the officers at the general, and no one knew what to do; one said this, and another that, until it was finally decided that they and the general should get into the boats and withdraw to Astrakhan. But the rascally [sharpshooters] of Chernyy Yar stood on the walls and towers, turning their weapons on us and opened fire; some of them ran out of the fortress and cut us off from the boats, so that we had no means of escape. In the meantime those curs of ours who had gone over to the Cossacks came up from behind. We numbered about eighty men, officers, noblemen, and clerks. Murder at once began. Then, however, Stenka Razin ordered that no more officers were to be killed, saying that there must be a few good men among them who should be pardoned, whilst those others who had not lived in amity with their men should be condemned to well-deserved punishment by the Ataman[1] and his *Krug*. A

---

[1] **Ataman**: A Cossack political and military leader, in this case Stenka Razin himself. Atamans were usually elected by the Cossack groups they led.

Krug is a meeting convened by the order of the Ataman, at which the Cossacks stand in a circle with the standard in the center; the Ataman then takes his place beside his best officers, to whom he divulges his wishes, ordering them to make these known to the common brothers and to hear their opinion on the matter. . . .

A *Krug* was accordingly called and Stenka asked his chiefs how the general and his officers had treated the soldiers under their command. Thereupon the unscrupulous curs [sharpshooters], as well as soldiers, unanimously called out that there was not one of them who deserved to remain alive, and they all asked that their father Stepan [i.e., Stenka] Timofeyevich Razin should order them to be cut down. This was granted with the exception of General Knyaz Semem Ivanovich Lvov, whose life was specially spared by Stenka himself. The officers were now brought in order of rank out of the tower, into which they hand been thrown bound hand and foot the previous day, their ropes were cut and they were led outside the gate. When all the bloodthirsty curs had lined up, each was eager to deal his former superior the first blow, one with the sword, another with the lance, another with the scimitar, and others again with martels, so that as soon as an officer was pushed into the ring, the curs immediately killed him with their many wounds; indeed, some were cut to pieces and straightaway thrown into the Volga. My stepfather, Paul Rudolf Beem, and Lt. Col. Wundrum and many other officers, senior and junior, were cut down before my eyes.

My own time had not yet come: this I could tell by the wonderful way in which God rescued me, for as I — half-dead — now awaited the final blow, my [former] orderly, a young soldier, came and took me by my bound arms and tried to take me down the hill. As I was already half-dead, I did not move and did not know what to do, but he came back and took me by the arms and led me, bound as I was, through the throng of curs, down the hill into the boat and immediately cut my arms free, saying that I should rest in peace here and that he would be responsible for me and do his best to save my life. . . . Then my guardian angel told me not to leave the boat, and left me. He returned in the evening and brought me a piece of bread which I enjoyed since I had had nothing to eat for two days.

The following day all our possessions were looted and gathered together under the main flag, so that both our bloodthirsty curs and the Cossacks got their share.

READING AND DISCUSSION QUESTIONS

1. What is Fabritius's attitude toward Stenka and his followers? Why?
2. What do his descriptions of the soldiers suggest about why they deserted?
3. Why, on the basis of Fabritius's account, do you think Peter the Great reformed his army?
4. What does Fabritius's account suggest to you about the political structure of Razin's army?

DOCUMENT 17-2

FREDERICK II (THE GREAT) AND FREDERICK WILLIAM I
Letters Between a Son and Father
1728

Frederick William I (r. 1713–1740) and his grandfather, Frederick William the Great Elector (r. 1640–1688), were most responsible for elevating Prussia to the status of a major European power. Both men realized that Prussia's security rested almost solely on the strength of its army, and both, especially Frederick William I, devoted immense sums and energy to make the army the best, if not the largest, in Europe. Frederick William's eldest son, the future Frederick the Great (r. 1740–1788), would eventually demonstrate his military genius, but as a young man he seemed far more interested in the cultural, rather than the military, arts, greatly displeasing his notoriously difficult father.

FREDERICK, PRINCE OF PRUSSIA TO HIS FATHER, FREDERICK WILLIAM I, SEPTEMBER 11, 1728

I have not ventured for a long time to present myself before my dear papa, partly because I was advised against it, but chiefly because I anticipated an

---

James Harvey Robinson, *Readings in European History* (Lexington, Mass.: Ginn & Co., 1934).

even worse reception than usual and feared to vex my dear papa still further by the favor I have now to ask; so I have preferred to put it in writing.

I beg my dear papa that he will be kindly disposed toward me. I do assure him that after long examination of my conscience I do not find the slightest thing with which to reproach myself; but if, against my wish and will, I have vexed my dear papa, I hereby beg most humbly for forgiveness, and hope that my dear papa will give over the fearful hate which has appeared so plainly in his whole behavior and to which I cannot accustom myself. I have always thought hitherto that I had a kind father, but now I see the contrary. However, I will take courage and hope that my dear papa will think this all over and take me again into his favor. Meantime I assure him that I will never, my life long, willingly fail him, and in spite of his disfavor I am still, with most dutiful and childlike respect, my dear papa's Most obedient and faithful servant and son.
Frederick

FREDERICK WILLIAM I TO FREDERICK, PRINCE OF PRUSSIA

A bad, obstinate boy, who does not love his father, for when one does one's best, and especially when one loves one's father, one does what he wishes not only when he is standing by but when he is not there to see. Moreover you know I cannot stand an effeminate fellow who has no manly tastes, who cannot ride or shoot (to his shame be it said!), is untidy about his person, and wears his hair curled like a fool instead of cutting it; and that I have condemned all these things a thousand times, and yet there is no sign of improvement. For the rest, haughty, offish as a country lout, conversing with none but a favored few instead of being affable and popular, grimacing like a fool, and never following my wishes out of love for me but only when forced into it, caring for nothing but to have his own way, and thinking nothing else is of any importance.

This is my answer.
Frederick William

READING AND DISCUSSION QUESTIONS

1. What, according to Frederick William I, are properly masculine virtues and pursuits? What do these suggest about his personality and priorities?

2. What, if any, statements are there in Prince Frederick's letter that might indicate why his father was so mad at him? Are there any clues in Frederick William I's reply? If so, what are they?

DOCUMENT 17-3

A Song to Lost Lands: Russia's Conquest by the Mongols

ca. 1240–1300

During the period 880–1200, a Russian principality developed in what is the Ukraine, its capital at Kiev. This poem recounts the glories of that state and the might of its princes, to whom even the Eastern Roman Empire paid homage, as well as the beauty of the lands it ruled. The "great misfortune" to which the unknown author refers in the final line of this excerpt was the Mongol conquest of the Kievan state in 1240. The Mongols were a nomadic people from north-central Asia who, between 1160 and 1250 conquered a vast swath of Asia and eastern Europe, stretching from China to Poland.

O Russian land, brightest of the bright,
most beautifully adorned,
thou art marvelous to us, with thy many beauties.
Marvelous are thy numerous lakes,
thy rivers and venerated springs,
steep mountains, high hills,
oak forests, beautiful fields,
many beasts and countless birds,
great cities, wonderful villages, and monastery gardens,
honorable boyars[2] and countless lords,
Christian churches and stern princes.
Thou, Russian land, art rich in wealth

"Orison on the Downfall of Russia," in Serge A. Zenkovsky, ed., *Medieval Russia's Epics, Chronicles and Tales* (New York: 1963), 173–174.

[2] **boyars:** The greatest nobles.

Thou spreadest from Hungary to Poland and Bohemia,
from Bohemia to the land of the Yatvags,[3]
from the land of the Yatvags to the Lithuanians and Germans,
from the land of the Germans to Karelia,[4]
from Karelia to Ustiug[5]
where live the pagan Toymians,
and beyond the breathing sea,
and from the sea to the Bulgars,[6]
from the Bulgars to the Burtasians,
from the Burtasians to the Cheremiss, and
from the Cheremiss to the Mordvians.[7]
All these vast areas and the people that live on them
were subjugated by God to the Christian people (of Russia)
and to Great Prince Vsevolod[8]
and to his father, Yury,[9] Prince of Kiev,
and to his grandfather, Vladimir Monomakh,[10]
with whose name the Kumans[11] frightened their children in their cradles,
and in whose reign the Lithuanians
did not dare show themselves from their swamps,
and in whose reign the Hungarians fortified
the stone walls of their cities with their iron gates
so that great Vladimir might not pass through.
And at that time the Germans did rejoice
in being so far (from the Russians) beyond the sea.
And the Burtasians, Cheremiss, Votiaks,[12] and Mordvians

---

[3] **Yatvags**: A non-Slavic people who inhabited the Baltic region.

[4] **Karelia**: The isthmus between the Gulf of Finland and Lake Ladoga; the Karelians were Finns.

[5] **Ustiug**: A settlement in northeastern corner of the modern-day Russian province of Vologda.

[6] **Bulgars**: A nomadic people originating in central Asia, perhaps of Turkic descent. They settled in the Caucasus, and along the north shore of the Black Sea.

[7] **Burtasians . . . Cheremiss . . . Mordvians**: Finnish peoples living in eastern Russia.

[8] **Vsevolod**: Vsevolod III, r. 1176–1212.

[9] **Yury**: Yuri Dolgoruki, r. 1154–1157.

[10] **Vladimir Monomakh**: Vladimir II Monomakh, r. 1113–1125; a ruthless ruler under whom the Kievan reached its highest power.

[11] **Kumans**: A Turkic people, settled in the lower Don, Donets, and Volga river basins.

[12] **Votiaks**: Another Finnish people, who inhabited the region between the Baltic and upper Volga river basin.

worked hard to pay tribute to Vladimir the Great.
And even the Emperor of Byzantium, Manuel,
fearing lest Vladimir the Great take Constantinople,
was sending rich presents to him.
And so it used to be.
But now a great misfortune has befallen the Russian land. . . .

READING AND DISCUSSION QUESTIONS

1. If the princes of Kiev were as powerful as the poet claims, what are
    some reasons the state may have succumbed to the Mongols?

2. Who, aside from the Mongols, were the chief beneficiaries of Kiev's
    collapse, and why?

DOCUMENT 17-4

PETER THE GREAT

Edicts and Decrees: Imposing Western Styles on the Russians

1699–1723

*Peter the Great's reign (1682–1725) marked Russia's emergence as a major
European power. Russia defeated Sweden in the grueling Great Northern
War (1700–1721) and acquired a "window on Europe" at the head of the
Gulf of Finland, where Peter built a new capital, St. Petersburg. In order to
defeat the Swedes, who had routed his ill-trained army at Narva in 1700,
Peter had reformed and modernized his military along western European
lines. His enthusiasm for western technology and tactics extended also to
other realms, including education, dress, and economic programs, as can be
seen from the following excerpts.*

L. Jay Oliva, *Peter the Great* (Englewood Cliffs, NJ: Prentice-Hall, 1970).

DECREE ON THE NEW CALENDAR, 1699

It is known to His Majesty that not only many European Christian lands, but also Slavic nations which are in total accord with our Eastern Orthodox Church . . . agree to count their years from the eighth day after the birth of Christ, that is from the first day of January, and not from the creation of the world,[13] because of the many difficulties and discrepancies of this reckoning. It is now the year 1699 from the birth of Christ, and from the first of January will begin both the new year 1700 and a new century; and so His Majesty has ordered, as a good and useful measure, that from now on time will be reckoned in government offices and dates be noted on documents and property deeds, starting from the first of January 1700. And to celebrate this good undertaking and the new century . . . in the sovereign city of Moscow . . . let the reputable citizens arrange decorations of pine, fir, and juniper trees and boughs along the busiest main streets and by the houses of eminent church and lay persons of rank. . . . Poorer persons should place at least one shrub or bough on their gates or on their house. . . . Also . . . as a sign of rejoicing, wishes for the new year and century will be exchanged, and the following will be organized: when fireworks are lit and guns fired on the great Red Square, let the boyars [nobles], the Lords of the Palace, of the Chamber, and the Council, and the eminent personages of Court, Army, and Merchant ranks, each in his own grounds, fire three times from small guns, if they have any, or from muskets and other small arms, and shoot some rockets into the air.

DECREE ON THE INVITATION OF FOREIGNERS, 1702

Since our accession to the throne all our efforts and intentions have tended to govern this realm in such a way that all of our subjects should, through our care for the general good, become more and more prosperous. For this end we have always tried to maintain internal order, to defend the state against invasion, and in every possible way to improve and to extend trade. With this purpose we have been compelled to make some necessary and salutary changes in the administration, in order that our subjects might more easily gain a knowledge of matters of which they were before ignorant, and become more skillful in their commercial relations.

---

[13] **agree to count their years . . . world**: Before January 1, 1700, the Russian calendar started from the date of the creation of the world, which was reckoned at 5508 B.C.E. The year began on September 1.

We have therefore given orders, made dispositions, and founded institutions indispensable for increasing our trade with foreigners, and shall do the same in the future. Nevertheless we fear that matters are not in such a good condition as we desire, and that our subjects cannot in perfect quietness enjoy the fruits of our labors, and we have therefore considered still other means to protect our frontier from the invasion of the enemy, and to preserve the rights and privileges of our State, and the general peace of all Christians. . . .

To attain these worthy aims, we have endeavored to improve our military forces, which are the protection of our State, so that our troops may consist of well-drilled men, maintained in perfect order and discipline. In order to obtain greater improvement in this respect, and to encourage foreigners, who are able to assist us in this way, as well as artisans profitable to the State, to come in numbers to our country, we have issued this manifesto, and have ordered printed copies of it to be sent throughout Europe. . . . And as in our residence of Moscow, the free exercise of religion of all other sects, although not agreeing with our church, is already allowed, so shall this be hereby confirmed anew in such manner that we, by the power granted to us by the Almighty, shall exercise no compulsion over the consciences of men, and shall gladly allow every Christian to care for his own salvation at his own risk.

An Instruction to Russian Students Abroad Studying Navigation, 1714

1. Learn how to draw plans and charts and how to use the compass and other naval indicators.
2. Learn how to navigate a vessel in battle as well as in a simple maneuver, and learn how to use all appropriate tools and instruments; namely, sails, ropes, and oars, and the like matters, on row boats and other vessels.
3. Discover . . . how to put ships to sea during a naval battle. . . . Obtain from foreign naval officers written statements, bearing their signatures and seals, of how adequately you are prepared for naval duties.
4. If, upon his return, anyone wishes to receive from the Tsar greater favors, he should learn, in addition to the above enumerated instructions, how to construct those vessels [aboard] which he would like to demonstrate his skills.
5. Upon his return to Moscow, every foreign-trained Russian should bring with him at his own expense, for which he will later be reimbursed, at

least two experienced masters of naval science. They [the returnees] will be assigned soldiers, one soldier per returnee, to teach them what they have learned abroad. . . .

DECREE ON WESTERN DRESS, 1701

Western dress shall be worn by all the boyars, members of our councils and of our court . . . gentry of Moscow, secretaries . . . provincial gentry, gosti,[14] government officials, streltsy,[15] members of the guilds purveying for our household, citizens of Moscow of all ranks, and residents of provincial cities . . . excepting the clergy and peasant tillers of the soil. The upper dress shall be of French or Saxon cut, and the lower dress . . . — waistcoat, trousers, boots, shoes, and hats — shall be of the German type. They shall also ride German saddles. Likewise the womenfolk of all ranks, including the priests', deacons', and church attendants' wives, the wives of the dragoons, the soldiers, and the streltsy, and their children, shall wear Western dresses, hats, jackets, and underwear — undervests and petticoats — and shoes. From now on no one of the abovementioned is to wear Russian dress or Circassian[16] coats, sheepskin coats, or Russian peasant coats, trousers, boots, and shoes. It is also forbidden to ride Russian saddles, and the craftsmen shall not manufacture them or sell them at the marketplaces.

DECREE ON SHAVING, 1705

Henceforth, in accordance with this, His Majesty's decree, all court attendants . . . provincial service men, government officials of all ranks, military men, all the gosti, members of the wholesale merchants' guild, and members of the guilds purveying for our household must shave their beards and moustaches. But, if it happens that some of them do not wish to shave their beards and moustaches, let a yearly tax be collected from such persons; from court attendants. . . . Special badges shall be issued to them from the Administrator of Land Affairs of Public Order . . . which they must wear. . . . As for the peasants, let a toll of two half-copecks[17] per beard be collected at the town gates each time they enter or leave a town; and do not let the peasants pass the town gates, into or out of town, without paying this toll.

---

[14] **gosti**: Merchants who often served the tsar in some capacity.
[15] **streltsy**: Members of the imperial guard stationed in Moscow.
[16] **Circassian**: Circassia was a Russian territory between the Caspian and Black Seas.
[17] **half-copecks**: One-twentieth a ruble, the basic unit of Russian money.

Decree on Promotion to Officer's Rank, 1714

Since there are many who promote to officer rank their relatives and friends — young men who do not know the fundamentals of soldiering, not having served in the lower ranks — and since even those who serve [in the ranks] do so for a few weeks or months only, as a formality; therefore . . . let a decree be promulgated that henceforth there shall be no promotion [to officer rank] of men of noble extraction or of any others who have not first served as privates in the Guards. This decree does not apply to soldiers of lowly origin who, after long service in the ranks, have received their commissions through honest service or to those who are promoted on the basis of merit, now or in the future. . . .

Statute for the College of Manufactures,[18] 1723

His Imperial Majesty is diligently striving to establish and develop in the Russian Empire such manufacturing plants and factories as are found in other states, for the general welfare and prosperity of his subjects. He [therefore] most graciously charges the College of Manufactures to exert itself in devising the means to introduce, with the least expense, and to spread in the Russian Empire these and other ingenious arts, and especially those for which materials can be found within the empire. . . .

His Imperial Majesty gives permission to everyone, without distinction of rank or condition, to open factories wherever he may find suitable. . . .

Factory owners must be closely supervised, in order that they have at their plants good and experienced [foreign] master craftsmen, who are able to train Russians in such a way that these, in turn, may themselves become masters, so that their produce may bring glory to the Russian manufactures. . . .

By the former decrees of His Majesty commercial people were forbidden to buy villages [i.e., to own serfs], the reason being that they were not engaged in any other activity beneficial for the state save commerce; but since it is now clear to all that many of them have started to found manufacturing establishments and build plants, . . . which tend to increase the welfare of the state . . . therefore permission is granted both to the gentry and to men of commerce to acquire villages for these factories without hindrance. . . .

---

[18] **College of Manufactures**: One of several administrative boards created by Peter in 1717. Modeled on Swedish practice.

In order to stimulate voluntary immigration of various craftsmen from other countries into the Russian Empire, and to encourage them to establish factories and manufacturing plants freely and at their own expense, the College of Manufactures must send appropriate announcements to the Russian envoys accredited at foreign courts. The envoys should then, in an appropriate way, bring these announcements to the attention of men of various professions, urge them to come to settle in Russia, and help them to move.

READING AND DISCUSSION QUESTIONS

1. Why do you think Peter decreed that the nobles, merchants, and townspeople wear German, rather than French, clothes, seeing that the French kings and their palaces were objects of emulation throughout Europe?

2. What does Peter's decree encouraging foreign soldiers and artisans to emigrate to Russia and his Statute for the College of Manufactures suggest about the state of its military forces and economy as of the early 1700s?

3. Why didn't Russia have a navy prior to 1700?

4. What, according to Peter, was wrong with the system of promotion in the Russian army, and how did he intend to redress it? What does his decree on promotion suggest about the power and benefits granted to the Russian nobility?

COMPARATIVE QUESTIONS

1. In what ways were the absolutist states of eastern Europe — Russia, Austria, and Prussia — and their societies similar to France? In what ways did they differ, and how do you account for those differences?

2. What do Peter the Great's decrees about clothes and beards and Frederick William I's letter to his son suggest about their personalities and their methods of ruling?

3. In 1240, Kiev quickly succumbed to Mongol invaders; by the early eighteenth century Peter the Great was able to defeat the Swedes,

expand his empire, and bring Russia into the ranks of the great european powers. What had the Romanov rulers, especially Peter, learned from past events, and how had they reformed their state, society, and military forces?

4. According to the principles set forth in John Locke's *Second Treatise of Civil Government* (Document 16-4), was Stenka Razin's bloody revolt justified?

CHAPTER 18

Toward a New Worldview

1540–1789

L earning in the medieval period focused on studying ancient texts such as the Bible and Aristotle and then using that knowledge to draw conclusions about the world. The Polish astronomer Nicolaus Copernicus (1473–1543) was one of the first thinkers to dispute effectively archaic ideas on astronomy, spurring a centuries-long challenge to the system of scientific and mathematical thinking that had shaped the Western world since antiquity. By the eighteenth century, the spirit of scientific inquiry had spread to human affairs. Philosophers and scientists of the European "Enlightenment," particularly in France, began to question forms of social and political organization. Some thinkers rejected the legitimacy of absolutism and divine right. In the climate of the age, especially beginning in the eighteenth century, even absolutist monarchs made efforts to incorporate new political ideas, though with varying degrees of enthusiasm and success.

DOCUMENT 18-1

NICOLAUS COPERNICUS

From Commentariolus

ca. 1519

For over a thousand years Europeans widely believed that the Earth was the center of the universe, based on the work of the Greek philosopher Aristotle and his follower, Ptolemy. This aligned with Scripture and the Christian belief that humans were the center of creation. Copernicus theorized that a

---

Nicolaus Copernicus, "The Commentariolus," in Edward Rosen, *Three Copernican Treatises*, 3d ed. (New York: Octagon, 1971), 57–59.

sun-centered system made for easier, more precise calculations of planetary and stellar movement, both important for accurate calendars and oceanic navigation. Fearful of how the Catholic Church might react to his theory, Copernicus only published his work in 1542, shortly before his death and almost twenty years after writing this private letter.

Our ancestors assumed, I observe, a large number of celestial spheres for this reason especially, to explain the apparent motion of the planets by the principle of regularity. For they thought it altogether absurd that a heavenly body, which is a perfect sphere, should not always move uniformly. They saw that by connecting and combining regular motions in various ways they could make any body appear to move to any position.

Callippus and Eudoxus,[1] who endeavored to solve the problem by the use of concentric spheres, were unable to account for all the planetary movements; they had to explain not merely the apparent revolutions of the planets but also the fact that these bodies appear to us sometimes to mount higher in the heavens, sometimes to descend; and this fact is incompatible with the principle of concentricity. Therefore it seemed better to employ eccentrics and epicycles, a system which most scholars finally accepted.

Yet the planetary theories of Ptolemy and most other astronomers, although consistent with the numerical data, seemed likewise to present no small difficulty. For these theories were not adequate unless certain equants were also conceived; it then appeared that a planet moved with uniform velocity neither on its deferent nor about the center of its epicycle. Hence a system of this sort seemed neither sufficiently absolute nor sufficiently pleasing to the mind.

Having become aware of these defects, I often considered whether there could perhaps be found a more reasonable arrangement of circles, from which every apparent inequality would be derived and in which everything would move uniformly about its proper center, as the rule of absolute motion requires. After I had addressed myself to this very difficult and almost insoluble problem, the suggestion at length came to me how it could be solved with fewer and much simpler constructions than were formerly used, if some assumptions (which are called axioms) were granted me. They follow in this order.

---

[1] **Callippus and Eudoxus**: A pair of ancient astronomers; Callippus died in about 300 B.C.E., and Eudoxus, his teacher, about 350 B.C.E.

Assumptions

1. There is no one center of all the celestial circles or spheres.
2. The center of the earth is not the center of the universe, but only of gravity and of the lunar sphere.
3. All the spheres revolve about the sun as their mid-point, and therefore the sun is the center of the universe.
4. The ratio of the earth's distance from the sun to the height of the firmament[2] is so much smaller than the ratio of the earth's radius to its distance from the sun that the distance from the earth to the sun is imperceptible in comparison with the height of the firmament.
5. Whatever motion appears in the firmament arises not from any motion of the firmament, but from the earth's motion. The earth together with its circumjacent elements performs a complete rotation on its fixed poles in a daily motion, while the firmament and highest heaven abide unchanged.
6. What appear to us as motions of the sun arise not from its motion but from the motion of the earth and our sphere, with which we revolve about the sun like any other planet. The earth has, then, more than one motion.
7. The apparent retrograde and direct motion of the planets arises not from their motion but from the earth's. The motion of the earth alone, therefore, suffices to explain so many apparent inequalities in the heavens.

Having set forth these assumptions, I shall endeavor briefly to show how uniformity of the motions can be saved in a systematic way. However, I have thought it well, for the sake of brevity, to omit from this sketch mathematical demonstrations, reserving these for my larger work. But in the explanation of the circles I shall set down here the lengths of the radii; and from these the reader who is not unacquainted with mathematics will readily perceive how closely this arrangement of circles agrees with the numerical data and observations.

Accordingly, let no one suppose that I have gratuitously asserted, with the Pythagoreans,[3] the motion of the earth; strong proof will be found in

---

[2] **firmament**: The sky, specifically the eighth sphere, beyond the planetary spheres, in which the stars could be found.

[3] **Pythagoreans**: Ancient practitioners of geometry — followers of Pythagoras, for whom the Pythagorean theorem is named — who found mystical significance in numbers.

my exposition of the circles. For the principal arguments by which the natural philosophers attempt to establish the immobility of the earth rest for the most part on the appearances; it is particularly such arguments that collapse here, since I treat the earth's immobility as due to an appearance.

READING AND DISCUSSION QUESTIONS

1. What proof does Copernicus offer to support his theory about the layout of the solar system?

2. In what ways does Copernicus seek to set himself apart from the ancient astronomers he mentions, and why might this be important?

3. Based on the structure of this letter, to whom does Copernicus seem to be explaining his theory?

DOCUMENT 18-2

FRANCIS BACON
On Superstition and the Virtue of Science
1620

Trained as a lawyer, Sir Francis Bacon (1561–1626) served in the court of the English king James I (r. 1603–1625) and conducted numerous experiments designed to illuminate the natural world. Bacon argued for a new method of observation and reasoning based on drawing conclusions from specific examples rather than on theory or, worse, on superstition. Most of the scientists (known in their day as natural philosophers) of the seventeenth century were religious men as well, and Bacon was no exception.

The discoveries which have hitherto been made in the sciences are such as lie close to vulgar notions, scarcely beneath the surface. In order to penetrate

Francis Bacon, "Aphorisms Concerning the Interpretation of Nature and the Kingdom of Man," in James Spedding, *The Works of Francis Bacon*, Vol. 8 (Boston: Taggard and Thompson, 1864), 70–126.

into the inner and further recesses of nature, it is necessary that both notions and axioms [be] derived from things by a more sure and guarded way, and that a method of intellectual operation be introduced altogether better and more certain. . . .

There is no soundness in our notions, whether logical or physical. Substance, quality, action, passion, essence itself are not sound notions; much less are heavy, light, dense, rare, moist, dry, generation, corruption, attraction, repulsion, element, matter, form, and the like; but all are fantastical and ill-defined. . . .

There are and can be only two ways of searching into and discovering truth. The one flies from the senses and particulars to the most general axioms, and from these principles, the truth of which it takes for settled and immovable, proceeds to judgment and the discovery of middle axioms. And this way is now in fashion. The other derives axioms from the senses and particulars, rising by a gradual and unbroken ascent, so that it arrives at the most general axioms last of all. This is the true way, but as yet untried. . . .

It is not to be forgotten that in every age natural philosophy has had a troublesome adversary and hard to deal with — namely, superstition and the blind and immoderate zeal of religion. For we see among the Greeks that those who first proposed to man's uninitiated ears the natural causes for thunder and for storms were thereupon found guilty of impiety. Nor was much more forbearance shown by some of the ancient fathers of the Christian Church to those who, on most convincing grounds (such as no one in his senses would now think of contradicting), maintained that the earth was round and, of consequence, asserted the existence of the antipodes.[4]

Moreover, as things now are, to discourse of nature is made harder and more perilous by the summaries and systems of the schoolmen; who, having reduced theology into regular order as well as they were able, and fashioned it into the shape of an art, ended in incorporating the contentious and thorny philosophy of Aristotle, more than was fit, with the body of religion. . . .

---

[4] **maintained that the earth was round . . . antipodes**: Bacon refers to an ancient debate relating to the shape of the Earth; if the Earth was round, some Greek theorists argued, then there would be lands (or ocean) on the side of the world directly opposite the one they inhabited. The debate was largely mooted by the fifteenth-century voyages of European explorers, culminating in the 1492 discovery of the new world. The theorists were proven correct.

Lastly, some are weakly afraid lest a deeper search into nature should transgress the permitted limits of sobermindedness; wrongfully wresting and transferring what is said in Holy Writ [the Christian Bible] against those who pry into sacred mysteries to the hidden things of nature, which are barred by no prohibition. Others, with more subtlety, surmise and reflect that if secondary causes are unknown everything can be more readily referred to the divine hand and rod, — a point in which they think religion greatly concerned; which is, in fact, nothing else but to seek to gratify God with a lie. Others fear from past example that movements and changes in philosophy will end in assaults on religion; and others again appear apprehensive that in the investigation of nature something may be found to subvert, or at least shake, the authority of religion, especially with the unlearned.

But these two last fears seem to me to savor utterly of carnal wisdom; as if men in the recesses and secret thoughts of their hearts doubted and distrusted the strength of religion, and the empire of faith over the senses, and therefore feared that the investigation of truth in nature might be dangerous to them. But if the matter be truly considered, natural philosophy is, after the word of God, at once the surest medicine against superstition and the most approved nourishment for faith; and therefore she is rightly given to religion as her most faithful handmaid, since the one displays the will of God, the other his power. . . .

READING AND DISCUSSION QUESTIONS

1. If, as Bacon argues, that moving from specific observations to general truths "by a gradual and unbroken ascent" is the "true way, but as yet untried," what reasons might he have for thinking it is a better way?

2. What reasons would Bacon have for referring to settled arguments instead of ongoing ones in order to make his points?

3. What does Bacon's relationship to religion suggest about the larger relationship between science and faith in the seventeenth century?

DOCUMENT 18-3

BARON DE MONTESQUIEU

From The Spirit of Laws: On the Separation of Governmental Powers

1748

The writings of Frenchman Charles de Secondat (1689–1755), better known as Baron Montesquieu, were composed as the spirit of the Enlightenment swept over Europe in the early eighteenth century. Montesquieu's political writings, excerpted here, were concerned with the makeup of the state and the effect of a government on the choices available to those it ruled. Rather than turn to ancient writers for evidence — Aristotle had produced a similar work, the Politics *— Montesquieu culled his examples from contemporary European experience. His work was highly influential and was heavily quoted by the American revolutionaries twenty years after his death.*

In every government there are three sorts of power: the legislative; the executive in respect to things dependent on the law of nations; and the executive in regard to matters that depend on the civil law.

By virtue of the first, the prince or magistrate enacts temporary or perpetual laws, and amends or abrogates those that have been already enacted. By the second, he makes peace or war, sends or receives embassies, establishes the public security, and provides against invasions. By the third, he punishes criminals, or determines the disputes that arise between individuals. The latter we shall call the judiciary power, and the other simply the executive power of the state.

The political liberty of the subject is a tranquillity of mind arising from the opinion each person has of his safety. In order to have this liberty, it is requisite the government be so constituted as one man need not be afraid of another.

When the legislative and executive powers are united in the same person, or in the same body of magistrates, there can be no liberty; because

Baron de Montesquieu, *The Spirit of Laws,* trans. T. Nugent (New York: Hafner, 1949), 151–152.

apprehensions may arise, lest the same monarch or senate should enact tyrannical laws, to execute them in a tyrannical manner.

Again, there is no liberty, if the judiciary power be not separated from the legislative and executive. Were it joined with the legislative, the life and liberty of the subject would be exposed to arbitrary control; for the judge would be then the legislator. Were it joined to the executive power, the judge might behave with violence and oppression.

There would be an end of everything, were the same man or the same body, whether of the nobles or of the people, to exercise those three powers, that of enacting laws, that of executing the public resolutions, and of trying the causes of individuals.

Most kingdoms in Europe enjoy a moderate government because the prince who is invested with the two first powers leaves the third to his subjects. In Turkey, where these three powers are united in the Sultan's person, the subjects groan under the most dreadful oppression.

In the republics of Italy, where these three powers are united, there is less liberty than in our monarchies. Hence their government is obliged to have recourse to as violent methods for its support as even that of the Turks; witness the state inquisitors, and the lion's mouth into which every informer may at all hours throw his written accusations.

READING AND DISCUSSION QUESTIONS

1. What attitude toward representative government — as opposed to monarchy — does Montesquieu display in this excerpt? Hint: the "Italian republics" are the ones with no powerful central monarch.

2. How does Montesquieu's definition of liberty (see the third paragraph) differ from ours today? Does his understanding reflect his status as a nobleman?

3. What reasons might a French author have for discussing political organization and not citing France in his examples?

DOCUMENT 18-4

JEAN-JACQUES ROUSSEAU

From The Social Contract: *On Popular Sovereignty and the General Will*

1762

Jean-Jacques Rousseau (1712–1778) was born in Swiss Geneva — not France — and came from the common, not the aristocratic, class. As a young man, Rousseau traveled to Paris seeking to make a name for himself as a writer and theorist. These factors, combined with Rousseau's prickly personality, made him something of an outsider in Enlightenment social circles. His 1762 work on political theory, The Social Contract, *was part of an extended argument in the seventeenth and eighteenth centuries over who, if anyone, had the right to change the form of government, and from where the government derived its power.*

Since no man has any natural authority over his fellowmen, and since force is not the source of right, conventions remain as the basis of all lawful authority among men. [Book I, Chapter 4].

Now, as men cannot create any new forces, but only combine and direct those that exist, they have no other means of self-preservation than to form by aggregation a sum of forces which may overcome the resistance, to put them in action by a single motive power, and to make them work in concert.

This sum of forces can be produced only by the combination of many; but the strength and freedom of each man being the chief instruments of his preservation, how can he pledge them without injuring himself, and without neglecting the cares which he owes to himself? This difficulty, applied to my subject, may be expressed in these terms.

"To find a form of association which may defend and protect with the whole force of the community the person and property of every associate, and by means of which each, coalescing with all, may nevertheless obey only himself, and remain as free as before." Such is the fundamental problem of which the social contract furnishes the solution. . . .

Jean-Jacques Rousseau, *The Social Contract*, in *Translations and Reprints from the Original Sources of European History* (Philadelphia: University of Pennsylvania Press, 1902), 1/6:14–16.

If then we set aside what is not of the essence of the social contract, we shall find that it is reducible to the following terms: "Each of us puts in common his person and his whole power under the supreme direction of the general will, and in return we receive every member as an indivisible part of the whole." [Book I, Chapter 6].

But the body politic or sovereign, deriving its existence only from the contract, can never bind itself, even to others, in anything that derogates from the original act, such as alienation of some portion of itself, or submission to another sovereign. To violate the act by which it exists would be to annihilate itself, and what is nothing produces nothing. [Book I, Chapter 7].

It follows from what precedes, that the general will is always right and always tends to the public advantage; but it does not follow that the resolutions of the people have always the same rectitude. Men always desire their own good, but do not always discern it; the people are never corrupted, though often deceived, and it is only then that they seem to will what is evil. [Book II, Chapter 3].

The public force, then, requires a suitable agent to concentrate it and put it in action according to the directions of the general will, to serve as a means of communication between the state and the sovereign, to effect in some manner in the public person what the union of soul and body effects in a man. This is, in the State, the function of government, improperly confounded with the sovereign of which it is only the minister.

What, then, is the government? An intermediate body established between the subjects and the sovereign for their mutual correspondence, charged with the execution of the laws and with the maintenance of liberty both civil and political. [Book III, Chapter 1].

It is not sufficient that the assembled people should have once fixed the constitution of the state by giving their sanction to a body of laws; it is not sufficient that they should have established a perpetual government, or that they should have once for all provided for the election of magistrates. Besides the extraordinary assemblies which unforeseen events may require, it is necessary that there should be fixed and periodical ones which nothing can abolish or prorogue; so that, on the appointed day, the people are rightfully convoked by the law, without needing for that purpose any formal summons. [Book III, Chapter 13].

So soon as the people are lawfully assembled as a sovereign body, the whole jurisdiction of the government ceases, the executive power is suspended, and the person of the meanest citizen is as sacred and inviolable as that of the first magistrate, because where the represented are, there is no longer any representative. [Book III, Chapter 14].

These assemblies, which have as their object the maintenance of the social treaty, ought always to be opened with two propositions, which no one should be able to suppress, and which should pass separately by vote. The first: "Whether it pleases the sovereign to maintain the present form of government." The second: "Whether it pleases the people to leave the administration to those at present entrusted with it."

I presuppose here what I believe I have proved, viz., that there is in the State no fundamental law which cannot be revoked, not even this social compact; for if all the citizens assembled in order to break the compact by a solemn agreement, no one can doubt that it could be quite legitimately broken. [Book III, Chapter 18].

READING AND DISCUSSION QUESTIONS

1. What might Rousseau mean when he says "force is not the source of right"?

2. From where does Rousseau see a government deriving its legitimacy, and on what basis?

3. How does Rousseau's concept of the "general will" relate to the concept of majority rule in a representative government?

4. In what way might the concept of dissolving an unrepresentative government be a dangerous one, particularly in a world of hereditary monarchs?

DOCUMENT 18-5

CATHERINE II

Grand Instruction to the Legislative Commission

1767

Catherine II of Russia (r. 1762–1796) was not Russian by birth but was the daughter of a Prussian (German) noble who arranged her marriage to the

Catherine II, "The Grand Instruction to the Commissioners Appointed to Frame a New Code of Laws for the Russian Empire," in James Cracraft, ed., *Major Problems in the History of Imperial Russia* (Lexington, Mass.: D. C. Heath, 1994), 200–205.

future tsar of Russia in 1745. Her husband, Peter III, was weak, and, in his brief six-month reign, managed to alienate much of his nobility. In July 1762, he was overthrown and replaced with his wife. Catherine was well-educated, even corresponding with the controversial and prominent Enlightenment writers Denis Diderot and Voltaire. Although she attempted to reconcile her individual power with Enlightenment ideals, under her rule, Russia was the most autocratic state in Europe.

6. Russia is a European state.

7. This is clearly demonstrated by the following observations: the alterations which Peter the Great undertook in Russia succeeded with greater ease because the manners which prevailed at that time, and had been introduced amongst us by a mixture of different nations and the conquest of foreign territories, were quite unsuitable to the climate. Peter the First,[5] by introducing the manners and customs of Europe among the *European* people in his domains, found at that time such means [success] as even he himself did not expect. . . .

9. The Sovereign is absolute; for there is no other authority but that which centers in his single person that can act with a vigor proportionate to the extent of such a vast Dominion. . . .

13. What is the true end of Monarchy? Not to deprive people of their natural liberty but to correct their actions, in order to attain the Supreme Good. . . .

15. The intention and end of Monarchy is the glory of the Citizens, of the State, and of the Sovereign. . . .

66. All laws which aim at the extremity of rigor, may be evaded. It is moderation which rules a people, and not excess of severity.

67. Civil liberty flourishes when the laws deduce every punishment from the peculiar nature of every crime. The application of punishment ought not to proceed from the arbitrary will or mere caprice of the Legislator, but from the nature of the crime. . . .

68. Crimes are divisible into four classes: against religion, against manners [morality], against the peace, against the security of the citizens. . . .

74. I include under the first class of crimes [only] a direct and immediate attack upon religion, such as sacrilege, distinctly and clearly defined

---

[5] **Peter the First**: Peter I ruled Russia between 1682 and 1725, and is usually called "the Great" for his expansion of Russia's territory and attempts to introduce European manners.

by law. . . . In order that the punishment for the crime of sacrilege might flow from the nature of the thing, it ought to consist in depriving the offender of those benefits to which we are entitled by religion; for instance, by expulsion from the churches, exclusion from the society of the faithful for a limited time, or for ever. . . .

76. In the second class of crimes are included those which are contrary to good manners.

77. Such [include] the corruption of the purity of morals in general, either publick or private; that is, every procedure contrary to the rules which show in what manner we ought to enjoy the external conveniences given to man by Nature for his necessities, interest, and satisfaction. The punishments of these crimes ought to flow also from the nature of the thing [offense]: deprivation of those advantages which Society has attached to purity of morals, [for example], monetary penalties, shame, or dishonor . . . expulsion from the city and the community; in a word, all the punishments which at judicial discretion are sufficient to repress the presumption and disorderly behavior of both sexes. In fact, these offenses do not spring so much from badness of heart as from a certain forgetfulness or mean opinion of one's self. To this class belong only the crimes which are prejudicial to manners, and not those which at the same time violate publick security, such as carrying off by force and rape; for these are crimes of the fourth class.

78. The crimes of the third class are those which violate the peace and tranquillity of the citizens. The punishments for them ought also to flow from the very nature of the crime, as for instance, imprisonment, banishment, corrections, and the like which reclaim these turbulent people and bring them back to the established order. Crimes against the peace I confine to those things only which consist in a simple breach of the civil polity.

79. The penalties due to crimes of the fourth class are peculiarly and emphatically termed Capital Punishments. They are a kind of retaliation by which Society deprives that citizen of his security who has deprived, or would deprive, another of it. The punishment is taken from the nature of the thing, deduced from Reason, and the sources of Good and Evil. A citizen deserves death when he has violated the publick security so far as to have taken away, or attempted to take away, the life of another. Capital punishment is the remedy for a distempered society. If publick security is violated with respect to property, reasons may be produced to prove that the offender ought not

in such a case suffer capital punishment; but that it seems better and more conformable to Nature that crimes against the publick security with respect to property should be punished by deprivation of property. And this ought inevitably to have been done, if the wealth of everyone had been common, or equal. But as those who have no property are always most ready to invade the property of others, to remedy this defect corporal punishment was obliged to be substituted for pecuniary. What I have here mentioned is drawn from the nature of things, and conduces to the protection of the liberty of the citizens. . . .

348. The rules of Education are the fundamental institutes which train us up to be citizens. . . .

350. It is impossible to give a general education to a very numerous people and to bring up all the children in schools; for that reason, it will be proper to establish some general rules which may serve by way of advice to all parents.

351. Every parent is obliged to teach his children the fear of God as the beginning of all Wisdom, and to inculcate in them all those duties which God demands from us in the Ten Commandments and in the rules and traditions of our Orthodox Eastern Greek religion.[6]

352. Also to inculcate in them the love of their Country, and to ensure they pay due respect to the established civil laws, and reverence the courts of judicature in their Country as those who, by the appointment of God, watch over their happiness in this world.

353. Every parent ought to refrain in the presence of his children not only from actions but even from words that tend to injustice and violence, as for instance, quarreling, swearing, fighting, every sort of cruelty, and such like behavior; and not to allow those who are around his children to set them such bad examples. . . .

511. A Monarchy is destroyed when a Sovereign imagines that he displays his power more by changing the order of things than by adhering to it, and when he is more fond of his own imaginations than of his will, from which the laws proceed and have proceeded.

512. It is true there are cases where Power ought and can exert its full influence without any danger to the State. But there are cases also where it ought to act according to the limits prescribed by itself.

---

[6] **Orthodox Eastern Greek religion**: Russia had been converted to Christianity by missionaries from Constantinople, not Rome, and as such was part of a different religious heritage than western Europe.

513. The supreme art of governing a State consists in the precise knowledge of that degree of power, whether great or small, which ought to be exerted according to the different exigencies of affairs. For in a Monarchy the prosperity of the State depends, in part, on a mild and condescending government. . . .

522. Nothing more remains now for the Commission to do but to compare every part of the laws with the rules of this Instruction.

READING AND DISCUSSION QUESTIONS

1. Based on the document, what is the relation between state power and religious belief in Catherine's Russia?

2. In what ways does the document reflect Catherine's desire to change Russia, and what hints do you see that she might have limited success?

3. How does Catherine define her role in the Russian government?

4. Based on the included excerpts, describe Catherine's intentions with her "Grand Instruction."

COMPARATIVE QUESTIONS

1. Nicolaus Copernicus and Francis Bacon were separated by a lifetime (Copernicus died almost twenty years before Bacon was born). What similarities can you see between how they thought, and in what ways did they differ?

2. What differences do you see between Montesquieu's and Rousseau's theories about the nature of government and how it ought to interact with its citizens? Where do they seem to be in agreement?

3. When compared with Montesquieu and Rousseau, how "enlightened" was Catherine the Great? How might her desire for reform be constrained in ways that theirs were not?

4. Through all the documents in this chapter, how do you see the role of tradition changing in how Europeans justified their knowledge and how they were ruled (or ruled, in Catherine's case).

5. Where else and in what context might you have heard Montesquieu's ideas?

CHAPTER 19

The Expansion of Europe in the Eighteenth Century

I n the early modern era (ca. 1500–1800), the economic policy followed by most European states was mercantilism, a system that encouraged overseas colonization. The benefit was twofold: furnishing commodities that could not be produced in the parent country, and providing consumer markets for manufactured goods from the parent country. During the 1700s, mercantilism helped fuel a prolonged imperial conflict between France and Great Britain. The two rivals fought over North America, the Caribbean sugar islands, control of the Atlantic slave trade, and trade with India. The eventual outcome was the establishment of British rule over most of North America and much of India, as well as the involuntary transportation of millions of Africans to the Americas. By the latter half of the century, however, men like Anne-Robert Jacques Turgot and Adam Smith were criticizing the tenets of mercantilism, and opposition to the slave trade on humanitarian grounds began to emerge.

DOCUMENT 19-1

ANNE-ROBERT JACQUES TURGOT
Abolishment of the French Guilds
1774

Anne-Robert Jacques Turgot (1727–1781), a French philosopher, economist, and statesman, came from a wealthy Parisian merchant family. He was a friend of the great Enlightenment philosopher Voltaire and a contributor to the Encyclopedia. *Turgot was an early advocate of free trade and, during*

"Preamble to Turgot's Edict Abolishing Guilds," in James Harvey Robinson, ed., *Readings in European History* (Boston: Ginn, 1904), 2:389.

his two years (1774–1776) as controller-general of the French state's finances, devoted much of his energy to dismantling mercantilistic policies. He attempted without success to remove all tariffs, duties, and taxes on grain, which, ground and baked into bread, was the most important component of the poor's diet.

In almost all the towns the exercise of the different arts and trades is concentrated in the hands of a small number of masters, united in corporations,[1] who alone can, to the exclusion of all other citizens, make or sell the articles belonging to their particular industry. Any person who, by inclination or necessity, intends following an art or trade can only do so by acquiring the mastership after a probation as long and vexatious as it is superfluous. By having to satisfy repeated exactions, the money he had so much need of in order to start his trade or open his workshop has been consumed in mere waste. . . .

Citizens of all classes are deprived both of the right to choose the workmen they would employ, and of the advantages they would enjoy from competition operating toward improvements in manufacture and reduction in price. Often one cannot get the simplest work done without its having to go through the hands of several workmen of different corporations, and without enduring the delays, tricks, and exaction which the pretensions of the different corporations, and the caprices of their arbitrary and mercenary directors, demand and encourage. . . .

Among the infinite number of unreasonable regulations, we find in some corporations that all are excluded from them except the sons of masters, or those who marry the widows of masters. Others reject all those whom they call "strangers," — that is, those born in another town. In many of them for a young man to be married is enough to exclude him from the apprenticeship, and consequently from the mastership. The spirit of monopoly which has dictated the making of these statutes has been carried out to the excluding of women even from the trades the most suitable to their sex, such as embroidery, which they are forbidden to exercise on their own account. . . .

God, by giving to man wants, and making his recourse to work necessary to supply them, has made the right to work the property of every

---

[1] **corporations:** These corporations, or "guilds," were craft unions in specific trades that regulated and controlled membership, work rules, and prices.

man, and this property is the first, the most sacred, the most imprescriptible of all. . . .

It shall be free to all persons, of whatever quality or condition they may be, even to all foreigners, to undertake and to exercise in all our kingdom, and particularly in our good city of Paris, whatever kind of trade and whatever profession of art or industry may seem good to them; for which purpose we now extinguish and suppress all corporations and communities of merchants and artisans, as well as all masterships and guild directories. We abrogate all privileges, statutes, and regulations of the said corporations, so that none of our subjects shall be troubled in the exercise of his trade or profession by any cause or under any pretext whatever.

READING AND DISCUSSION QUESTIONS

1. Why did Turgot find guilds objectionable? What monopolistic practices did he accuse them of?

2. What does his observation that the guilds excluded "women even from the trades the most suitable to their sex, such as embroidery" suggest about contemporary perceptions about differences between the sexes?

3. What does Turgot's invocation of God in his next-to-final paragraph suggest about his views on religion?

DOCUMENT 19-2

CAPTAIN WILLEM BOSMAN
On the Slave Trade in Guinea
ca. 1700

African American slavery was key to the economic development of not only the southern colonies of British North America but also the sugar industry in

Willem Bosman, "A New and Accurate Description . . ." (London: 1721), in David Northrup, ed., *The Atlantic Slave Trade* (Lexington, Mass.: D. C. Heath, 1994), 72–73.

the West Indies and Brazil. Indeed, most of the slaves transported to the Americas during the period 1620–1850 went to those destinations (rather than to North America) due chiefly to the appalling mortality rate among slaves engaged in sugar production. As enslaved Africans died, more were imported to replenish the labor force. During the seventeenth century, the Dutch dominated the Atlantic slave trade. Captain Willem Bosman was sent to West Africa as a representative of the Dutch West India Company. He spent fourteen years there and published a detailed account of the trade in human beings.

Not a few in our country fondly imagine that parents here sell their children, men their wives, and one brother the other. But those who think so, do deceive themselves; for this never happens on any other account but that of necessity, or some great crime; but most of the slaves that are offered to us, are prisoners of war, which are sold by the victors as their booty.

When these slaves come to Fida,[2] they are put in prison all together; and when we treat concerning buying them, they are all brought out together in a large plain; where, by our surgeons, whose province it is, they are thoroughly examined, even to the smallest member, and that naked both men and women, without the least distinction or modesty. . . .

The invalids and the maimed being thrown out, as I have told you, the remainder are numbered, and it is entered who delivered them. In the meanwhile, a burning iron, with the arms or name of the companies, lies in the fire, with which ours are marked on the breast. This is done that we may distinguish them from the slaves of the English, French, or others (which are also marked with their mark), and to prevent the Negroes [i.e., the traders] exchanging them for worse, at which they have a good hand. I doubt not but this trade seems very barbarous to you, but since it is followed by mere necessity, it must go on; but we yet take all possible care that they are not burned too hard, especially the women, who are more tender than the men.

We are seldom long detained in the buying of these slaves, because their price is established, the women being one fourth or fifth part cheaper than the men. The disputes which we generally have with the owners of

---

[2] **Fida**: It is not clear to what place Bosman is referring; Fida is in Chad, hundreds of miles from the West African coast, where slaves were loaded onboard ships.

these slaves are, that we will not give them such goods as they ask for them, especially the *boesies* [cowry shells] (as I have told you, the money of this country) of which they are very fond, though we generally make a division on this head, in order to make one part of the goods help off another; because those slaves which are paid for in *boesies*, cost the company one half more than those bought with other goods. . . .

When we have agreed with the owners of the slaves, they are returned to their prison; where, from that time forwards, they are kept at our charge, cost us two pence a day a slave; which serves to subsist them, like our criminals, on bread and water: so that to save charges, we send them on board our ships with the very first opportunity, before which their masters strip them of all they have on their backs; so that they come to us stark naked, as well women as men: in which condition they are obliged to continue, if the master of the ship is not so charitable (which he commonly is) as to bestow something on them to cover their nakedness.

You would really wonder to see how these slaves live on board; for though their number sometimes amounts to six or seven hundred, yet by the careful management of our masters of ships, they are so [well] regulated, that it seems incredible. And in this particular our nation exceeds all other Europeans; for as the French, Portuguese, and English slave-ships are always foul and stinking; on the contrary, ours are for the most part clean and neat.

The slaves are fed three times a day with indifferent good victuals, and much better than they eat in their own country. Their lodging place is divided into two parts; one of which is appointed for the men, the other for the women, each sex being kept apart. Here they lie as close together as it is possible for them to be crowded. . . .

READING AND DISCUSSION QUESTIONS

1. What does Bosman's matter-of-fact description of his activities as a slave trader suggest about contemporary European attitudes toward slavery?

2. What most shocks you in the description of slave trading in West Africa, and why is it shocking?

3. Which of the author's statements suggest that he might have been responding to criticism of the slave trade? Where (or who) might that criticism have come from?

DOCUMENT 19-3

OLAUDAH EQUIANO

From The Interesting Narrative of
Olaudah Equiano

1789

Olaudah Equiano (ca. 1745–1797), likely born in Essaka (present-day Nigeria), was kidnapped as a child from his home, sold and resold several times in Africa, and eventually transported to Virginia by way of Barbados. Equiano was in many respects fortunate; for an extended time he was the slave of a British naval officer who took him to sea, where he learned reading, writing, and arithmetic, and became a capable sailor. He was able to purchase his freedom in 1766. A Christian convert, Equiano wrote his autobiography in large part to publicize the horrors of the trade and the plight of millions of enslaved Africans. It proved very popular and became one of the foundational texts for the abolitionist movement on both sides of the Atlantic. There is a heated scholarly debate as to whether Equiano was in fact born in Africa; some historians argue that he was North American.

One day, when all our people were gone out to their works as usual, and only I and my dear sister were left to mind the house, two men and a woman got over our walls, and in a moment seized us both, and, without giving us time to cry out, or make resistance, they stopped our mouths, and ran off with us into the nearest wood. Here they tied our hands, and continued to carry us as far as they could, till night came on, when we reached a small house, where the robbers halted for refreshment, and spent the night. We were then unbound, but were unable to take any food; and, being quite overpowered by fatigue and grief, our only relief was some sleep, which allayed our misfortune for a short time. The next morning we left the house, and continued travelling all the day. For a long time we had kept [to] the woods, but at last we came to a road which I believed I knew. I now had some hopes of being delivered; for we had advanced but a little way before I discovered some people at a distance, on which I began to cry out for their assistance; but my cries had no other effect that to make them

Olaudah Equiano, *The Interesting Narrative of Olaudah Equiano* (London, 1789).

tie me faster and stop my mouth, and then they put me in a large sack. They also stopped my sister's mouth, and tied her hands; and in this manner we proceeded till we were out of sight of these people. When we went to rest the following night, they offered us some victuals, but we refused it; and the only comfort we had was in being in one another's arms all that night, and bathing each other with our tears. But alas! we were soon deprived of even the small comfort of weeping together.

The next day proved a day of greater sorrow that I had yet experienced; for my sister and I were then separated, while we lay clasped in each other's arms. It was in vain that we besought them not to part us; she was torn from me, and immediately carried away, while I was left in a state of distraction not to be described. I cried and grieved continually; and for several days did not eat anything but what they forced into my mouth. At length, after many days' travelling, during which I had often changed masters, I got into the hands of a chieftain, in a very pleasant country. This man had two wives and some children, and they all used me extremely well, and did all they could to comfort me; particularly the first wife, who was something like my mother. Although I was a great many days' journey from my father's house, yet these people spoke exactly the same language with us. . . .

From the time I left my own nation, I always found somebody that understood me till I came to the sea coast. The languages of different nations did not totally differ, nor were they so copious as those of the Europeans,[3] particularly the English. They were therefore easily learned; and, while I was journeying thus through Africa, I acquired two or three different tongues. In this manner I had been travelling for a considerable time, when, one evening, to my great surprise, whom should I see brought to the house where I was but my dear sister! As soon as she saw me, she gave a loud shriek, and ran into my arms — I was quite overpowered; neither of us could speak, but, for a considerable time, clung to each other in mutual embraces, unable to do anything but weep. Our meeting affected all who saw us; and, indeed, I must acknowledge, in honor of those sable destroyers of human rights, that I never met with any ill treatment, or saw any offered to their slaves, except tying them, when necessary, to keep them from running away.

When these people knew we were brother and sister, they indulged us to be together; and the man, to whom I suppose we belonged, lay with us,

---

[3] **nor were they so copious . . . Europeans:** Equiano meant that they had more limited vocabularies than the European languages, especially English.

he in the middle, while she and I held one another by the hands across his breast all night; and thus for a while we forgot our misfortunes, in the joy of being together; but even this small comfort was soon to have an end; for scarcely had the fatal morning appeared when she was again torn from me forever! I was now more miserable, if possible, than before. The small relief which her presence gave me from pain, was gone, and the wretchedness of my situation was redoubled by my anxiety after her fate, and my apprehensions lest her sufferings should be greater than mine, when I could not be with her to alleviate them. . . .

I continued to travel, sometimes by land, sometimes by water, through different countries and various nations, till, at the end of six or seven months after I had been kidnapped, I arrived at the sea coast. . . .

The first object which saluted my eyes when I arrived on the coast, was the sea, and a slave ship, which was then riding at anchor, and waiting for its cargo. These filled me with astonishment, which was soon converted into terror, when I was carried on board. I was immediately handled, tossed up to see if I were sound, by some of the crew, and I was now persuaded that I had gotten into a world of bad spirits, and that they were going to kill me. Their complexions, too, differing so much from ours, their long hair, and the language they spoke (which was very different from any I had ever heard), united to confirm me in this belief. Indeed, such were the horrors of my views and fears at the moment, that, if ten thousand worlds had been my own, I would have freely parted with them all to have exchanged my condition with that of the meanest slave in my own country. When I looked round the ship too, and saw a large furnace of copper boiling, and a multitude of black people of every description chained together, every one of their countenances expressing dejection and sorrow, I no longer doubted of my fate, and, quite overpowered with horror and anguish, I fell motionless on the deck and fainted. When I recovered a little, I found some black people about me, who I believed were some of those who had brought me on board, and had been receiving their pay; they talked to me in order to cheer me, but all in vain. I asked them if we were not to be eaten by these white men with horrible looks, red faces, and long hair. They told me I was not, and one of the crew brought me a small portion of spirituous liquor in a wine glass; but being afraid of him, I would not take it out of his hand. One of the blacks therefore took it from him and gave it to me, and I took a little down my palate, which, instead of reviving me, as they thought it would, threw me into the greatest consternation at the strange feeling it produced, having never tasted any such liquor before. Soon after this, the blacks who brought me on board went off, and left me abandoned to despair. . . .

At last, when the ship we were in, had got in all her cargo, they made ready with many fearful noises, and we were all put under deck, so that we could not see how they managed the vessel. But this disappointment was the least of my sorrow. The stench of the hold while we were on the coast was so intolerably loathsome, that it was dangerous to remain there for any time, and some of us had been permitted to stay on the deck for the fresh air; but now that the whole ship's cargo was confined together, it became absolutely pestilential. The closeness of the place, and the heat of the climate, added to the number in the ship, which was so crowded that each had scarcely room to turn himself, almost suffocated us. This produced copious perspirations, so that the air soon became unfit for respiration, from a variety of loathsome smells, and brought on a sickness among the slaves, of which many died — thus falling victims to the improvident avarice, as I may call it, of their purchasers. This wretched situation was again aggravated by the galling of the chains, now became insupportable, and the filth of the necessary tubs,[4] into which the children often fell, and were almost suffocated. The shrieks of the women, and the groans of the dying, rendered the whole a scene of horror almost inconceivable. Happily, perhaps, for myself, I was soon reduced so low here that it was thought necessary to keep me almost always on deck, and from my extreme youth I was not put in fetters. In this situation I expected every hour to share the fate of my companions, some of whom were almost daily brought upon deck at the point of death, which I began to hope would soon put an end to my miseries. Often did I think of the many inhabitants of the deep much more happy than myself. I envied them [for] the freedom they enjoyed, and as often wished I could change my condition for theirs. Every circumstance I met with, served only to render my state more painful, and heightened my apprehensions, and my opinion of the cruelty of the whites.

One day they had taken a number of fishes; and when they had killed and satisfied themselves with as many as they thought fit, to our astonishment who were on deck, rather than give any of them to us to eat, as we expected, they tossed the remaining fish into the sea again, although we begged and prayed for some as well we could, but in vain. . . .

---

[4] **necessary tubs**: For urinating and defecating.

One day, when we had a smooth sea and a moderate wind, two of my wearied countrymen who were chained together (I was near them at the time), preferring death to such a life of misery, somehow made through the nettings and jumped into the sea; immediately, another quite dejected fellow, who, on account of his illness, was suffered to be out of irons, also followed their example; and I believe many more would have soon done the same, if they had not been prevented by the ship's crew, who were instantly alarmed. . . .

At last we came in sight of the island of Barbadoes, at which the whites on board gave a great shout, and made many signs of joy to us. We did not know what to think of this; but as the vessel grew nearer, we plainly saw the harbor, and other ships of different kinds and sizes, and we soon anchored among them, off Bridgetown. Many merchants and planters now came on board, though it was in the evening. They put us in separate parcels, and examined us attentively. They also made us jump, and pointed to the land, signifying we were to go there. We thought by this, we should be eaten by these ugly men, as they appeared to us; and, when soon after we were all put down under deck again, there was much dread and trembling among us, and nothing but bitter cries to be heard all the night from these apprehensions, insomuch, that at last the white people got some old slaves from the land to pacify us. They told us we were not to be eaten, but to work, and were soon to go on land, where we would see many of our country people. This report eased us much. And sure enough, soon after we were landed, there came to us Africans of all languages.

We were immediately conducted to the merchant's yard, where we were all pent up together, like so many sheep in a fold, without regard to sex or age. As every object was new to me, everything I saw filled me with surprise. What struck me first, was, that the houses were built with bricks and stories, and every other respect different from those I had seen in Africa; but I was still more astonished on seeing people on horseback.[5] I did not know what this could mean; and, indeed, I thought these people were full of nothing but magical arts. While I was in this astonishment, one of my fellow prisoners spoke to a countryman of his, about the horses, who said they were the same kind they had in their country. I understood them, though they were from a distant part of Africa; and I thought it odd I had not seen any horses there; but afterwards, when I came to converse

---

[5] **people on horseback**: Horses were unknown in much of West Africa owing to their susceptibility to sleeping sickness.

with different Africans, I found they had many horses amongst them, and much larger than those I then saw.

We were not many days in the merchant's custody, before we were sold in the usual manner, which is this: On a signal given (as the beat of a drum), the buyers rush at once into the yard where the slaves are confined, and make a choice of that parcel they like best. The noise and clamor with which this is attended, and the eagerness visible in the countenances of the buyers, serve not a little to increase the apprehension of terrified Africans, who may well be supposed to consider them as the ministers of that destruction to which they think themselves devoted. In this manner, without scruple, are relations and friends separated, most of them never to see each other again.

I remember, in the vessel in which I was brought over, in the men's apartment, there were several brothers, who, in the sale, were sold in different lots; and it was very moving on this occasion, to see and hear their cries at parting. O, ye nominal Christians! might not an African ask you — Learned you this from your God, who says unto you, Do unto all men as you would men should do unto you? Is it not enough that we are torn from our country and friends, to toil for your luxury and lust of gain? Must every tender feeling be likewise sacrificed to your avarice? Are the dearest friends and relations, now rendered more dear by their separation from their kindred, still to be parted from each other, and thus prevented from cheering the gloom of slavery, with the small comfort of being together, and mingling their sufferings and sorrows? Why are parents to lose their children, brothers their sisters, or husbands their wives? Surely, this is a new refinement in cruelty, which, while it has no advantage to atone for it, thus aggravates distress, and adds fresh horrors even to the wretchedness of slavery.

READING AND DISCUSSION QUESTIONS

1. Equiano makes a very clear distinction between the behavior of his African captors and that the crew of the slave ship on which he was transported. From whom did he receive worse treatment? What examples would you cite to contrast his treatment in Africa and while aboard the slave ship?

2. On what grounds does Equiano appeal to his white European audience to cease the horrors of the slave trade?

DOCUMENT 19-4

ADAM SMITH

From The Wealth of Nations: *A Natural Law of Economy*

1776

Adam Smith (1723–1790) is widely regarded as the father of modern economics. His most famous work, An Inquiry Into the Nature and Causes of the Wealth of Nations, *from which the following extracts are drawn, was a sustained critique of mercantilism. Smith was not the first economist to advocate free trade, but he was certainly the most famous and persuasive. At the time* The Wealth of Nations *appeared, government policies throughout Europe were still firmly mercantilistic, but over the following decades, Smith's arguments gained more adherents, especially in Britain, and his theories formed the basis for classical liberal economics.*

To take an example, therefore, from a very trifling manufacture; but one in which the division of labor has been very often taken notice of, the trade of the pin-maker; a workman not educated to this business (which the division of labor has rendered a distinct trade), nor acquainted with the use of the machinery employed in it (to the invention of which the same division of labor has probably given occasion), could scarce, perhaps, with his utmost industry, make one pin in a day, and certainly could not make twenty. But in the way in which this business is now carried on, not only the whole work is a peculiar trade, but it is divided into a number of branches, of which the greater part are likewise peculiar trades. One man draws out the wire, another straights it, a third cuts it, a fourth points it, a fifth grinds it at the top for receiving the head; to make the head requires two or three distinct operations; to put it on, is a peculiar business, to whiten the pins is another; it is even a trade by itself to put them into the paper; and the important business of making a pin is, in this manner, divided into about eighteen distinct operations, which, in some manufactories, are all performed by distinct hands, though in others the same man

Adam Smith, in Edwin Cannan, ed., *The Wealth of Nations* (New York: Modern Library, 1937), 4–5, 423, 425–426.

will sometimes perform two or three of them. I have seen a small manufactory of this kind where ten men only were employed, and where some of them consequently performed two or three distinct operations. But though they were very poor, and therefore but indifferently accommodated with the necessary machinery, they could, when they exerted themselves, make among them about twelve pounds of pins in a day. There are in a pound upwards of four thousand pins of a middling size. Those ten persons, therefore, could make among them upwards of forty-eight thousand pins in a day. Each person, therefore, making a tenth part of forty-eight thousand pins, might be considered as making four thousand eight hundred pins in a day. But if they had all wrought separately and independently, and without any of them having been educated to this peculiar business, they certainly could not each of them have made twenty, perhaps not one pin in a day; that is, certainly, not the two hundred and fortieth, perhaps not the four thousand eight hundredth part of what they are at present capable of performing, in consequence of a proper division and combination of their different operations.

In every other art and manufacture, the effects of the division of labor are similar to what they are in this very trifling one: though, in many of them, the labor can neither be so much subdivided, nor reduced to so great a simplicity of operation. The division of labor, however, so far as it can be introduced, occasions, in every art, a proportionable increase of the productive powers of labor. The separation of different trades and employments from one another, seems to have taken place, in consequence of this advantage. This separation too is generally carried furthest in those countries which enjoy the highest degree of industry and improvement; what is the work of one man in a rude state of society, being generally that of several in an improved one. . . .

. . . As every individual, therefore, endeavors as much as he can both to employ his capital in the support of domestic industry, and so to direct that industry that its produce may be of the greatest value; every individual necessarily labors to render the annual revenue of the society as great as he can. He generally, indeed, neither intends to promote the public interest, nor knows how much he is promoting it. By preferring the support of domestic to that of foreign industry, he intends only his own security; and by directing that industry in such a manner as its produce may be of the greatest value, he intends only his own gain, and he is in this, as in many other cases, led by an invisible hand to promote an end which was no part of his intention. Nor is it always the worse for the society that it was no part of it. By pursuing his own interest he frequently promotes that of the society more effectually than when he really intends to promote it. I have never known much good done by those who affected to trade for the public good. It is an affectation, indeed, not very common among merchants, and very few words need be employed in dissuading them from it. . . .

The natural advantages which one country has over another in producing particular commodities are sometimes so great, that it is acknowledged by all the world to be in vain to struggle with them. By means of glasses, hotbeds, and hotwalls, very good grapes can be raised in Scotland, and very good wine too can be made of them at about thirty times the expense for which at least equally good can be brought from foreign countries. Would it be a reasonable law to prohibit the importation of all foreign wines, merely to encourage the making of claret and burgundy in Scotland? But if there would be a manifest absurdity in turning towards any employment, thirty times more of the capital and industry of the country, than would be necessary to purchase from foreign countries an equal quantity of the commodities wanted, there must be an absurdity, though not altogether so glaring, yet exactly of the same kind, in turning towards any such employment a thirtieth, or even a three hundredth part more of either. Whether the advantages which one country has over another, be natural or acquired, is in this respect of no consequence. As long as the one country has those advantages, and the other wants them, it will always be more advantageous for the latter, rather to buy of the former than to make. It is an acquired advantage only, which one artificer has over his neighbor, who exercises another trade; and yet they both find it more advantageous to buy of one another, than to make what does not belong to their particular trades. . . .

READING AND DISCUSSION QUESTIONS

1. What did Smith mean by "the division of labor," and why was he so firmly in favor of it?

2. Smith claimed that by pursuing their own selfish interests, individuals "frequently promote that of the society more effectually than when [they] really intend to promote it." In other words, the pursuit of individual wealth can benefit the whole of society. On what does he base this argument? Is it convincing? Why or why not?

3. Mercantilism advocated national self-sufficiency in the belief that trade with rivals was a win-lose situation: one party would benefit, the other would suffer. What does the final paragraph of Smith's suggest about his take on mercantilism in this regard?

DOCUMENT 19-5

ARTHUR YOUNG

On the Expediency of Forming New Colonies
1772

While Turgot and Smith advocated the relaxation or abolition of govern-
ment and guild regulations, mercantilism remained the economic orthodoxy
in Europe throughout the eighteenth century, so the following excerpt by
Arthur Young is more representative of contemporary thought than either of
the other men's writings. Young himself was a prolific author on numerous
subjects, especially agriculture, and a fervent advocate of the improvements
described in the text as the "agricultural revolution." In the excerpt here, he
lays out his position on Britain's overseas colonies and their role in Britain's
standing as a European power.

There is a too common prejudice to be combated with upon the very
mention of such a plan as that of a new colony. It is directly said, are we
not plagued with enough colonies, not to want any more? Have we not
colonies enough? Yes, doubtless, too many bad ones; and for that reason
we should plant more good ones. If the old settlements of Britain are
grown populous out of proportion to the benefits they yield her; if her
American trade is at a stand [i.e., stagnant] rather than on the increase; if
there is in idea the least danger of her losing their allegiance; if these evils
threaten at the very time when the nation most requires (in consequence
of her immense drains of treasure, and her debts) an increase of that beneficial traffick she has for so many years enjoyed by their means; surely it
behooves her to look a little into futurity, and prepare for the worst of
events. All the evils, inconveniences, and forward conduct Britain has
experienced from her subjects in America, should never blind her so
much as to put her out of conceit with colonies in general; she has
received, and continues to receive, too much benefit from those which
were planted in a proper climate, to allow of such unjust and undistin-
guishing ideas. Every thing that she has met with of that sort came, as I

Arthur Young, *Political essays concerning the present state of the British Empire, par-*
ticularly respecting 1. Natural advantages and disadvantages . . . VI. Commerce. (London: W. Strahan and T. Cadell, 1772), 444–448.

have before attempted to prove, from those which she very unpolitically settled in an improper climate; and the greater the evils which result from such a mistake, the greater the expediency of planting new colonies to supply the deficiency of such ill-concerted old ones. For it is going back strangely, if our colonies do not increase in value when the necessities [i.e., the demand] are so greatly increased in this nation. Thus, there cannot be a fairer argument, than to answer the proposers of such plans as this, by referring to the old colonies, with such speeches as, *we now have more than we know how to manage already*. Since every thing which proves the force of that truth, proves the expediency of not relying on such unmanageable settlements [*sic*]. And I should likewise observe, that this necessity of extending our views, is in great proportion to the want of policy in Britain. If her present system is continued much longer, her trade, her riches, her navigation, and her power, will sink very low, unless some expedient of this sort is devised and executed, to supply the immense vacancy she will then experience. But let her conduct be ever so just to her old colonies, we have already found, that she can scarcely hope for fully supplying them with manufactures; and even if she did, that the time would at last come, when she must expect a period [i.e., an end] to their allegiance. I do not, however, venture to assert, that the necessity of planting new colonies would be by any means so great, if she vigorously determined to make the most of her old ones; but her present system appears so very contrary, that there can be no imputation of sketching mere impracticable ideas, in proposing the means of remedying the evils that will arise from such mistaken politics.

It should never be forgotten in all such disquisitions concerning plantations [colonies], that Britain does, and will perpetually, colonize. The question is not, whether the surplus of her population will emigrate or stay at home? — but whether they shall go to old and disadvantageous[6] settlements, or to new and beneficial ones? Since to one or the other they will certainly go, or stay in Britain to be hanged or starved.

---

[6] **old and disadvantageous**: Here Young inserted a footnote that reads "I use this term [i.e, disadvantageous] in general, because so much greater a proportion go to the northern than the southern settlements." He meant that most emigration from Britain went to the northern colonies in America, which, in contrast to the tobacco colonies of the Chesapeake Bay region or South Carolina, which exported rice and indigo, produced little of value for sale in Britain (although large quantities of foodstuffs to feed the slaves in Britain's West Indian sugar colonies). Nor were they a large market for British manufactures.

The prodigious consequence to Great Britain of all tropical productions, and the small, or rather no share she possesses of the European consumption, might alone prove to her the expediency of planting new colonies, which would supply her own consumption, and enable her to acquire a share in that of foreigners. . . . It has already been proposed, to increase the productions of the British sugar islands; but it does not follow, that a proposition of settling new colonies to cultivate even the same articles, is therefore useless. The Dutch raise much sugar in Surinam, and might raise much more; but that has not prevented them from forming a vast many sugar works in Java, even for European consumption. Their India ships of late years scarce come home without sugar being a part of their cargo. The French raise coffee in the West Indies to a vast amount; but has that hindered them from greatly extending the culture of it in the isles? It is a weak objection to say, that colonies rival one another by such means; which cannot disadvantageously be the case, except in very cheap staples: but the tropical productions [principally coffee and sugar] are all dear. Britain, in respect of tropical vegetables, can rival none but foreigners; for she has no exportation of them, but, on the contrary, a vast importation in sugar itself. New colonies could not rival the old ones by selling that commodity cheaper; and if they were able to do that, it sufficiently proves the benefit of them. Our own consumption would be served on easier terms, and we should have some chance of an exportation. But while Britain has such an enemy as France, so periodically (I may almost say) to contend with, it will be very far from bad politics to have tropical colonies in other parts of the world besides the West Indies, where the French are confessedly so much stronger[7] than she is.

Nor should we forget the vast difference between planting colonies at a time when every circumstance relating to them is perfectly understood, and in an age before experience could have given that knowledge. We at present see the immense difference between colonies in northern climates and southern ones. Our extended commerce and increase of luxury point out the commodities which colonies ought to yield. Will you plant a tract of lands which produces wheat, barley, oats, and wool, or one which yields spices, sugar, and wine? This knowledge, I say, is, or might be very common at present. And yet, in the name of common sense, must not that very

---

[7] **the French are . . . stronger**: Here Young's footnote reads, "The events of the last war prove nothing against this assertion. Britain's superiority was that of her fleet; — but the islands of the two nations left to themselves, — which would then have fell?"

question have been asked in the year 1750? We then possessed the Bahama Islands, and Nova Scotia, — both uncultivated; — the expence of the one already fixed in having a civil establishment [i.e., a colonial government]; — that of the other to form; — the one extremely fertile in the tropical productions, the other scarcely yielding the necessaries of life, but peculiarly situated for rivaling us in our Newfoundland fishery. If any person was ignorant of the fact, would it be possible for him to conceive that we chose the latter?

It would be difficult in any person to prove, that the settling [of] new colonies which produce sugar, coffee, spices, tea, &c. &c. would be of any detriment to Great Britain. Sugar is the only tropical production of which we raise enough to supply even our own consumption. Our importation of all others from foreigners is immense; by which means the balance of many trades is against us, to the great loss of the nation, — and to the considerable increase of foreign navigation [i.e., trade] and naval power. What an infinite difference there is between emigrations to our old northern colonies, which produce nothing but rivalry, — and to new ones, which yield those commodities that we at present purchase with our specie of [i.e., from] foreigners?

But there are other colonies besides those of *planting*, which it is in the power of Britain to form, and which are of immense consequence to any trading and manufacturing nation. They consist in the possession of coasts of populous islands, inhabited by the people generally denominated, wherever they are found, *Indians*. The Dutch possess most of the coasts of several of the largest islands in the world, such as Borneo, which is three times as large as Great Britain, Java, and others, which are inhabited by very numerous nations. The consequences of the command of such coasts are immense. A monopoly is gained of all the rich products the inhabitants can produce, which are purchased at very reasonable rates with European manufactures [i.e., goods]; the consumption of which is taught and extended among them by an hundred means. Nor are Indians in hot countries (the only ones whose production we want[8]) ever able to make any head against the force and arms of Europeans.

It is not at present suitable to inquire, whether the complaints of the British manufacturers of a decay in their business, is true or not; — but we may suppose them somewhat well founded, from the mere general view of the increasing industry of other nations: that we are undersold in many

---

[8] **the only ones . . . want**: Young seems to have forgotten or ignored the lucrative trade in furs from Canada and Hudson's Bay.

articles of consequence, appeared clearly enough when I inquired into the state of our manufactures. Now, as our old markets fall off, is it not necessary to gain new ones? Must not our people decrease, if we do not? And where but in colonies are such markets to be found? Our old settlements, it is true, yet take off large quantities; but in proportion to the increasing benefits of the southern ones, we lose by the increasing rivalship of the northern: So that upon the whole the exportation has been some years at a stand[still]; and I have already attempted to prove, that there is the greatest reason to fear a very considerable decrease, according to the present system of British conduct. In such a situation, can anything be more expedient that to endeavour to open new markets for our manufactures, where we need not fear either the rivalship of the settlers, or that of foreigners? Markets in which the purchasers can and will pay those prices which will never be gained in Europe.

Such a market, at the distance of a thousand leagues, is much more advantageous than an European one. A large portion of those commodities which Europe takes of us is carried from this island in foreign ships, by which means we lose the freight, the building, fitting out, victualling [i.e., provisioning], &c. of the shipping, and that valuable article, the employment and maintenance of the seamen: All these we fully enjoy in the case of our commodities transported in our own bottoms [i.e., ships]; and consequently such an exportation is infinitely more valuable than any other. Add to this, that such colonies as I have sketched can only be formed at a vast distance from Britain, and of course all those articles I just mentioned would be tenfold greater than in an exportation to any part of Europe. There is no comparison in the national benefits resulting from a voyage of a ship of five hundred tons to Chinas, or to Portugal, for instance: These benefits increase in direct proportion to the length of the voyage.

I have frequently reflected upon the execution of these ideas, and imagined the objections which would most probably be made to them, but none that ever struck me were of the least real weight. I have already considered that extremely weak one, of our having more old colonies than we know what to do with, and shewn that one of the principal motives for engaging in these undertakings results from that very fact. Those who plume themselves upon a regard to public economy, may object the expence, but in all such cases that is the weakest of all please: If the execution would be attended with great advantage, it deserves the expence, and any person of the most ordinary capacity may, by throwing a careless eye over the parliamentary grants, discover that it is the principle of the British government to expend the public money for those purposes which advance

the public good. I shall draw no invidious comparisons between such ex-
pences as these, and some to which the nation is very well reconciled.

Other[s] object, that we have trade, commerce, manufactures, and
riches enough, and that excess of wealth will be our ruin; that the public
is excessively poor, but individuals immensely rich; the very contrary of
which ought to be the case. I must allow that I have known such arguments advanced with a wit and liveliness that has pleased, but very far from
having convinced me. For supposing the facts, viz. public poverty, and private wealth, what have they to do in reference to each other? Will any one
be so [fool]hardy as to assert, that the wealth of individuals causes the
poverty of the public[?] From whence come those riches which the public
really enjoys? From whence comes the ability of the public to be so very
poor? Surely from private wealth. Public riches are but another name for
the product of taxes. Upon what are taxes laid? Upon private consumption; that is, upon private wealth. There is only one tax in Britain that is
not laid upon consumption, and that is, the land-tax, which is but a fifth of
the whole. So that this plea, that we have trade enough and too much
riches among individual, is a very idle one, and nothing but the mere sport
of imagination. While we are a trading and a naval power, and burdened
with vast debts, trade, navigation, and riches, are essential to our being:
and those riches should flow from the pockets of individuals, or they will
never come to the coffers of the public. — It would be disgracing the
understanding of the reader to go through all the commonplace rubbish
that is usually urged in answer to such propositions as these. I know but
few arguments against them that are founded even in a *shew* of reason,
much less any that are built upon reason itself.

All naval enterprises, particularly those which relate to the settlement
of new colonies, however adventurous and daring, are of high importance
to such a maritime power as Britain. It is inconceivable what vigor,
alacrity, and spirit, is exerted by private adventurers, who fail in quest of
new countries, and a new means of growing rich. This country, above all
others, should hold such adventures in the highest repute, since the foundation of all the power and consequence she enjoys was laid in the noble
spirit of adventure of the last two centuries. Thanks to those gallant, brave,
and daring private adventurers, for all the colonies at present in the possession of Britain, and all that advantageous commerce carried on [there]
by their means. I am very far, however, from insinuating, that such new colonies as are at present wanted by Britain should be left to take the chance
of private discovery and settlement; and for two very material reasons:
first, they would never be undertaken at all; this age being totally deficient

in that noble spirit which actuated the Columbuses, the Magellans, the Gamas, the Drakes, and the Cavendishes, of the last age: and, *secondly*, temporary reasons might occasion the settling of improper tracts and countries, which would require the same trouble and expence as the best in the world. A nobleman of very great fortune, and the spirit of the last age, indeed would be a very proper person to undertake and direct such expeditions, under the supposition that the instructions which he gave his people were such as promised public as well as private benefits, and that in relation to only one point, viz. the fixing in hot climates alone. But the countenance and support of the government would in all cases be necessary.

READING AND DISCUSSION QUESTIONS

1. What does Young's essay suggest about the demand for sugar in Britain and the rest of Europe?

2. Young condemned Britain's government for "want of policy" toward its colonies, and warns that "[i]f her present system is continued much longer, her trade, her riches, her navigation, and her power, will sink very low"? What examples does Young provide that suggest this might happen, or is already occurring?

3. Among the products Britain "harvested" from "hot climates" were slaves. Why might Young have refrained from listing them along with "sugar, coffee, spices, tea, &c."?

4. Young was writing on the eve of the American Revolution and appears to have foreseen the possible loss of the thirteen colonies. On the basis of his statements, how do you think he would he have felt about the loss of the northern colonies (New England, New York, Pennsylvania, and Delaware), and why? How about the southern colonies (Georgia, the Carolinas, Virginia, and Maryland)? Why?

COMPARATIVE QUESTIONS

1. What do you think Adam Smith would say about "the spirit of monopoly" of which Turgot complains?

2. How might Adam Smith reply to Equaino's plea for the abolition of the slave trade?

3. How does Turgot's definition of "property" differ from that of John Locke, as expressed in the *Second Treatise of Civil Government* (Document 16–4)?

4. What might Smith say about Young's advocacy of acquiring new colonies? Would he approve or disapprove, and on what grounds?

5. What differences do you see in Bosman's and Equiano's reports of the slave trade, and how do you account for them? Might the time at which each was written have anything to do with the authors' attitudes toward the trade? Explain.

CHAPTER 20

The Changing Life of the People

W hile there are abundant sources about modern life, from letters and diaries to financial records and opinion polls (to mention only a few), other periods are markedly less recorded. For the social historian, the task of understanding how the "ordinary people" of early modern Europe lived — to say nothing of what they thought — is quite challenging. Most of the nonelite in the seventeenth and eighteenth centuries were illiterate and thus left no self-composed evidence of their existence. Historians studying the period have to rely on the limited writings left by common people or try to interpret their lives through the lens of the better-off classes. This, in effect, may distort the reality of the everyman's daily existence. The documents in this chapter contain a sampling of both elite and nonelite sources.

DOCUMENT 20-1

EDMOND WILLIAMSON
Births and Deaths in an English Gentry Family
1709–1720

Little is known of Edmond Williamson. He lived in Bedfordshire, one of the "Home Counties" surrounding London. The mere fact that he was literate and kept a diary suggests that he was a man of means, as does his mention of the servants present at his wife's childbirths. Despite their brevity, his

---

Edmond Williamson, "An Account of the Birth of My Children by My Second Wife (1709–1720)," in Walter Arnstein, ed., *The Past Speaks*, 2d ed. (Lexington, Mass.: D. C. Heath, 1993), 2:33–34.

diary entries reveal that proximity of death was a central fact of life, even in the lives of the affluent. Three of Williamson's seven children died at birth or shortly afterward, and a fourth succumbed to smallpox before the age of three. Williamson's wife died as well, just a month after the birth of her last child.

1709

March 29. My wife fell into labor and a little after 9 in the morning was delivered of a son. Present: aunt Taylor, cousin White, sister Smith, cousin Clarkson, widow Hern, Mrs. Howe, midwife, Mr[s]. Wallis, nurse, Mrs. Holms, Eleanor Hobbs, servants.

April 4. He was baptised by Doctor Battle by the name of John. . . .

[April] 16. The child died about 1 o'clock in the morning.

1711

Sept. 17. My said wife was delivered of a son just before 4 in the morning. Present: Mrs. Thomas Molyneux's lady and maid, Mrs. Mann, midwife, Margaret Williamson, nurse, Susan Nuthall, servant.

Oct. 4. He was baptised by Mr. Trabeck by the name of Talbot after my grandmother's name. Sir John Talbot and John Pulteny esquire were gossips [godfathers], with my sister Smith godmother. . . .

1713

June 9. About 8 at night my said wife began her labor.

[June] 10. Half an hour after 1 in the morning was brought to bed of a son. Present: Mrs. Molyneux, Mrs. Bisset, Mrs. Mann, midwife, Nurse Williamson, Susan Nuthall and Betty Ginger, servants.

[June] 30. Baptised by Mr. Mompesson of Mansfield by the name of Edmond. . . .

1715

March 7. My said wife was brought to bed of a daughter 10 minutes before 6 in the morning. Present: Mrs. Molyneux, Mrs. Mann, midwife, Nurse Williamson, Mary Evans, Mary Cole and Mary Wheeler, servants.

[March] 29. Was baptised by Dr. Mandivel, chancellor of Lincoln, by the name of Christian.

1716

March 9. My wife was delivered of a daughter at 7 at night. Present: aunt Taylor, Mrs. Molyneux, Mrs. Oliver, Mrs. Mann, midwife, Mary Smith, nurse, Jane Kensey, and Mary Wheeler, servants.

[March] 31. Was baptised by Mr. Widmore, the reader of St. Margaret's, by the name of Elizanna. . . . Registered in St. Margaret's, Westminster, as all the rest were.

April 27. Died, was buried in the new chapel yard in the Broadway.

1718

Jan. 21. [Mrs. Williamson:] I was brought to bed of a son about 2 in the morning, Mrs. Mann, midwife, nurse Chatty, dry-nurse, present; Mrs. Taylor, Mrs. White and Mrs. Molyneux, Jane Beadle; servants: Mary Wells, Jane Griffith, Edmond Kinward. He was baptised by Mr. Widmore, reader of St. Margaret's, Westminster, by the name of Francis. . . .

1719

Feb. 21. [Mrs. Williamson:] I was brought to bed of a son between 6 and 7 in the evening, Mrs. Mann, midwife, nurse Chatty, dry-nurse; present: aunt Taylor, Mrs. Molyneux and Jane Beadle; servants: Rebecca Shippy, Betty Hall and Mathew Dowect.

March 7. He was baptised by Mr. Widmore, reader of St. Margaret's, Westminster, by the name of William. . . .

[Undated] Died and buried at Hadley.

1720

June. My wife brought to bed of a daughter, but the child did not live a minute.

July 21. My wife died and was buried at Isleworth.

Sept. 9. [Francis] died of the smallpox at Nurse Ward's.

READING AND DISCUSSION QUESTIONS

1. What does the Williamsons' account of the births of their children suggest about pregnancy in early eighteenth century England? What factors would account for this?

2. What does Williamson's record of the deaths of his children suggest about the incidence of infant mortality in early modern Europe?

3. Apart from labor, births, and deaths, what else did Williamson record, and what does this tell us?

4. In what ways did the ritual of childbirth in early-eighteenth-century England differ from that in modern developed countries? What could account for the differences?

DOCUMENT 20-2

JOHN LOCKE

Some Thoughts Concerning Education

1693

John Locke's (1632–1704) intellectual curiosity and influence ranged wide, from political theory to the nature of human consciousness, from economics to, in this piece, education. Originally composed as a series of letters to a friend who had sought Locke's advice concerning his son's education, "Some Thoughts" constitutes a companion piece to his "Essay Concerning Human Understanding" (1690), in which he argued that the mind at birth was a "blank slate" upon which ideas were imprinted, and that all knowledge was derived from sensory experience and reasoning. These concepts were at the core of Enlightenment beliefs in human rationality and progress.

The well educating of their children is so much the duty and concern of parents, and the welfare and prosperity of the nation so much depends on it, that I would have every one lay it seriously to heart; and after having well examined and distinguished what fancy, custom, or reason advises in the case, set his helping hand to promote every where that way of training up youth, with regard to their several conditions, which is the easiest, shortest, and likeliest to produce virtuous, useful, and able men in their distinct callings; tho' that most to be taken care of is the gentleman's calling. For if

---

From *English Philosophers of the Seventeenth and Eighteenth Centuries* (New York: P. F. Collier & Son, 1910).

those of that rank are by their education once set right, they will quickly bring all the rest into order. . . .

A sound mind in a sound body, is a short, but full description of a happy state in this world. He that has these two, has little more to wish for; and he that wants either of them, will be but little the better for any thing else. Men's happiness or misery is most part of their own making. He, whose mind directs not wisely, will never take the right way; and he, whose body is crazy and feeble, will never be able to advance in it. I confess, there are some men's constitutions of body and mind so vigorous, and well framed by nature, that they need not much assistance from others; but by the strength of their natural genius, they are from their cradles carried towards what is excellent; and by the privilege of their happy constitutions, are able to do wonders. But examples of this kind are but few; and I think I may say, that of all the men we meet with, nine parts of ten are what they are, good or evil, useful or not, by their education. 'Tis that which makes the great difference in mankind. The little, or almost insensible impressions on our tender infancies, have very important and lasting consequences: and there 'tis, as in the fountains of some rivers, where a gentle application of the hand turns the flexible waters in channels, that make them take quite contrary courses; and by this direction given them at first in the source, they receive different tendencies, and arrive at last at very remote and distant places. . . .

I have said he here [as opposed to "she" or "they"], because the principal aim of my discourse is, how a young gentleman should be brought up from his infancy, which in all things will not so perfectly suit the education of daughters; though where the difference of sex requires different treatment, 'twill be no hard matter to distinguish. . . .

[*Locke provides extensive advice on healthy eating and drinking habits for children.*]

As the strength of the body lies chiefly in being able to endure hardships, so also does that of the mind. And the great principle and foundation of all virtue and worth is placed in this: that a man is able to deny himself his own desires, cross his own inclinations, and purely follow what reason directs as best, tho' the appetite lean the other way.

The great mistake I have observed in people's breeding their children, has been, that this has not been taken care enough of in its due season: that the mind has not been made obedient to discipline, and pliant to reason, when at first it was most tender, most easy to be bowed. Parents being wisely ordained by nature to love their children, are very apt, if reason watch not that natural affection very warily, are apt, I say, to let it run into fondness. They love their little ones and it is their duty; but they often, with them, cherish their faults too. . . .

It seems plain to me, that the principle of all virtue and excellency lies in a power of denying ourselves the satisfaction of our own desires, where reason does not authorize them. This power is to be got and improved by custom, made easy and familiar by an early practice. If therefore I might be heard, I would advise, that, contrary to the ordinary way, children should be used to submit their desires, and go without their longings, even from their very cradles. The first thing they should learn to know, should be, that they were not to have anything because it pleased them, but because it was thought fit for them. If things suitable to their wants were supplied to them, so that they were never suffered to have what they once cried for, they would learn to be content without it, would never, with bawling and peevishness, contend for mastery, nor be half so uneasy to themselves and others as they are, because from the first beginning they are not thus handled. If they were never suffered to obtain their desire by the impatience they expressed for it, they would no more cry for another thing, than they do for the moon.

Those therefore that intend ever to govern their children, should begin it whilst they are very little, and look that they perfectly comply with the will of their parents. Would you have your son obedient to you when past a child; be sure then to establish the authority of a father as soon as he is capable of submission, and can understand in whose power he is. If you would have him stand in awe of you, imprint it in his infancy; and as he approaches more to a man, admit him nearer to your familiarity; so shall you have him your obedient subject (as is fit) whilst he is a child, and your affectionate friend when he is a man. For methinks they mightily misplace the treatment due to their children, who are indulgent and familiar when they are little, but severe to them, and keep them at a distance, when they are grown up: for liberty and indulgence can do no good to children; their want of judgment makes them stand in need of restraint and discipline; and on the contrary, imperiousness and severity is but an ill way of treating men, who have reason of their own to guide them; unless you have a mind to make your children, when grown up, weary of you, and secretly to say within themselves, When will you die, father? . . .

This being laid down in general, as the course that ought to be taken, 'tis fit we now come to consider the parts of the discipline to be used, a little more particularly. I have spoken so much of carrying a strict hand over children, that perhaps I shall be suspected of not considering enough, what is due to their tender age and constitutions. But that opinion will vanish, when you have heard me a little farther: for I am very apt to think, that great severity of punishment does but very little good, nay, great harm in education; and I believe it will be found that . . . those children who have been most chastised, seldom make the best men. All that I have hitherto contended for, is, that whatsoever rigor is necessary, it is more to be used, the younger children are; and having by a due application wrought its effect, it is to be relaxed, and changed into a milder sort of government. . . .

Beating them, and all other sorts of slavish and corporal punishments, are not the discipline fit to be used in the education of those we would have wise, good, and ingenuous men; and therefore very rarely to be applied, and that only in great occasions, and cases of extremity. On the other side, to flatter children by rewards of things that are pleasant to them, is as carefully to be avoided. He that will give to his son apples or sugar-plumbs, or what else of this kind he is most delighted with, to make him learn his book, does but authorize his love of pleasure, and cocker up that dangerous propensity, which he ought by all means to subdue and stifle in him. . . .

[Locke warns against the bad influence of servants upon children.]

Having named company, I am almost ready to throw away my pen, and trouble you no farther on this subject: for since that does more than all precepts, rules, and instructions, methinks 'tis almost wholly in vain to make a long discourse of other things, and to talk of that almost to no purpose. For you will be ready to say, what shall I do with my son? If I keep him always at home, he will be in danger to be my young master; and if I send him abroad, how is it possible to keep him from the contagion of rudeness and vice, which is every where so in fashion? In my house he will perhaps be more innocent, but more ignorant too of the world; wanting there change of company, and being used constantly to the same faces, he will, when he comes abroad, be a sheepish or conceited creature.

I confess both sides have their inconveniences. Being abroad, 'tis true, will make him bolder, and better able to bustle and shift among boys of his own age; and the emulation of school-fellows often puts life and industry into young lads. But still you can find a school, wherein it is possible for the master to look after the manners of his scholars, and can shew as great effects of his care of forming their minds to virtue, and their carriage to good breeding, as of forming their tongues to the learned languages. . . .

Virtue is harder to be got than a knowledge of the world; and if lost in a young man, is seldom recovered. Sheepishness and ignorance of the world, the faults imputed to a private education, are neither the necessary consequences of being bred at home, nor if they were, are they incurable evils. Vice is the more stubborn, as well as the more dangerous evil of the two; and therefore in the first place to be fenced against. If that sheepish softness which often enervates those who are bred like fondlings [fools] at home, be carefully to be avoided, it is principally so for virtue's sake; for fear lest such a yielding temper should be too susceptible of vicious impressions, and expose the novice too easily to be corrupted. A young man before he leaves the shelter of his father's house, and the guard of a tutor, should be fortified with resolution, and made acquainted with men, to secure his virtues, lest he should be led into some ruinous course, or fatal precipice, before he is sufficiently acquainted with the dangers of conversation, and has steadiness enough not to yield to every temptation. Were it not for this, a young man's bashfulness and ignorance in the world, would not so much need an early care. Conversation would cure it in a great measure; or if that will not do it early enough, it is only a stronger reason for a good tutor at home. For if pains be to be taken to give him a manly air and assurance betimes, it is chiefly as a fence to his virtue when he goes into the world under his own conduct. . . .

[Locke urges parents to choose tutors for their children discriminately, as children learn by example.]

Curiosity in children . . . ought to be encouraged in them, not only as a good sign, but as the great instrument nature has provided to remove that ignorance they were born with; and which, without this busy inquisitiveness, will make them dull and useless creatures. . . .

That which every gentleman . . . desires for his son, besides the estate he leaves him, is contained . . . in these four things, virtue, wisdom, breeding, and learning. . . .

I place virtue as the first and most necessary of those endowments that belong to a man or a gentleman; as absolutely requisite to make him valued and beloved by others, acceptable or tolerable to himself. Without that, I think, he will be happy neither in this nor the other world.

You will wonder, perhaps, that I put learning last, especially if I tell you I think it the least part. This may seem strange in the mouth of a bookish man; and this making usually the chief, if not only bustle and stir about children, this being almost that alone which is thought on, when people talk of education, makes it the greater paradox. When I consider, what ado is made about a little Latin and Greek, how many years are spent in it, and what a noise and business it makes to no purpose, I can hardly forbear thinking that the parents of children still live in fear of the school-master's rod, which they look on as the only instrument of education; as a language or two to be its whole business. How else is it possible that a child should be chained to the oar seven, eight, or ten of the best years of his life, to get a language or two, which, I think, might be had at a great deal cheaper rate of pains and time, and be learned almost in playing? . . .

Reading and writing and learning I allow to be necessary, but yet not the chief business. I imagine you would think him a very foolish fellow, that should not value a virtuous or a wise man infinitely before a great scholar. . . .

To conclude this part . . . , his tutor should remember, that his business is not so much to teach him all that is knowable, as to raise in him a love and esteem of knowledge; and to put him in the right way of knowing and improving himself when he has a mind to it.

Teach him to get a mastery over his inclinations, and submit his appetite to reason. This being obtained, and by constant practice settled into habit, the hardest part of the task is over. To bring a young man to this, I know nothing which so much contributes as the love of praise and commendation, which should therefore be instilled into him by all arts imaginable. Make his mind as sensible of credit and shame as may be; and when you have done that, you have put a principle into him, which will influence his actions when you are not by, to which the fear of a little smart of a rod is not comparable, and which will be the proper stock whereon afterwards to graff the true principles of morality and religion.

READING AND DISCUSSION QUESTIONS

1. Why does Locke advocate beginning a child's education at the earliest possible age?

2. What is Locke's opinion on the education of young women? What in the letter suggests his beliefs on sexual difference and gender roles?

3. What are Locke's views about the need for disciplining children and the nature of discipline to be used?

DOCUMENT 20-3

MARY WORTLEY MONTAGU

On Smallpox Inoculations

ca. 1717

Mary Wortley Montagu (1689–1762) was the daughter of an English aristocrat and married a member of the landed gentry. An unusually well-educated woman, Montagu was the sole female contributor to Joseph Addison's renowned political journal The Spectator. *She narrowly survived the often fatal smallpox disease in 1715. In 1716, while accompanying her diplomat husband in Constantinople, Montagu witnessed the common procedure of smallpox inoculation. She subsequently had both of her children inoculated, and, upon returning to England, championed the procedure despite strong anti-"Oriental" sentiment against it. The following letter was written to a close friend, but its substance was made public in the 1720s.*

A propos of distempers, I am going to tell you a thing, that will make you wish yourself here. The small-pox, so fatal, and so general amongst us, is here entirely harmless, by the invention of engrafting, which is the term they give it. There is a set of old women, who make it their business to perform the operation, every autumn, in the month of September, when the great heat is abated. People send to one another to know if any of their family has a mind to have the small-pox; they make parties for this purpose, and when they are met (commonly fifteen or sixteen together) the old woman comes with a nut-shell full of the matter of the best sort of small-pox, and asks what vein you please to have opened. She immediately rips open that you offer to her, with a large needle (which gives you no more pain than a common scratch) and puts into the vein as much matter as can lie upon the head of her needle, and after that, binds up the little wound with a hollow bit of shell, and in this manner opens four or five veins. The Grecians have commonly the superstition of opening one in the middle of the forehead, one in each arm, and one on the breast, to mark the sign of the Cross; but this has a very ill effect, all these wounds leaving little scars, and is not done by those that are not superstitious, who chuse to have them in the legs, or that part of the arm that is concealed. The children or young patients play together all the rest of the day, and are in perfect health to the eighth [day]. Then the fever begins to seize them, and they keep their beds two days, very seldom three. They have very rarely above twenty or thirty [pockmarks] in their faces, which never mark [i.e., leave scars] and in eight days time they are as well as before their illness. Where they are wounded [i.e., where pock marks appear], there remains running sores during the distemper, which I don't doubt is a great relief to it. Every year, thousands undergo this operation, and the French Ambassador says pleasantly, that they take the small-pox here by way of diversion, as they take the waters[1] in other countries. There is no example of any one that has died in it, and you may believe I am well satisfied of the safety of this experiment, since I intend to try it on my dear little son. I am patriot enough to take the pains to bring this useful invention into fashion in England, and I should not fail to write to some of our doctors very particularly about it, if I knew any one of them that I thought had virtue enough to destroy such a considerable branch of their revenue, for the good of mankind. But that distemper is too beneficial to them, not to expose to all their resentment, the hardy weight that should undertake to put an end to it. Perhaps if I live to return, I may, however, have courage to war with them. Upon this occasion, admire the heroism in the heart of

Your friend, etc. etc.

READING AND DISCUSSION QUESTIONS

1. What does Montagu's observation "I am patriot enough to take the pains to bring this useful invention into fashion in England" suggest about her sense of nationalism?

2. What does her subsequent comment that "I should not fail to write to some of our doctors very particularly about it, if I knew any one of them that I thought had virtue enough to destroy such a considerable branch of their revenue, for the good of mankind," suggest about her attitude toward the medical profession?

---

[1] **take the waters**: Upper-class men and women across Europe routinely visited spas with mineral waters or hot springs, like Bath in England, to "take the waters." Such trips combined medicinal and recreational motives.

3. What does Montagu's letter suggest about upper-class women's education and empowerment in early modern English society? Do you think she was representative of all women? Of all upper-class women? Why or why not?

4. What are some of the likely reasons English doctors dismissed the smallpox inoculation that was so successful abroad?

DOCUMENT 20-4

JOHN WESLEY

From A Plain Account of the People Called Methodists: *The Ground Rules for Methodism*

1749

John Wesley (1703–1791), the son of an Anglican clergyman, was himself trained to the ministry. He found little solace in the Anglicanism of his youth, however, and endured years of spiritual yearning until, in 1738, he had a religious awakening. His resulting theological message was quite simple: salvation was possible for all. The appeal of Wesley's message, coupled with his tireless preaching, often to huge crowds outdoors, quickly brought him a large following. These followers became known as "Methodists," after a Bible study group Wesley attended while at Oxford University.

THE NATURE, DESIGN, AND GENERAL RULES OF THE UNITED SOCIETIES

1. About ten years ago my brother [Charles Wesley] and I were desired to preach in many parts of London. We had no view therein but, so far as we were able (and we knew God could work by whomsoever it pleased Him) to convince those who would hear, what true Christianity was, and to persuade them to embrace it.

John Wesley, "A Plain Account of the People Called Methodists" (1749), in Walter Arnstein, ed., *The Past Speaks*, 2d ed. (Lexington, Mass.: D. C. Heath, 1993), 2:87–89.

2. The points we chiefly insisted upon were four: First, that orthodoxy or right opinions is, at best, but a very slender part of religion, if it can be allowed to be any part of it at all; that neither does religion consist in negatives, in bare harmlessness of any kind, nor merely in externals in doing good or using the means of grace, in works of piety (so called) or of charity: that it is nothing short of or different from the mind that was in Christ, the image of God stamped upon the heart, inward righteousness attended with the peace of God and joy in the Holy Ghost.

    Secondly, that the only way under heaven to this religion is to repent and believe the gospel, of (as the apostle words it) repentance toward God and faith in our Lord Jesus Christ.

    Thirdly, that by this faith, he that worketh not, but believeth in Him that justifieth the ungodly, is justified freely by His grace, through the redemption which is in Jesus Christ.

    And lastly, that being justified by faith we taste of the heaven to which we are going; we are holy and happy; we tread down sin and fear, and sit in heavenly places with Christ Jesus.

3. Many of those who heard this, began to cry out, that we brought strange things to their ears: that this was doctrine which they never heard before, or, at least, never regarded. They searched the scriptures, whether these things were so, and acknowledged the truth as it is in Jesus. Their hearts also were influenced as well as their understandings, and they determined to follow Jesus Christ and Him crucified.

4. Immediately [those who accepted this new way] were surrounded with difficulties. All the world rose up against them; neighbors, strangers, acquaintances, relations, friends began to cry out amain, "Be not righteous overmuch: why shouldst thou destroy thyself? Let not much religion make thee mad." . . .

Directions Given to the Band Societies

You are supposed to have the faith that "overcometh the world." To you, therefore, it is not grievous:

I. Carefully to abstain from doing evil; in particular:
    1. Neither to buy nor sell anything at all on the Lord's day.
    2. To taste no spiritous liquor, no dram of any kind, unless prescribed by a physician.
    3. To be at a word [i.e., to be honest] both in buying and selling.
    4. To pawn nothing, no, not to save life.

5. Not to mention the fault of any behind his back, and to stop those short that do.

6. To wear no needless ornaments, such as rings, earrings, necklaces, lace, ruffles.

7. To use no needless self-indulgence, such as taking snuff or tobacco, unless prescribed by a physician.

II. Zealously to maintain good works; in particular:

1. To give alms of such things as you possess, and that to the uttermost of your power.

2. To reprove all that sin in your sight, and that in love and meekness of wisdom.

3. To be patterns of diligence and frugality, of self-denial, and taking up the cross daily.

III. Constantly to attend on all the ordinances of God; in particular:

1. To be at church and at the Lord's table every week, and at every public meeting of the bands.

2. To attend the ministry of the word every morning unless distance, business or sickness prevent.

3. To use private prayer every day; and family prayer, if you are at the head of a family.

4. To read the scriptures, and meditate therein, at every vacant hour. And

5. To observe, as days of fasting or abstinence, all Fridays in the year. . . .

READING AND DISCUSSION QUESTIONS

1. What, according to Wesley, is the *only* means of obtaining salvation? What is the true nature of religion?

2. Wesley admits that soon after Methodism's establishment, "the world rose up against them . . . to cry out amain, 'Be not righteous overmuch: why shouldst thou destroy thyself? Let not much religion make thee mad.'" Why do you think Methodists were so vehemently criticized?

3. Wesley maintains in his second paragraph, that "orthodoxy or right opinions is, at best, but a very slender part of religion . . . ; that neither does religion consist in negatives, in bare harmlessness of any kind, nor merely in externals in doing good or using the means of grace, in works of piety (so called) or of charity." Why, then, does he proceed to

put forward his own "right opinions" through a set of rules that consist in large part of "negatives" (what Methodists should *not* do), and things that they should do, most of which could be described as "works of piety or of charity"?

4. Critics of Methodism have argued that it was a barely disguised tool of social control, promulgated by both traditional landed elites and the growing British urban middle class as a means of keeping the rapidly expanding urban working class obedient and subdued despite appalling living and working conditions in early industrial cities. Why do you think this charge has been made? Is it persuasive? Why or why not?

COMPARATIVE QUESTIONS

1. What does the familiarity with inoculation in the Ottoman Empire and European civilization's relative ignorance of the procedure suggest about the state of medical knowledge in the Muslim and Christian worlds?

2. What can be gleaned from Williamson's and Wesley's accounts about the prevalence and nature of religious belief in eighteenth-century England?

3. What do Williamson's and Montagu's accounts suggest about the state and extent of medical knowledge in eighteenth-century Europe?

4. What can be gleaned from Williamson's, Locke's, and Montagu's accounts about attitudes toward children in the late seventeenth and eighteenth centuries?

CHAPTER 21

The Revolution in Politics

1775–1815

B y the late eighteenth century, the industrious yet often impoverished citizens who brought wealth to their nations began to voice their displeasure over the economic conditions and political structures in western Europe. In France, Louis XV (r. 1715–1774) had inherited Louis XIV's imperial ambitions, and spent much of the century unsuccessfully battling Britain for a world empire, finally bankrupting the state. In 1789, Louis XVI (r. 1774–1792) was unable to resolve the issues that confronted him, and gave in to noble pressure to summon the Estates General, the French representative body that had last met in 1614. The Estates General failed to meet its citizens' needs. The French Revolution (1789–1815) that followed had an enormous impact on the debate over rights, liberty, and equality that had long-term, global reverberations. While the Revolution itself was initially quite conservative, women and enslaved peoples seized the moment to articulate their conceptions of universal rights.

DOCUMENT 21-1

COMMISSIONERS OF THE THIRD ESTATE

OF THE CARCASSONNE

From Cahier de Doleances

1789

Assuming the throne in 1774, Louis XVI inherited a bankrupt government that spent half its income just to pay the interest on the national debt. The Cahiers de Doleances (Notebooks of Grievances) *were an attempt to dis-*

Commissioners of Carcassonne, in James Harvey Robinson, ed., *Readings in European History* (Boston: Ginn, 1904), 2:397–399.

cover and catalog the issues the king would need to resolve at the meeting
of the Estates General in order to get approval for new taxes. Long denied
any formal avenue of complaint, the Third Estate — everyone not nobility
or clergy — responded with a flood of complaints and suggestions that sur-
prised Louis and his advisors. While phrased in respectful language, the
Cahiers *illuminate a society at odds with the absolutism of Louis XVI's*
predecessors.

The third estate of the electoral district of Carcassonne,[1] desiring to give to
a beloved monarch, and one so worthy of our affection, the most unmis-
takable proof of its love and respect, of its gratitude and fidelity, desiring to
cooperate with the whole nation in repairing the successive misfortunes
which have overwhelmed it, and with the hope of reviving once more its
ancient glory, declares that the happiness of the nation must, in their opinion, depend upon that of its king, upon the stability of the monarchy, and
upon the preservation of the orders which compose it and of the fundamental laws which govern it.

Considering, too, that a holy respect for religion, morality, civil liberty,
and the rights of property, a speedy return to true principles, a careful
selection and due measure in the matter of the taxes, a strict proportional-
ity in their assessment, a persistent economy in government expenditures,
and indispensable reforms in all branches of the administration, are the
best and perhaps the only means of perpetuating the existence of the
monarchy;

The third estate of the electoral district of Carcassonne very humbly
petitions his Majesty to take into consideration these several matters,
weigh them in his wisdom, and permit his people to enjoy, as soon as may
be, fresh proofs of that benevolence which he has never ceased to exhibit
toward them and which is dictated by his affection for them.

In view of the obligation imposed by his Majesty's command that the
third estate of this district should confide to his paternal ear the causes of
the ills which afflict them and the means by which they may be remedied
or moderated, they believe that they are fulfilling the duties of faithful subjects and zealous citizens in submitting to the consideration of the nation,
and to the sentiments of justice and affection which his Majesty entertains
for his subjects, the following:

---

[1] **Carcassonne:** A town in southern France, near the Mediterranean coast.

1. Public worship should be confined to the Roman Catholic apostolic religion,[2] to the exclusion of all other forms of worship; its extension should be promoted and the most efficient measures taken to reestablish the discipline of the Church and increase its prestige.

2. Nevertheless the civil rights of those of the king's subjects who are not Catholics should be confirmed, and they should be admitted to positions and offices in the public administration, without however extending this privilege — which reason and humanity alike demand for them — to judicial or police functions or to those of public instruction.

3. The nation should consider some means of abolishing the annates[3] and all other dues paid to the holy see, to the prejudice and against the protests of the whole French people. . . .

[The holding of multiple church positions should be prohibited, monasteries reduced in numbers, and holidays suppressed or decreased.]

7. The rights which have just been restored to the nation should be consecrated as fundamental principles of the monarchy, and their perpetual and unalterable enjoyment should be assured by a solemn law, which should so define the rights both of the monarch and of the people that their violation shall hereafter be impossible.

8. Among these rights the following should be especially noted: the nation should hereafter be subject only to such laws and taxes as it shall itself freely ratify.

9. The meetings of the Estates General of the kingdom should be fixed for definite periods, and the subsidies judged necessary for the support of the state and the public service should be voted for no longer a period than to the close of the year in which the next meeting of the Estates General is to occur.

10. In order to assure to the third estate the influence to which it is entitled in view of the number of its members, the amount of its contributions to the public treasury, and the manifold interests which it has

---

[2] **apostolic religion**: "Apostolic" meant that the leaders of the Roman Catholic church claimed to have received their authority in succession from one of the original twelve Christian apostles, specifically Peter. Of the Protestant churches, only the Church of England could claim apostolic succession.

[3] **annates**: Refers to the practice of claiming the first year's profits from a church district, or see, for the bishop who oversaw that district.

to defend or promote in the national assemblies, its votes in the assembly should be taken and counted by head.

11. No order, corporation, or individual citizen may lay claim to any pecuniary exemptions. . . . All taxes should be assessed on the same system throughout the nation.

12. The due exacted from commoners holding fiefs[4] should be abolished, and also the general or particular regulations which exclude members of the third estate from certain positions, offices, and ranks which have hitherto been bestowed on nobles either for life or hereditarily. A law should be passed declaring members of the third estate qualified to fill all such offices for which they are judged to be personally fitted.

13. Since individual liberty is intimately associated with national liberty, his Majesty is hereby petitioned not to permit that it be hereafter interfered with by arbitrary orders for imprisonment. . . .

14. Freedom should be granted also to the press, which should however be subjected, by means of strict regulations, to the principles of religion, morality, and public decency. . . .

60. The third estate of the district of Carcassonne places its trust, for the rest, in the zeal, patriotism, honor, and probity of its deputies in the National Assembly in all matters which may accord with the beneficent views of his Majesty, the welfare of the kingdom, the union of the three estates, and the public peace.

READING AND DISCUSSION QUESTIONS

1. What implications would this document have for a system of government based on absolute royal authority?

2. What position do the commissioners take toward the relationship of government and religion?

3. What economic reforms does the *Cahier* propose, and how might those affect the social structure of France?

---

[4] **fiefs**: Medieval gifts of land in return for military service. With the rise of professional armies, many fiefholders were expected to make cash payments instead.

DOCUMENT 21-2

EDWARD RIGBY

On the Taking of the Bastille and Its Aftermath

1789

The Bastille was the French royal prison, a massive structure in the heart of Paris that served as a physical reminder of the monarchy's power. On the 14th of July, 1789, as the National Assembly debated at Versailles, the citizens of Paris seized arms and cannons from a retired soldier's home and forced their way into the Bastille. The fall of the Bastille became the symbolic turning point of the Revolution, still celebrated every year in France. Edward Rigby, an English physician, was traveling through France at the time and wrote this account.

July 14. A Canadian Frenchman, whom we found in the crowd and who spoke good English, was the first who intimated to us that it had been resolved to attack the Bastille. We smiled at the gentleman, and suggested the improbability of undisciplined citizens taking a citadel which had held out against the most experienced troops in Europe; little thinking it would be actually in the hands of the people before night. From the commencement of the struggle on Sunday evening there had been scarcely any time in which the firing of guns had not been heard in all quarters of the city, and, as this was principally produced by exercising the citizens in the use of the musket, in trying cannon, etc., it excited, except at first, but little alarm. Another sound equally incessant was produced by the ringing of bells to call together the inhabitants in different parts of the city. These joint sounds being constantly iterated, the additional noise produced by the attack on the Bastille was so little distinguished that I doubt not it had begun a considerable time, and even been completed, before it was known to many thousands of the inhabitants as well as to ourselves.

We ran to the end of the Rue St. Honore.[5] We here soon perceived an immense crowd proceeding towards the Palais Royal with acceleration of

Edward Rigby, in J. M. Thompson, ed., *English Witnesses of the French Revolution* (Oxford: Basil Blackwell, 1938), 55–60.

[5] **Rue St. Honore**: A street in central Paris, near the royal palace.

an extraordinary kind, but which sufficiently indicated a joyful event, and, as it approached we saw a flag, some large keys, and a paper elevated on a pole above the crowd, in which was inscribed "La Bastille est prise et les portes sont ouvertes." ["The Bastille is taken and the gates are open."] The intelligence of this extraordinary event thus communicated, produced an impression upon the crowd really indescribable. A sudden burst of the most frantic joy instantaneously took place; every possible mode in which the most rapturous feelings of joy could be expressed, were everywhere exhibited. Shouts and shrieks, leaping and embracing, laughter and tears, every sound and every gesture, including even what approached to nervous and hysterical affection, manifested, among the promiscuous crowd, such an instantaneous and unanimous emotion of extreme gladness as I should suppose was never before experienced by human beings. . . .

The crowd passed on to the Palais Royal, and in a few minutes another succeeded. Its approach was also announced by loud and triumphant acclamations, but, as it came nearer, we soon perceived a different character, as though bearing additional testimony to the fact reported by the first crowd, the impression by it on the people was of a very different kind. A deep and hollow murmur at once pervaded them, their countenances expressing amazement mingled with alarm. We could not at first explain these circumstances; but as we pressed more to the center of the crowd we suddenly partook of the general sensation, for we then, and not till then, perceived two bloody heads raised on pikes, which were said to be the heads of the Marquis de Launay, Governor of the Bastille, and of Monsieur Flesselles, Prevot des Marchands.[6] It was a chilling and a horrid sight! An idea of savageness and ferocity was impressed on the spectators, and instantly checked those emotions of joy which had before prevailed. Many others, as well as ourselves, shocked and disgusted at this scene, retired immediately from the streets. . . .

The night approached; the crowd without continued agitated. Reports of a meditated attack upon the city that night by a formidable army under the command of the Count d'Artois and the Marechal Broglie[7] were in circulation, and gained such credit as to induce the inhabitants to take

---

[6] **Prevot des Marchands**: Literally the Provost of Merchants, the holder of this title was effectively the mayor of Paris.

[7] **Count d'Artois . . . Marechal Broglie**: The Comte (Count) d'Artois was the brother of Louis XVI, and later ruled France as Charles X between 1824 and 1830. Marechal (Marshal, a rank above general) Broglie was a distinguished French soldier who opposed the Revolution and commanded a foreign army trying to suppress it in 1792.

measures for opposing them. Trees were cut down and thrown across the principal approaches to the city; the streets were impaved, and the stones carried to the tops of houses which fronted the streets through which the troops might pass (for the fate of Pyrrhus[8] was not unknown to the French) and the windows in most parts of the city were illuminated. The night passed with various indications of alarm; guns were firing continually; the tocsin sounded unceasingly; groups of agitated citizens passed hastily along, and parties of the Milice Bourgeoise [citizens' militia] (for such was the name already assumed by those who had taken arms the day before) paraded the streets. . . .

I went (July 15) and was led by the sound of an approaching crowd towards the end of the Rue St. Honore, and there I witnessed a most affecting spectacle. The Bastille had been scarcely entered and the opposition subdued, when an eager search began to find out and liberate every unhappy captive immured within its walls. Two wretched victims of the detestable tyranny of the old Government had just been discovered and taken from some of the most obscure dungeons of this horrid castle, and were at this time conducted by the crowd to the Palais Royal. One of these was a little feeble old man, I could not learn his history; he exhibited an appearance of childishness and fatuity; he tottered as he walked, and his countenance exhibited little more than the smile of an idiot. . . . The other was a tall and rather robust old man; his countenance and whole figure interesting in the highest degree; he walked upright, with a firm and steady gait; his hands were folded and turned upwards, he looked but little at the crowd; the character of his face seemed a mixture of surprise and alarm, for he knew not whither they were leading him, he knew not what fate awaited him; his face was directed towards the sky, but his eyes were but little open. . . . He had a remarkably high forehead, which, with the crown of his head, was completely bald; but he had a very long beard, and on the back of his head the hair was unusually abundant. . . . His dress was an old greasy reddish tunic; the color and the form of the garb were probably some indication of what his rank had been; for we afterwards learned that he was a Count d'Auche, that he had been a major of cavalry, and a young man of some talent, and that the offense for which he had sustained this long imprisonment had been his having written a pamphlet against the

---

[8] **Pyrrhus**: Pyrrhus was the ancient king of Epirus who defeated the Romans in a series of battles in 280 and 279 B.C.E., losing so many men in the process that he had to give up his hopes of conquest. It is from Pyrrhus that we get the term "Pyrrhic victory."

Jesuits.[9] Every one who witnessed this scene probably felt as I did, an emotion which partook of horror and detestation of the Government which could so obdurately as well as unjustly expose human beings to such sufferings; and of pity for the miserable individuals before us. . . .

It had been reported that the King was to come to Paris on the Thursday (July 16), and great crowds filled the streets through which it was expected he would pass: but his coming did not take place till the Friday (July 17). We were very desirous of witnessing the spectacle of the monarch thus, I might almost say, led captive. The spectacle was very interesting, though not from the artificial circumstances which have usually given distinction to royal processions. The impression made on the spectator was not the effect of any adventitious splendor of costly robes or glittering ornaments — the appearance of the King was simple, if not humble; the man was no longer concealed in the dazzling radiance of the sovereign. . . . The streets were lined with the armed bourgeois, three deep — forming a line, as we were assured, of several miles extent. The procession began to pass the place where we were at a quarter past three. The first who appeared were the city officers and the police guards; some women followed them, carrying green branches of trees which were fancifully decorated; then more officers; then the Prevot des Marchands[10] and different members of the city magistracy. Many of the armed bourgeois followed on horseback; then some of the King's officers, some on horseback and some on foot; then followed the whole body of the Etats Generaux [Estates General] on foot, the noblesse, clergy, and Tiers-Etats [Third Estate], each in their peculiar dresses. That of the noblesse was very beautiful; they wore a peculiar kind of hat with large white feathers, and many of them were tall, elegant young men. The clergy, especially the bishops and some of the higher orders, were most superbly dressed; many of them in lawn dresses, with pink scarfs and massive crosses of gold hanging before them. The dress of the Tiers-Etats was very ordinary, even worse than that of the

---

[9] **the Jesuits**: A militant Catholic order, the Society of Jesus was founded in the wake of the Protestant Reformation and dedicated to the spread of Catholicism. In officially Catholic France, denouncing them would have been a political offense, though it is likely that Rigby and the crowd were mistaken about either the reason for the count's imprisonment or the fact that he was a prisoner in the Bastille at all. No political prisoners were liberated when the Bastille fell, only five common criminals and two madmen.

[10] **the Prevot des Marchands**: Possibly the successor of the man whose head was last seen on a pike

inferior order of gownsmen at the English universities. More of the King's officers followed; then the King in a large plain coach with eight horses. After this more bourgeois; then another coach and eight horses with other officers of state; than an immense number of the bourgeois, there having been, it was said, two hundred thousand of them in arms. The countenance of the King was little marked with sensibility, and his general appearance by no means indicated alarm. He was accustomed to throw his head very much back on his shoulders, which, by obliging him to look upwards, gave a kind of stupid character to his countenance by increasing the apparent breadth of his face, by preventing that variation of expression which is produced by looking about. He received neither marks of applause nor insult from the populace, unless their silence could be construed into a negative sort of disrespect. Nor were any insults shown to the noblesse or clergy, except in the instance of the Archbishop of Paris, a very tall thin man. He was very much hissed, the popular clamor having been excited against him by a story circulated of his having encouraged the King to use strong measures against the people, and of his attempting to make an impression on the people by a superstitious exposure of a crucifix. He looked a good deal agitated, and whether he had a leaden eye or not I know not, but it certainly loved the ground. The warm and enthusiastic applause of the people was reserved for the Tiers-Etat. . . . Vivent les Tiers-Etats! Vive la Liberte! ["Long live the Third Estate! Long live liberty!] were loudly iterated as they passed. . . .

On the Saturday (July 18) we visited more of the public places, but the most interesting object, and which attracted the greatest number of spectators, was the Bastille. We found two hundred workmen busily employed in the destruction of this castle of despotism. We saw the battlements tumble down amidst the applauding shouts of the people. I observed a number of artists taking drawings of what from this time was to have no existence but on paper. . . .

And this reminds me of our having a second time seen the other prisoner, the feeble old man. He was placed conspicuously at a window opposite the house where we saw the King pass, and at that time he was brought forward and made to wave his hat, having a three colored cockade[11] on it.

---

[11] **three colored cockade:** The tricolor — red, white, and blue — was the symbol of the Revolution, and an insult to the king as he passed.

READING AND DISCUSSION QUESTIONS

1. Based on reading Rigby's account, what seemed to be the mood of the citizenry of Paris in July 1789? What was their attitude toward their former rulers?

2. How might a royalist have interpreted these same events? Where do the author's sympathies seem to lie and why might he feel as he does?

3. How much do these events seem to indicate a planned revolution, with specific goals, and how much do they indicate the Third Estate's relief at change without much thought for the future nature of French government?

DOCUMENT 21-3

NATIONAL ASSEMBLY OF FRANCE

From Declaration of the Rights of Man and of the Citizen

1789

After the fall of the Bastille, rumors that the nobility were plotting to use foreign mercenaries to suppress the Revolution swept through the French countryside. In an effort to quell the "great fear," the National Assembly abolished feudalism and released the "Declaration of the Rights of Man," which laid out the basic principles upon which their government would be founded. While Enlightenment thinkers had used reason to critique social practices and customs but rarely produced actual reforms, the French revolutionaries applied the spirit of reason to practical politics. It is a measure of their success that their ideas about a citizen's relationship with their government no longer seem so radical.

The representatives of the French people, organized as a National Assembly, believing that the ignorance, neglect, or contempt of the rights of man

James Harvey Robinson, ed., *Readings in European History* (Boston: Ginn, 1904), 2:409–411.

are the sole cause of public calamities and of the corruption of governments, have determined to set forth in a solemn declaration the natural, inalienable, and sacred rights of man, in order that this declaration, being constantly before all the members of the social body, shall remind them continually of their rights and duties; in order that the acts of the legislative power, as well as those of the executive power, may be compared at any moment with the objects and purposes of all political institutions and may thus be more respected; and, lastly, in order that the grievances of the citizens, based hereafter upon simple and incontestable principles, shall tend to the maintenance of the constitution and redound to the happiness of all. Therefore the National Assembly recognizes and proclaims, in the presence and under the auspices of the Supreme Being, the following rights of man and of the citizen:

ARTICLE 1. Men are born and remain free and equal in rights. Social distinctions may be founded only upon the general good.

2. The aim of all political association is the preservation of the natural and imprescriptible rights of man. These rights are liberty, property, security, and resistance to oppression.

3. The principle of all sovereignty resides essentially in the nation. No body nor individual may exercise any authority which does not proceed directly from the nation.

4. Liberty consists in the freedom to do everything which injures no one else; hence the exercise of the natural rights of each man has no limits except those which assure to the other members of the society the enjoyment of the same rights. These limits can only be determined by law.

5. Law can only prohibit such actions as are hurtful to society. Nothing may be prevented which is not forbidden by law, and no one may be forced to do anything not provided for by law.

6. Law is the expression of the general will. Every citizen has a right to participate personally, or through his representative, in its formation. It must be the same for all, whether it protects or punishes. All citizens, being equal in the eyes of the law, are equally eligible to all dignities and to all public positions and occupations, according to their abilities, and without distinction except that of their virtues and talents.

7. No person shall be accused, arrested, or imprisoned except in the cases and according to the forms prescribed by law. Any one soliciting, transmitting, executing, or causing to be executed, any arbitrary order, shall be punished. But any citizen summoned or arrested in virtue of the law shall submit without delay, as resistance constitutes an offense.

8. The law shall provide for such punishments only as are strictly and obviously necessary, and no one shall suffer punishment except it be legally inflicted in virtue of a law passed and promulgated before the commission of the offense.

9. As all persons are held innocent until they shall have been declared guilty, if arrest shall be deemed indispensable, all harshness not essential to the securing of the prisoner's person shall be severely repressed by law.

10. No one shall be disquieted on account of his opinions, including his religious views, provided their manifestation does not disturb the public order established by law.

11. The free communication of ideas and opinions is one of the most precious of the rights of man. Every citizen may, accordingly, speak, write, and print with freedom, but shall be responsible for such abuses of this freedom as shall be defined by law.

12. The security of the rights of man and of the citizen requires public military forces. These forces are, therefore, established for the good of all and not for the personal advantage of those to whom they shall be intrusted.

13. A common contribution is essential for the maintenance of the public forces and for the cost of administration. This should be equitably distributed among all the citizens in proportion to their means.

14. All the citizens have a right to decide, either personally or by their representatives, as to the necessity of the public contribution; to grant this freely; to know to what uses it is put; and to fix the proportion, the mode of assessment and of collection and the duration of the taxes.

15. Society has the right to require of every public agent an account of his administration.

16. A society in which the observance of the law is not assured, nor the separation of powers defined, has no constitution at all.

17. Since property is an inviolable and sacred right, no one shall be deprived thereof except where public necessity, legally determined, shall clearly demand it, and then only on condition that the owner shall have been previously and equitably indemnified.

READING AND DISCUSSION QUESTIONS

1. Who, according to the authors of this document, make up the "nation"? What is the basis of the government they propose?

2. In what ways is this declaration revolutionary, and in what ways does it continue the status quo?

3. What sort of balance does the declaration attempt to strike between the rights and responsibilities of citizens?

DOCUMENT 21-4

MARY WOLLSTONECRAFT

From A Vindication of the Rights of Women

1792

The French Constitution of 1791, drafted by the same National Assembly that passed the "Declaration of the Rights of Man," confined full citizenship to a limited number of property-holding men. While many Enlightenment ideals that underlay the Revolution had developed in salons overseen by upper-class women, prevailing thought held that women lacked the intellectual and emotional capacity to participate in politics. The English radical Mary Wollstonecraft disagreed. Her response was A Vindication of the Rights of Women, *written to French diplomat Charles Talleyrand, who had recently advocated a very limited and domestic education for women.*

My own sex, I hope, will excuse me, if I treat them like rational creatures, instead of flattering their fascinating graces, and viewing them as if they were in a state of perpetual childhood, unable to stand alone. I earnestly wish to point out in what true dignity and human happiness consists — I wish to persuade women to endeavor to acquire strength, both of mind and body, and to convince them that the soft phrases, susceptibility of heart, delicacy of sentiment, and refinement of taste, are almost synonymous with epithets of weakness, and that those beings who are only the objects of pity will soon become objects of contempt.

Dismissing those soft pretty feminine phrases, which the men condescendingly use to soften our slavish dependence, and despising that

Mary Wollstonecraft, A *Vindication of the Rights of Women* (1792), ed. Carol H. Poston (New York: W. W. Norton, 1975), 9–10, 27, 31.

weak elegancy of mind, exquisite sensibility, and sweet docility of manners, supposed to be the sexual characteristics of the weaker vessel, I wish to shew that elegance is inferior to virtue, that the first object of laudable ambition is to obtain a character as a human being, regardless of the distinction of sex.

Youth is the season for love in both sexes; but in those days of thoughtless enjoyment provision should be made for the more important years of life, when reflection takes place of sensation. The woman who has only been taught to please will soon find that her charms are oblique sunbeams and that they cannot have much effect on her husband's heart when they are seen every day, when the summer is passed and gone. Will she then have sufficient native energy to look into herself for comfort, and cultivate her dormant faculties? or, is it not more rational to expect that she will try to please other men?

Why must the female mind be tainted by coquettish arts to gratify the sensualist and prevent love from subsiding into friendship, or compassionate tenderness, when there are not qualities on which friendship can be built? Let the honest heart shew itself, and reason teach passion to submit to necessity; or, let the dignified pursuit of virtue and knowledge raise the mind above those emotions. . . .

If then women are not a swarm of ephemeron triflers, why should they be kept in ignorance under the specious name of innocence? . . . As to the argument respecting the subjection in which the sex has ever been held, it retorts on man. The many have always been enthralled by the few; and monsters, who scarcely have shown any discernment of human excellence, have tyrannized over thousands of their fellow-creatures. . . . China is not the only country where a living man has been made a God. Men have submitted to superior strength to enjoy with impunity the pleasure of the moment; women have only done the same, and therefore till it is proved that the courtier, who servilely resigns the birthright of a man, is not a moral agent, it cannot be demonstrated that woman is essentially inferior to man because she has always been subjugated.

READING AND DISCUSSION QUESTIONS

1. How might a man and a woman read this document differently? Is it addressed to men or women?

2. In what ways does Wollstonecraft accept that women are inferior? Does this weaken or strengthen her argument?

3. Based on Wollstonecraft's argument, what can you discern about a stereotypical woman of the time? How does she behave? How do men respond to her?

4. Of what is the title of Wollstonecraft's argument reminiscent? If this was not merely coincidence, what was the author's purpose?

DOCUMENT 21-5

FRANÇOIS DOMINIQUE TOUSSAINT L'OUVERTURE

A Black Revolutionary Leader in Haiti

1797

The French Revolution had an impact in the new world as well, as represen-tatives of the oppressed slaves on the Caribbean sugar-growing islands seized the opportunity to make their voices heard. In 1792, after French colonial rulers arrested the leader of a Caribbean slave delegation in Paris, freed slave Toussaint Breda (who later changed his name to "L'Ouverture," as he had "opened" the way) emerged as the leader of a massive Haitian revolt. The revolutionaries faced not only the French plantation owners, but British and Spanish forces hoping to capture the lucrative island amid the turmoil.

The impolitic and incendiary discourse of Vaublanc[12] has not affected the blacks nearly so much as their certainty of the projects which the propri-etors of San Domingo are planning: insidious declarations should not have any effect in the eyes of wise legislators who have decreed liberty for the nations. But the attempts on that liberty which the colonists propose are all the more to be feared because it is with the veil of patriotism that they cover their detestable plans. We know that they seek to impose some of

---

François Dominique Toussaint L'Ouverture, Letter, in C. L. R. James, *The Black Jacobins*, 2d ed. (New York: Vintage Books, 1963), 195–197.

[12] **Vaublanc**: The count of Vaublanc was a royalist and proponent of freeing the slaves and giving them citizenship, in opposition to L'Ouverture's more moderate views.

them on you by illusory and specious promises, in order to see renewed in this colony its former scenes of horror. Already perfidious emissaries have stepped in among us to ferment the destructive leaven prepared by the hands of liberticides [i.e., murderers of liberty]. But they will not succeed. I swear it by all that liberty holds most sacred. My attachment to France, my knowledge of the blacks, make it my duty not to leave you ignorant either of the crimes which they meditate or the oath that we renew, to bury ourselves under the ruins of a country revived by liberty rather than suffer the return of slavery.

It is for you, Citizens Directors, to turn from over our heads the storm which the eternal enemies of our liberty are preparing in the shades of silence. It is for you to enlighten the legislature, it is for you to prevent the enemies of the present system from spreading themselves on our unfortunate shores to sully it with new crimes. Do not allow our brothers, our friends, to be sacrificed to men who wish to reign over the ruins of the human species. But no, your wisdom will enable you to avoid the dangerous snares which our common enemies hold out for you. . . .

I send you with this letter a declaration which will acquaint you with the unity that exists between the proprietors of San Domingo who are in France, those in the United States, and those who serve under the English banner. You will see there a resolution, unequivocal and carefully constructed, for the restoration of slavery; you will see there that their determination to succeed has led them to envelop themselves in the mantle of liberty in order to strike it more deadly blows. You will see that they are counting heavily on my complacency in lending myself to their perfidious views by my fear for my children. It is not astonishing that these men who sacrifice their country to their interests are unable to conceive how many sacrifices a true love of country can support in a better father than they, since I unhesitatingly base the happiness of my children on that of my country, which they and they alone wish to destroy.

I shall never hesitate between the safety of San Domingo and my personal happiness; but I have nothing to fear. It is to the solicitude of the French Government that I have confided my children. . . . I would tremble with horror if it was into the hands of the colonists that I had sent them as hostages; but even if it were so, let them know that in punishing them for the fidelity of their father, they would only add one degree more to their barbarism, without any hope of ever making me fail in my duty. . . . Blind as they are! They cannot see how this odious conduct on their part can become the signal of new disasters and irreparable misfortunes, and that far from making them regain what in their eyes liberty for all has made them lose, they expose themselves to a total ruin and the colony to its inevitable destruction. Do they think that men who have been able to enjoy the blessing of liberty will calmly see it snatched away? They supported their chains only so long as they did not know any condition of life more happy than that of slavery. But to-day when they have left it, if they had a thousand lives they would sacrifice them all rather than be forced into slavery again. But no, the same hand which has broken our chains will not enslave us anew. France will not revoke her principles, she will not withdraw from us the greatest of her benefits. She will protect us against all our enemies; she will not permit her sublime morality to be perverted, those principles which do her most honor to be destroyed, her most beautiful achievement to be degraded, and her Decree of 16 Pluviose[13] which so honors humanity to be revoked. But if, to re-establish slavery in San Domingo, this was done, then I declare to you it would be to attempt the impossible: we have known how to face dangers to obtain our liberty, we shall know how to brave death to maintain it.

This, Citizens Directors, is the morale of the people of San Domingo, those are the principles that they transmit to you by me.

My own you know. It is sufficient to renew, my hand in yours, the oath that I have made, to cease to live before gratitude dies in my heart, before I cease to be faithful to France and to my duty, before the god of liberty is profaned and sullied by the liberticides, before they can snatch from my hands that sword, those arms, which France confided to me for the defence of its rights and those of humanity, for the triumph of liberty and equality.

READING AND DISCUSSION QUESTIONS

1. Who is the intended audience of this document? What is L'Ouverture trying to convince them to do?

2. What reasons might persuade the French to reimpose slavery in Haiti, and what reasons might they have for defending its abolition?

---

[13] **Decree of 16 Pluviose**: In 1793, the French revolutionaries reorganized their calendar to remove the Christian elements; the event marking year one moved from the birth of Jesus to the adoption of the French constitution in 1792. The fifth month, roughly corresponding to April, known for its rains, became Pluviose, which loosely translates as "rainy." The specific decree to which L'Overture refers abolished slavery in French colonies in April 1794.

3. In what way is L'Ouverture seeking to find common ground with the French? Why?

COMPARATIVE QUESTIONS

1. How did the attitude of the people of France seem to change between the creation of the *Cahier de Doleances* and the fall of the Bastille?
2. In what ways did the points expressed in the *Cahier de Doleances* find their way into the "Declaration of the Rights of Man"? Were any points left out of the declaration? If so, why do you suppose they were excluded?
3. What similarities exist between the arguments of Mary Wollstonecraft and Toussaint L'Ouverture for their groups' inclusion in the new political order? What differences can you discern?
4. Based on "The Declaration of the Rights of Man," Mary Wollstonecraft's argument, and Toussaint L'Ouverture's letter, what were the limits on the liberty and equality promised by the Revolution?
5. In what ways does Rousseau's *Social Contract* (Document 18–4) seem to have influenced the writing of the *Cahier* and the "Declaration of the Rights of Man"? How have the citizens of France departed from his thinking?

CHAPTER 22

The Revolution in Energy and Industry

ca. 1780–1860

The term *Industrial Revolution* was coined almost 150 years ago to describe the technological, economic, and social transformations that took place first in Great Britain and then elsewhere in Europe and the United States. Between 1780 and 1850, traditional English society, in which the overwhelming majority of the population worked in rural agriculture, gave way to an industrial society wherein the majority lived in urban settings and worked in the manufacturing or service sectors. Although working and living conditions worsened in the short term, industrialization led to a vast expansion in the economy, providing jobs and goods for a rapidly growing population. Historians still debate whether "revolution" is an apt description for changes that took place over several decades, but there is little doubt that the consequences of those changes were profound.

DOCUMENT 22-1

JOHN AIKIN

From A Description of the Country: *Manchester Becomes a Thriving Industrial City*

1795

John Aikin was trained as a physician but is better known today as a writer and editor of biography. In 1795, Aikin published A Description of the

John Aikin, *A Description of the Country from Thirty to Forty Miles Round Manchester*, in Walter Arnstein, ed., *The Past Speaks*, 2d ed. (Lexington, Mass.: D. C. Heath, 1993), 2:148–149.

Country from Thirty to Forty Miles Round Manchester, *one of the most complete accounts of the center of Britain's cotton textile industry in its formative stages. As of 1773, Manchester was a market town of about 23,000 people but, blessed with ample water to drive mill wheels, it became a thriving manufacturing center. By 1801, when Britain conducted its first national census, Manchester's population topped 84,000.*

No exertions of the masters or workmen could have answered the demands of trade without the introduction of *spinning machines* [that spun cotton fibers into thread].

These were first used by the country people on a confined scale,[1] twelve spindles being thought a great matter; while the awkward posture required to spin on them was discouraging to grown up people, who saw with surprise children from nine to twelve years of age manage them with dexterity, whereby plenty was brought into families formerly overburthened with children, and the poor weavers were delivered from the bondage in which they had lain from the insolence of spinners. . . .

The improvements kept increasing, till the capital engines for twist [i.e., the machinery that twisted cotton fibers into thread] were perfected, by which thousands of spindles are put in motion by a water wheel,[2] and managed mostly by children, without confusion and with less waste of cotton than by the former methods. But the carding [wherein cotton fibers were combed out straight and parallel] and slubbing [wherein carded fibers were drawn together and twisted into yarn] preparatory to twisting required a greater range of invention. The first attempts were in carding engines, which are very curious, and now brought to a great degree of perfection; and an engine has been contrived for converting the carded wool [cotton] to slubbing, by drawing it to about the thickness of candlewick preparatory to throwing it into twist. . . .

These machines exhibit in their construction an aggregate of clockmaker's work and machinery most wonderful to behold. The cotton to be spun is introduced through three sets of rollers, so governed by the clock-

---

[1] **country people . . . scale**: The author refers to the cottage industry, in which individual families labored as a unit in their own homes to convert raw cotton into woven cloth.

[2] **water wheel**: Aikin is describing an early thread-spinning machine called a "water frame," owing to the water wheel that powered it. The water frame's invention is usually attributed to pioneer textile manufacturer Richard Arkwright.

work, that the set which first receives the cotton makes so many revolutions than the next in order, and these more than the last which feed the spindles, that it is drawn out considerably in passing through the rollers; being lastly received by spindles, which have every one on the bobbin a fly [an arm which revolves around the bobbin, adding additional twist to the thread] like that of a flax wheel. . . .

Upon these machines twist is made of any fineness [thickness] proper for warps [threads that run lengthwise on a loom]; but as it is drawn length way of the staple, it was not so proper for weft;[3] wherefore on the introduction of fine callicoes [coarse cotton cloth] and muslins [fine cotton cloth], mules[4] were invented, having a name expressive of their species, being a mixed machinery between jennies and the machines for twisting, and adapted to spin weft as fine as could be desired. . . .

These mules carry often to a hundred and fifty spindles, and can be set to draw weft to an exact fineness up to 150 hanks in the pound, of which muslin has been made, which for a while had a prompt sale; but the flimsiness of its fabric has brought the finer sorts into discredit, and a stagnation of trade damped the sale of the rest. . . .

The prodigious extension of the several branches of the Manchester manufactures has likewise greatly increased the business of several trades and manufactures connected with or dependent upon them. The making of paper at mills in the vicinity has been brought to great perfection, and now includes all kinds, from the strongest parcelling paper to the finest writing sorts, and that on which banker's bills are printed. To the ironmongers shops, which are greatly increased of late, are generally annexed smithies [blacksmiths], where many articles are made, even to nails. A considerable iron foundry is established in Salford, in which are cast most of the articles wanted in Manchester and its neighborhood, consisting chiefly of large cast wheels for the cotton machines; cylinders, boilers, and pipes for steam engines; cast ovens, and grates of all sizes. This work belongs to Batemen and Sharrard, gen[tle]men every way qualified for so great an undertaking. Mr. Sharrard is a very ingenious and able engi-

---

[3] **as it is drawn . . . weft**: Aiken suggests that thread produced by water frames lacked the flexibility and strength to be used for the weft, the threads that cross from side to side on a loom at right angles to the warp.

[4] **mules**: Samuel Crompton's "spinning mule" (1772), so called because, like its namesake, which combined the virtues of the donkey (nimbleness, endurance) with those of a horse (strength), it combined the productive capacity of the water frame with the spinning jenny's ability to spin the finest thread.

neer, who has improved upon and brought the steam engine to great perfection. . . .

The tin-plate workers have found additional employment in furnishing many articles for spinning machines; as have also the braziers in casting wheels for the motion-work of the rollers used in them; and the clock-makers in cutting them. Harness-makers have been much employed in making bands for carding engines, and large wheels for the first operation of drawing out the cardings, whereby the consumption of strong curried leather has been much increased. . . .

Within the last twenty or thirty years the vast increase of foreign trade has caused many of the Manchester manufacturers to travel abroad, and agents or partners to be fixed for a considerable time on the continent, as well as foreigners to reside at Manchester. And the town has now in every respect assumed the style and manners of one of the commercial capitals of Europe. . . .

READING AND DISCUSSION QUESTIONS

1. What is Aikin's reaction to the prevalence of child labor in the spinning mills he describes? What might this imply about English labor standards at the time?

2. Where was the demand that drove this "prodigious extension of the several branches of the Manchester manufactures" coming from, and why? Put another way, why were cotton textile producers and other manufacturers employing machinery to increase production, rather than relying on the traditional cottage industry?

3. Based on Aikin's account, what can be inferred about Britain's population and its purchasing power?

4. In addition to the water supply, what elements made Manchester an ideal location for manufacturing? What different businesses or work forces did manufacturers rely upon?

DOCUMENT 22-2

ROBERT MALTHUS

From An Essay on the Principle of Population

1798

Thomas Malthus (1766–1834) was an Anglican clergyman by training but was deeply interested in demography, or the study of human population. His 1798 book An Essay on the Principle of Population *is widely regarded as the foundational text on the subject, and his argument — that, unchecked by birth control, human populations increase faster than their food supplies — remains relevant today, as manufacturers, farmers, politicians, and scientists alike debate the Earth's ability to sustain a population of upwards of seven billion indefinitely.*

I have read some of the speculations on the perfectibility of man and of society with great pleasure. I have been warmed and delighted with the enchanting picture which they hold forth. I ardently wish for such happy improvements. But I see great, and, to my understanding, unconquerable difficulties in the way to them. These difficulties it is my present purpose to state; declaring, at the same time, that so far from exulting in them, as a cause of triumphing over the friends of innovation, nothing would give me greater pleasure than to see them completely removed. . . .

I think I may fairly make two postulata.

First, That food is necessary to the existence of man.

Secondly, That the passion between the sexes is necessary, and will remain nearly in its present state. . . .

Assuming, then, my postulata as granted, I say, that the power of population is indefinitely greater than the power in the earth to produce subsistence for man.

Population, when unchecked, increases in a geometrical ratio. Subsistence only increases in an arithmetical ratio. A slight acquaintance with numbers will show the immensity of the first power in comparison of the second.

Thomas Malthus, *An Essay on the Principle of Population,* in Walter Arnstein, ed., *The Past Speaks,* 2d ed. (Lexington, Mass.: D.C. Heath, 1993), 2:144–146.

By that law of our nature which makes food necessary to the life of man, the effects of these two unequal powers must be kept equal.

This implies a strong and constantly operating check on population from the difficulty of subsistence. This difficulty must fall some where; and must necessarily be severely felt by a large portion of mankind. . . .

The ultimate check to population appears then to be a want of food arising necessarily from the different ratios according to which population and food increase. But this ultimate check is never the immediate check, except in cases of actual famine.

The immediate check may be stated to consist in all those customs, and all those diseases which seem to be generated by a scarcity of the means of subsistence; and all those causes, independent of this scarcity, whether of a moral or physical nature, which tend prematurely to weaken and destroy the human frame.

In every country some of these checks are, with more or less force, in constant operation; yet, notwithstanding their general prevalence, there are few states in which there is not a constant effort in the population to increase beyond the means of subsistence. This constant effort as constantly tends to subject the lower classes of society to distress, and to prevent any great permanent melioration of their condition.

These effects, in the present state of society, seem to be produced in the following manner. We will suppose the means of subsistence in any country just equal to the easy support of its inhabitants. The constant effort toward population, which is found to act even in the most vicious societies, increases the number of people before the means of subsistence are increased. The food, therefore, which before supported eleven millions, must now be divided among eleven millions and a half. The poor consequently must live much worse, and many of them be reduced to severe distress. The number of laborers also being above the proportion of work in the market, the price of labor must tend to fall, while the price of provisions would at the same time tend to rise. The laborer therefore must do more work to earn the same as he did before. During this season of distress, the discouragements to marriage and the difficulty of rearing a family are so great, that the progress of population is retarded. In the meantime, the cheapness of labor, the plenty of laborers, and the necessity of an increased industry among them, encourage cultivators to employ more labor upon their land, to turn up fresh soil, and to manure and improve more completely what is already in tillage, till ultimately the means of subsistence may become in the same proportion to the population as at the period from which we set out. The situation of the laborer being then again tolerably comfortable, the restraints to population are in some degree loosened; and, after a short period, the same retrograde and progressive movements, with respect to happiness, are repeated. . . .

READING AND DISCUSSION QUESTIONS

1. Where might those speculations regarding "the perfectability of man and society in general" to which Malthus refers have originated? Does he agree or disagree with them, and on what grounds?

2. Why, according to Malthus, were there "few states in which there is not a constant effort in the population to increase beyond the means of subsistence"?

3. What does Malthus mean when he alludes to the cyclical "retrograde and progressive movements" regarding population decline and growth, "with respect to [human] happiness"?

4. If population is checked by the scarcity of food, what must occur in order for population to increase again? How might this requirement be problematic, if not in Malthus's time, then in our own?

DOCUMENT 22-3

Yorkshire Luddites Threaten the Owner of a Mechanized Factory
1811–1812

In the early nineteenth century, the new mechanization of textile manufacturing endangered the livelihoods of the handiworkers engaged in manual textile production. During the years 1811–1816, many English hosiery weavers found themselves replaced by stocking frames. Croppers, whose task was to finish woven cloth by cropping (shearing) it, were threatened by the introduction of the shearing frame. The workers retaliated by smashing the

G. D. H. Cole and A. W. Filson, eds., *British Working Class Documents: Selected Documents 1789–1875* (London: Macmillan, 1951), 113–115.

"detestable" machines that had claimed their jobs. They adopted the name "Luddites" after an (probably) apocryphal Edward "Ned" Ludd, lauded as the first to destroy a shearing frame. Hostile missives, like that which follows, were often sent to the owners of stocking or shearing frames, and make frequent reference to "King Ludd," a protector of the downtrodden.

Sir,

Information has just been given in, that you are a holder [owner] of those detestable Shearing Frames, and I was desired by my men to write to you, and give you fair warning to pull them down, and for that purpose I desire that you will understand I am now writing to you, you will take notice that if they are not taken down by the end of next week, I shall detach one of my lieutenants with at least 300 men to destroy them, and further more take notice that if you give us the trouble of coming thus far, we will increase your misfortunes by burning your buildings down to ashes. . . . We hope for assistance from the French Emperor[5] in shaking off the Yoke of the Rottenest, wickedest, and most Tyrannical Government that ever existed. . . . We will never lay down our arms till the House of Commons passes an act to put down all the machinery hurtfull [*sic*] to the Commonality and repeal that[6] to the Frame Breakers. . . .

Signed by the General of the Army of Redressers,

Ned Ludd, Clerk

READING AND DISCUSSION QUESTIONS

1. Why do you think the Luddites resorted to threats and violence rather than peacefully seeking redress through the political process?

2. Why, in a threat to an individual factory owner, do you think the anonymous author of this letter denounced Britain's government as "the Rottenest, wickedest, and most Tyrannical . . . that ever existed"?

3. Why might the Luddites have expected the French emperor Napoleon to be their savior?

---

[5] **assistance from the French Emperor**: Great Britain was engaged in a lengthy war against the French emperor, Napoleon Bonaparte.

[6] **repeal that**: In response to the wave of machine-breaking, Parliament made such crimes capital offenses.

DOCUMENT 22-4

ROBERT OWEN
A New View of Society
1813–1816

Robert Owen (1771–1858) first gained prominence as a successful textile manufacturer who treated his employees generously and beneficently. He later became a tireless promoter of educational reform, and was an early "utopian" socialist and trade union advocate, providing the inspiration for the founding of the Grand National Consolidated Trades Union in 1834. None of Owen's schemes for socialist communities succeeded, nor did the early trade unions, but his theories about educating children were very influential during his own lifetime and remain current today.

Any general character, from the best to the worst, from the most ignorant to the most enlightened, may be given to any community, even to the world at large, by the application of proper means; which means are to a great extent at the command and under the control of those who have influence in the affairs of men. According to the last returns under the Population Act, the poor and working classes of Great Britain and Ireland have been found to exceed fifteen millions of persons, or nearly three-fourths of the population of the British Islands.

The characters of these persons are now permitted to be very generally formed without proper guidance or direction, and, in many cases, under circumstances which directly impel them to a course of extreme vice and misery; thus rendering them the worst and most dangerous subjects in the empire; while the far greater part of the remainder of the community are educated upon the most mistaken principles of human nature, such, indeed, as cannot fail to produce a general conduct throughout society, totally unworthy of the character of rational beings.

The first thus unhappily situated are the poor and the uneducated profligate among the working classes, who are now trained to commit crimes, for the commission of which they are afterwards punished.

From the Avalon Project, Documents in Law, History and Diplomacy. http://avalon .law.yale.edu.

The second is the remaining mass of the population, who are now instructed to believe, or at least to acknowledge, that certain principles are unerringly true, and to act as though they were grossly false; thus filling the world with folly and inconsistency, and making society, throughout all its ramifications, a scene of insincerity and counteraction.

In this state the world has continued to the present time; its evils have been and are continually increasing; they cry aloud for efficient corrective measures, which if we longer delay, general disorder must ensue. . . .

Children are, without exception, passive and wonderfully contrived compounds; which, by an accurate previous and subsequent attention, founded on a correct knowledge of the subject, may be formed collectively to have any human character. And although these compounds, like all the other works of nature, possess endless varieties, yet they partake of that plastic quality, which, by perseverance under judicious management, may be ultimately molded into the very image of rational wishes and desires.

In the next place these principles cannot fail to create feelings which, without force or the production of any counteracting motive, will irresistibly lead those who possess them to make due allowance for the difference of sentiments and manners, not only among their friends and countrymen, but also among the inhabitants of every region of the earth, even including their enemies. With this insight into the formation of character, there is no conceivable foundation for private displeasure or public enmity. Say, if it be within the sphere of possibility that children can be trained to attain that knowledge, and at the same time to acquire feelings of enmity towards a single human creature? The child who from infancy has been rationally instructed in these principles, will readily discover and trace whence the opinions and habits of his associates have arisen, and why they possess them. At the same age he will have acquired reason sufficient to exhibit to him forcibly the irrationality of being angry with an individual for possessing qualities which, as a passive being during the formation of those qualities, he had not the means of preventing. Such are the impressions these principles will make on the mind of every child so taught; and, instead of generating anger or displeasure, they will produce commiseration and pity for those individuals who possess either habits or sentiments which appear to him to be destructive of their own comfort, pleasure, or happiness; and will produce on his part a desire to remove those causes of distress, and his own feelings of commiseration and pity may be also removed. The pleasure which he cannot avoid experiencing by this mode of conduct will likewise stimulate him to the most active endeavors to withdraw those circumstances which surround any part of mankind with causes of misery, and to replace them with others which have a tendency to increase happiness. He will then also strongly entertain the desire "to do good to all men," and even to those who think themselves his enemies. . . .

In the year 1784 the late Mr Dale, of Glasgow, founded a manufactory for spinning of cotton, near the falls of the Clyde, in the county of Lanark, in Scotland; and about that period cotton mills were first introduced into the northern part of the kingdom.

It was the power which could be obtained from the falls of water that induced Mr Dale to erect his mills in this situation; for in other respects it was not well chosen. The country around was uncultivated; the inhabitants were poor and few in number; and the roads in the neighborhood were so bad, that the Falls, now so celebrated, were then unknown to strangers.

It was therefore necessary to collect a new population to supply the infant establishment with laborers. This, however, was no light task; for all the regularly trained Scotch peasantry disdained the idea of working early and late, day after day, within cotton mills. Two modes then only remained of obtaining these laborers; the one, to procure children from the various public charities of the country; and the other, to induce families to settle around the works.

To accommodate the first, a large house was erected, which ultimately contained about 500 children, who were procured chiefly from workhouses and charities in Edinburgh. These children were to be fed, clothed, and educated; and these duties Mr Dale performed with the unwearied benevolence which it is well known he possessed. . . .

The benevolent proprietor spared no expense to give comfort to the poor children. The rooms provided for them were spacious, always clean, and well ventilated; the food was abundant, and of the best quality; the clothes were neat and useful; a surgeon was kept in constant pay, to direct how to prevent or cure disease; and the best instructors which the country afforded were appointed to teach such branches of education as were deemed likely to be useful to children in their situation. Kind and well-disposed persons were appointed to superintend all their proceedings. Nothing, in short, at first sight seemed wanting to render it a most complete charity.

But to defray the expense of these well-devised arrangements, and to support the establishment generally, it was absolutely necessary that the children should be employed within the mills from six o'clock in the morning till seven in the evening, summer and winter; and after these hours their education commenced. The directors of the public charities, from mistaken economy, would not consent to send the children under their care to cotton mills, unless the children were received by the proprietors at the ages of six, seven, and eight. And Mr Dale was under the necessity of accepting them at those ages, or of stopping the manufactory which he had commenced.

It is not to be supposed that children so young could remain, with the intervals of meals only, from six in the morning until seven in the evening, in constant employment, on their feet, within cotton mills, and afterwards acquire much proficiency in education. And so it proved; for many of them became dwarfs in body and mind, and some of them were deformed. Their labor through the day and their education at night became so irksome, that numbers of them continually ran away, and almost all looked forward with impatience and anxiety to the expiration of their apprenticeship of seven, eight, and nine years, which generally expired when they were from thirteen to fifteen years old. At this period of life, unaccustomed to provide for themselves, and unacquainted with the world, they usually went to Edinburgh or Glasgow, where boys and girls were soon assailed by the innumerable temptations which all large towns present, and to which many of them fell sacrifices.

Thus Mr Dale's arrangements, and his kind solicitude for the comfort and happiness of these children, were rendered in their ultimate effect almost nugatory. They were hired by him and sent to be employed, and without their labor he could not support them; but, while under his care, he did all that any individual, circumstanced as he was, could do for his fellow creatures. The error proceeded from the children being sent from the workhouses at an age much too young for employment. They ought to have been detained four years longer, and educated; and then some of the evils which followed would have been prevented.

If such be a true picture, not overcharged, of parish apprentices to our manufacturing system, under the best and most humane regulations, in what colors must it be exhibited under the worst? . . .

[Once Owen himself was put in charge of the factory,] the system of receiving apprentices from public charities was abolished; permanent settlers with large families were encouraged, and comfortable houses were built for their accommodation.

The practice of employing children in the mills, of six, seven, and eight years of age, was discontinued, and their parents advised to allow them to acquire health and education until they were ten years old. (It may be remarked, that even this age is too early to keep them at constant employment in manufactories, from six in the morning to seven in the evening. Far better would it be for the children, their parents, and for society, that the first should not commence employment until they attain the age of twelve, when their education might be finished, and their bodies would be more competent to undergo the fatigue and exertions required of them. When parents can be trained to afford this additional time to their children without inconvenience, they will, of course, adopt the practice now recommended.)

The children were taught reading, writing, and arithmetic, during five years, that is, from five to ten, in the village school, without expense to their parents. All the modern improvements in education have been adopted, or are in process of adoption. (To avoid the inconveniences which must ever arise from the introduction of a particular creed into a school, the children are taught to read in such books as inculcate those precepts of the Christian religion, which are common to all denominations.) They may therefore be taught and well-trained before they engage in any regular employment. Another important consideration is, that all their instruction is rendered a pleasure and delight to them; they are much more anxious for the hour of school-time to arrive than to end; they therefore make a rapid progress; and it may be safely asserted, that if they shall not be trained to form such characters as may be most desired, the fault will not proceed from the children; the cause will be in the want of a true knowledge of human nature in those who have the management of them and their parents.

READING AND DISCUSSION QUESTIONS

1. Why was Owen opposed to child labor?
2. What does Owen believe regarding human nature and behavior, especially as they pertain to the poor, criminal, or undereducated?
3. What purposes did Owen propose education served for the children of the working class?

COMPARATIVE QUESTIONS

1. What do you think Robert Owen thought of the Luddites, and why?
2. Compare Owen's views on child labor with those of John Aikin. What might account for the differences between the two?

3. What do you think Malthus would say about Owen's views on human nature? Why? What do you think John Locke (Document 16-4) would say about them and why?

4. How might Adam Smith (Document 19-4) respond to the new manufacturing processes and machinery that Aikin describes?

CHAPTER 23

Ideologies and Upheavals

1815–1850

The rapid social changes brought about by the Industrial Revolution in the early nineteenth century led to the rise of a number of competing ideologies, often proposed as responses to the appalling living and working conditions in early industrial cities. Protectionist legislation, favored by conservatives and mercantilists, sought to keep the prices of food and other items artificially high while controlling their distribution. Liberals, by contrast, sought an end to government controls to stimulate business and encourage free trade. Communists offered yet another solution — the seizure of the means and ownership of production by the working classes. For all the hardships wrought by industrialization, the population of England rose dramatically in nineteenth century. At the same time, the population of Ireland shrank from about eight million to scarcely six million during the 1840s as people fled the devastating conditions of the potato famine.

<hr>

DOCUMENT 23-1

<hr>

DAVID RICARDO
On Wages
1817

After Adam Smith, David Ricardo (1772–1823) is almost certainly the most famous classical liberal economist. A prolific writer on "political economy," Ricardo penned the 1817 treatise On the Principles of Political Economy and Taxation, *from which the following excerpt is drawn. Unlike Smith, who*

<hr>

The Works of David Ricardo, J. R. McCulloch, ed. (London: John Murray, 1881), 31, 50–58.

believed that free trade could benefit all, Ricardo argued that laws of supply
and demand applied to wages as well as to products. Given a surplus of
labor like that in nineteenth-century England, wages would inevitably sink.
In the wake of Ricardo's highly influential writings, economics became
widely known as "the dismal science."

Money, from its being a commodity obtained from a foreign country, from
its being the general medium of exchange between all civilized countries,
and from its being also distributed among those countries in proportions
which are ever changing with every improvement in commerce and
machinery, and with every increasing difficulty of obtaining food and necessaries for an increasing population, is subject to incessant variations. In
stating the principles which regulate exchangeable value and price, we
should carefully distinguish between those variations which belong to the
commodity itself, and those which are occasioned by a variation in the
medium in which value is estimated, or price expressed.

A rise in wages, from an alteration in the value of money, produces a
general effect [i.e., inflation] on price, and for that reason it produces no
real effect whatever on profits. On the contrary, a rise of wages, from the
circumstance of the laborer being more liberally rewarded, or from a difficulty of procuring the necessaries on which wages are expended, does not,
except in some instances, produce the effect of raising price, but has a
great effect in lowering profits. In the one case, no greater proportion of
the annual labor of the country is devoted to the support of the laborers; in
the other case, a larger portion is so devoted.

Labor, like all other things which are purchased and sold, and which
may be increased or diminished in quantity, has its natural and its market
price. The natural price of labor is that price which is necessary to enable
the laborers, one with another, to subsist and to perpetuate their race, without either increase or diminution.

The power of the laborer to support himself, and the family which
may be necessary to keep up the number of laborers, does not depend on
the quantity of money which he may receive for wages, but on the quantity
of food, necessaries, and conveniences become essential to him from
habit, which that money will purchase.[1] The natural price of labor, therefore, depends on the price of the food, necessaries, and conveniences

---

[1] **The quantity of food . . . purchase:** The concept of "real wages" or "purchasing
power." It is not the wage itself that matters, but what that wage can buy.

required for the support of the laborer and his family. With a rise in the price of food and necessaries, the natural price of labor will rise; with the fall in their price, the natural price of labor will fall.

With the progress of society the natural price of labor has always a tendency to rise, because one of the principal commodities by which its natural price is regulated [food], has a tendency to become dearer, from the greater difficulty of producing it. As, however, the improvements in agriculture, the discovery of new markets, whence provisions may be imported, may for a time counteract the tendency to a rise in the price of necessaries, and may even occasion their natural price to fall, so will the same causes produce the correspondent effects on the natural price of labor.

The natural price of all commodities, excepting raw produce and labor, has a tendency to fall, in the progress of wealth and population; for though, on one hand, they are enhanced in real value, from the rise in the natural price of the raw material of which they are made, this is more than counterbalanced by the improvements in machinery, by the better division and distribution of labor, and by the increasing skill, both in science and art, of the producers.

The market price of labor is the price which is really paid for it, from the natural operation of the proportion of the supply to the demand; labor is dear when it is scarce, and cheap when it is plentiful. However much the market price of labor may deviate from its natural price, it has, like commodities, a tendency to conform to it.

It is when the market price of labor exceeds its natural price, that the condition of the laborer is flourishing and happy, that he has it in his power to command a greater proportion of the necessaries and enjoyments of life, and therefore to rear a healthy and numerous family.

When, however, by the encouragement which high wages give to the increase of population, the number of laborers is increased, wages again fall to their natural price, and indeed from a reaction sometimes fall below it.

When the market price of labor is below its natural price, the condition of the laborers is most wretched: then poverty deprives them of those comforts which custom renders absolute necessaries. It is only after their privations have reduced their number, or the demand for labor has increased, that the market price of labor will rise to its natural price, and that the laborer will have the moderate comforts which the natural rate of wages will afford.

Notwithstanding the tendency of wages to conform to their natural rate, their market rate may, in an improving society, for an indefinite period, be constantly above it; for no sooner may the impulse, which an increased capital gives to a new demand for labor, be obeyed, than another increase of capital may produce the same effect; and thus, if the increase of capital be gradual and constant, the demand for labor may give a continued stimulus to an increase of people. . . .

Thus, then, with every improvement of society, with every increase in its capital, the market wages of labor will rise; but the permanence of their rise will depend on the question, whether the natural price of labor has also risen; and this again will depend on the rise in the natural price of those necessaries on which the wages of labor are expended. . . .

As population increases, these necessaries will be constantly rising in price, because more labor will be necessary to produce them. If, then, the money wages of labor should fall, whilst every commodity on which the wages of labor were expended rose, the laborer would be doubly affected, and would be soon totally deprived of subsistence. Instead, therefore, of the money wages of labor falling, they would rise; but they would not rise sufficiently to enable the laborer to purchase as many comforts and necessaries as he did before the rise in the price of those commodities. . . .

These, then, are the laws by which wages are regulated, and by which the happiness of far the greatest part of every community is governed. Like all other contracts, wages should be left to the fair and free competition of the market, and should never be controlled by the interference of the legislature.

The clear and direct tendency of the poor laws[2] is in direct opposition to these obvious principles: it is not, as the legislature benevolently intended, to amend the condition of the poor, but to deteriorate the condition of both poor and rich; instead of making the poor rich, they are calculated to make the rich poor; and whilst the present laws are in force, it is quite in the natural order of things that the fund for the maintenance of the poor should progressively increase till it has absorbed all the net revenue of the country, or at least so much of it as the state shall leave to us, after satisfying its own never-failing demands for the public expenditure.

This pernicious tendency of these laws is no longer a mystery, since it has been fully developed by the able hand of Mr. Malthus;[3] and every friend to the poor must ardently wish for their abolition.

---

[2] **poor laws**: The English Poor Law (1601) enabled local authorities to levy taxes (the "Poor Rates") for the assistance and relief of the deserving poor. As such, they amounted to a rudimentary social safety net.
[3] **Mr. Malthus**: Thomas Malthus, whose *Essay on the Principle of Population* (see Document 22-2) was a major influence on Ricardo's thought.

READING AND DISCUSSION QUESTIONS

1. Explain the difference between "natural price" and "market price."

2. Given a free market (that is to say no minimum wage laws or other government interference) for labor and a surplus of laborers, what would, according to Ricardo, happen to wages?

3. Why do you think Ricardo argues that the Poor Laws, which were intended "to amend the condition of the poor," conversely "deteriorate the condition of both poor and rich; instead of making the poor rich, they are calculated to make the rich poor"?

4. To what extent did the mechanization of manufacturing and the replacement of skilled handicraft workers by semi-skilled "machine tenders" reinforce Ricardo's argument?

DOCUMENT 23-2

KARL MARX AND FRIEDRICH ENGELS
From The Communist Manifesto
1848

Karl Marx (1818–1883) and Friedrich Engels (1820–1895) are credited as the founders of communism. In formulating their theories, Marx and Engels drew on the work of earlier economists, particularly Adam Smith and David Ricardo, and on Thomas Malthus's demographic theories, as well as their familiarity with living and working conditions in England's industrial centers. Their Communist Manifesto, *first published in London as a pamphlet (written in German), opens with the proclamation that "the history of all hitherto existing society is the history of class struggles." The authors predict the eventual triumph of the working class (proletariat) over the middle class (bourgeoisie) and the establishment of a classless society in which wealth is equally distributed.*

A specter is haunting Europe — the specter of communism. All the powers of old Europe have entered into a holy alliance to exorcise this specter:

Karl Marx and Friedrich Engels, *The Communist Manifesto*, in Arthur P. Mendel, *The Essential Works of Marxism* (New York: Bantam, 1961), 13–17, 19, 23, 40–44.

Pope and Czar, Metternich and Guizot,[4] French Radicals and German police-spies. . . .

Communism is already acknowledged by all European powers to be itself a power.

It is high time that Communists should openly, in the face of the whole world, publish their views, their aims, their tendencies, and meet this nursery tale of the specter of communism with a Manifesto of the party itself. . . .

The history of all hitherto existing society is the history of class struggles. . . .

Modern industry has established the world market, for which the discovery of America paved the way. This market has given an immense development to commerce, to navigation, to communication by land. This development has, in its turn, reacted on the extension of industry; and in proportion as industry, commerce, navigation, railways extended, in the same proportion the bourgeoisie developed, increased its capital, and pushed into the background every class handed down from the Middle Ages. . . .

The bourgeoisie, historically, has played a most revolutionary part.

The bourgeoisie, wherever it has got the upper hand, has put an end to all feudal, patriarchal, idyllic relations. It has pitilessly torn asunder the motley feudal ties that bound man to his "natural superiors," and has left remaining no other nexus between man and man than naked self-interest, than callous "cash payment." It has drowned the most heavenly ecstasies of religious fervor, of chivalrous enthusiasm, of philistine sentimentalism, in the icy water of egotistical calculation. It has resolved personal worth into exchange value, and in place of the numberless indefeasible chartered freedoms, has set up that single, unconscionable freedom — Free Trade. In a word, for exploitation, veiled by religious and political illusions, it has substituted naked, shameless, direct, brutal exploitation.

The bourgeoisie has stripped of its halo every occupation hitherto honored and looked up to with reverent awe. It has converted the physician, the lawyer, the priest, the poet, and the man of science into its paid wage-laborers.

The bourgeoisie has torn away from the family its sentimental veil and has reduced the family relation to a mere money relation. . . .

---

[4] **Metternich and Guizot**: Prince Klemens von Metternich (1773–1859) was foreign minister and chancellor of the Austrian Empire (1809–1848), and François Guizot (1787–1874) was a French politician who served at a variety of government posts, including prime minister from 1847 to 1848.

The bourgeoisie has subjected the country to the rule of the towns. It has created enormous cities, greatly increased the urban population as compared with the rural, and thus rescued a considerable part of the population from the idiocy of rural life. . . .

The bourgeoisie, during its rule of scarcely one hundred years, has created more massive and more colossal productive forces than have all preceding generations together. . . .

But not only has the bourgeoisie forged the weapons that bring death to itself; it has also called into existence the men who are to wield those weapons — the modern working class — the proletariat.

In proportion as the bourgeoisie, *i.e.*, capital, develops, in the same proportion the proletariat, the modern working class, develops — a class of laborers, who live only so long as they find work, and who find work only so long as their labor increases capital. These laborers, who must sell themselves piecemeal, are a commodity, like every other article of commerce, and are consequently exposed to all the vicissitudes of competition, to all the fluctuations of the market. . . .

Of all the classes that stand face to face with the bourgeoisie today, the proletariat alone is a really revolutionary class. The other classes decay and finally disappear in the face of modern industry; the proletariat is its special and essential product. . . .

The socialist and communist systems properly so called, those of Saint-Simon, Fourier, Owen,[5] and others, spring into existence in the early undeveloped period, described above, of the struggle between proletariat and bourgeoisie. . . .

Such fantastic pictures of future society, painted at a time when the proletariat is still in a very undeveloped state and has but a fantastic conception of its own position, correspond with the first instinctive yearnings of that class for a general reconstruction of society.

But these socialist and communist publications contain also a critical element. They attack every principle of existing society. . . .

---

[5] **Saint-Simon, Fourier, Owen**: Claude Henri de Rouvroy, comte de Saint-Simon (1760–1825), was an early advocate of socialism, as was Charles Fourier (1772–1837). Robert Owen (1771–1858) was an industrialist, utopian socialist, and trade union advocate. These socialist predecessors believed that capitalists and workers could overcome their antagonism and work cooperatively for the common good. As Marx and Engels believed "class struggle" to be the engine that drove history, they imply that these other socialists were naive to the point of delusionary, hence the "fantastic pictures" jibe that follows.

The Communists fight for the attainment of the immediate aims, for the enforcement of the momentary [i.e., current] interests of the working class; but in the movement of the present, they also represent and take care of the future of that movement. . . .

The Communists turn their attention chiefly to Germany, because that country is on the eve of a bourgeois revolution that is bound to be carried out under more advanced conditions of European civilization, and with a much more developed proletariat, than that of England was in the seventeenth, and of France in the eighteenth century, and because the bourgeois revolution in Germany will be but the prelude to an immediately following proletarian revolution.

In short, the Communists everywhere support every revolutionary movement against the existing social and political order of things.

In all these movements they bring to the fore, as the leading question in each, the property question, no matter what its degree of development at the time.

Finally, they labor everywhere for the union and agreement of the democratic parties of all countries.

The Communists disdain to conceal their views and aims. They openly declare that their ends can be attained only by the forcible overthrow of all existing social conditions. Let the ruling classes tremble at a Communistic revolution. The proletarians have nothing to lose but their chains. They have a world to win.

WORKING MEN OF ALL COUNTRIES, UNITE!

READING AND DISCUSSION QUESTIONS

1. What do Marx and Engels cite as their reasons for writing the *Manifesto*? What is its purpose?

2. How would you describe the power relationship between the bourgeoisie and the proletariat, and how is it changing?

3. Why, in a manifesto exhorting the proletariat to rise up against their bourgeoisie oppressors, do you think Marx and Engels devoted space to *praising* the latter? For example, "during its rule of scarcely one hundred years, [the bourgeoisie] has created more massive and more colossal productive forces than have all preceding generations together."

4. Why, according to Marx and Engels, was a working-class revolution against the capitalist middle class *inevitable*?

DOCUMENT 23-3

RICHARD COBDEN

A Denunciation of the Corn Laws

1838

Richard Cobden (1804–1865) was an English businessman and politician, one of the foremost nineteenth-century proponents of economic liberalism. In 1838, Cobden helped form the Anti-Corn Law League, a political action committee that fought for a repeal of the Corn Law, a tariff on imported grain that protected British producers from foreign competition but resulted in higher food prices. Despite Conservative Prime Minister Peel's introduction of a bill to eliminate the Corn Law over time, the Anti-Corn League's rabid popularity forced his 1846 resignation. Peel's liberal successors almost immediately repealed the Corn Law, cutting off emergency supplies of Indian corn to Ireland right at the height of the Irish Potato Famine.

With all sincerity I declare that I am for the total repeal of those taxes which affect the price of bread and provisions of every description, and I will not allow it to be said without denying it, that the three millions of people who have petitioned the House for the total repeal of those taxes are not sincere in their prayer. What are those taxes upon food? They are taxes levied upon the great body of the people, and the honorable gentlemen opposite, who show such sympathy for the working classes after they have made them paupers, cannot deny my right to claim on their behalf that those taxes should be a primary consideration.

I have heard them called protections; but taxes they are, and taxes they shall be in my mouth, as long as I have the honor of a seat in this House [i.e., the House of Commons, to which Cobden was speaking]. The bread tax is a tax primarily levied upon the poorer classes; it is a tax, at the lowest estimate, of 40 per cent above the price we should pay if there were a free trade in corn [i.e., grain]. The report upon the hand-loom weavers puts down 10 [shillings] as the estimated weekly earnings of a family, and states

Richard Cobden, in James Harvey Robinson and Charles Beard, eds., *Readings in Modern European History* (Boston: Ginn, 1909), 2:287–288.

that in all parts of the United Kingdom that will be found to be not an unfair estimate of the earnings of every laborer's family. It moreover states, that out of 10 [shillings] each family expends 5 [shillings] on bread. The tax of 40 per cent is therefore a tax of 2 [shillings] upon every laboring man's family earning 10 [shillings] a week, or 20 per cent upon their earnings. How does it operate as we proceed upwards in society? The man with 40 [shillings] a week pays an income tax of 5 per cent; the man of £250 a year pays but 1 per cent; and the nobleman or millionaire with an income of £200,000 a year, and whose family consumes no more bread than that of the agricultural laborer, pays less than one halfpenny in every £100. . . .

I will state generally, that, from both the manufacturing and agricultural districts, there was the most unimpeachable testimony that the condition of the great body of her Majesty's laboring subjects had deteriorated woefully within the last ten years, and more especially so within the three years last past; and furthermore, that in proportion as the price of the food of the people had increased, just so had their comforts been diminished. When they who sit in high places are oppressive and unjust to the poor, I am glad to see that there are men amongst us who, like Nathan of old, can be found to come forward and exclaim, "Thou art the man!" The religious people of the country have revolted against the infamous injustice of the bread tax, which is condemned by the immutable morality of the Scriptures. They have prepared and signed a petition to this House, in which they declare that these laws are a violation of the will of the Supreme Being, whose providence watches over his famishing children.

READING AND DISCUSSION QUESTIONS

1. Why might a prosperous manufacturer like Cobden, who could easily afford food for his own table, have been in the forefront of the movement against agricultural protectionism?

2. What does Cobden's invocation of scripture suggest about his religious beliefs? To whom would it appeal?

3. Who were the chief beneficiaries of the Corn Law, and why? Who suffered from it, and why?

4. Cobden and his associates believed that cheaper (freely traded) grain would encourage laborers to spend their remaining wages on other goods, thereby stimulating the economy. What, if any, problems can you foresee with this imagined trade relationship?

DOCUMENT 23-4

R. WILLIAM STEUART TRENCH

From Realities of Irish Life: *The Misery of the Potato Famine*

1847

As an Irish land agent, William Steuart Trench (1808–1872) was a first-hand witness to the ravages of the potato famine. A fungus, the potato blight, attacked the crop repeatedly during the years 1845–1848. The British government's limited efforts to provide help for the Irish were wholly inadequate. The Irish poor, whose diets consisted of little other than potatoes, were the victims of a Malthusian demographic disaster; between 1841 and 1851 Ireland's population fell between 20 and 25 percent. Estimates of the death toll range from around 750,000 to double that figure. Hundreds of thousands of the more fortunate Irish emigrated.

I did not see a child playing in the streets or on the roads; no children are to be seen outside the doors but a few sick and dying children. . . . In the districts which are now being depopulated by starvation, coffins are only used for the more wealthy. The majority were taken to the grave without any coffin, and buried in their rags: in some instances even the rags are taken from the corpse to cover some still living body.

. . . On arriving at Cappagh, in the first house I saw a dead child lying in a corner of the house, and two children, pale as death, with their heads hanging down upon their breasts sitting by a small fire. The father had died on the road coming home from work. One of the children, a lad seventeen years of age, had been found, in the absence of his mother, who was looking for food, lying dead, with his legs held out of the fire by the little child which I then saw lying dead. Two other children had also died. The mother and the two children still alive had lived on one dish of barley for the last four days. On entering another house the doctor said, "Look there, Sir, you can't tell whether they are boys or girls." Taking up a skeleton child, he said, "Here is the way it is with them all; their legs swing and rock like the legs of a doll, they have the smell of mice."

William Steuart Trench, *Realities of Irish Life* (London: Longmans, Green, 1868).

READING AND DISCUSSION QUESTIONS

1. Why do you think the British government failed to take effectual action to alleviate the famine?

2. The blight, which affected potato harvests throughout northern Europe, did not produce a similar catastrophe in Britain. Why might Britain have been spared?

COMPARATIVE QUESTIONS

1. In what ways did Thomas Malthus's theories in his *Essay on the Principle of Population* (Document 22-2) affect Ricardo's views about the supply and demand of labor?

2. What do you think Marx and Engels derived from Ricardo's essay "On Wages" in formulating their theory of class struggle?

3. In the eighteenth century, protectionism in the form of mercantilistic policies to discourage foreign trade and encourage domestic self-sufficiency was default economic policy. What do Marx and Engels's, Ricardo's, and Cobden's arguments suggest about early and mid-nineteenth century attitudes toward protectionism in Britain?

4. Describe the connections between the conditions of the Irish potato famine detailed in Trench's account and the economic philosophy outlined by David Ricardo.

CHAPTER 24

Life in the Emerging Urban Society in the Nineteenth Century

I n the second half of the nineteenth century, Britain's status as the only major industrialized nation vanished as Germany, France, the United States, and, to a lesser extent, Italy and Russia followed its lead. Like Britain earlier in the century, these nations experienced the rapid urbanization and the accompanying deplorable sanitary conditions. All witnessed the growth of the middle and working classes. However, public health and medical science had advanced significantly by the 1860s. The association between squalor and disease was better understood, and new iron pipe with threaded ends made possible the installation of sanitary water and sewage systems in cities. Politically, the expansion of the electorate in Britain, Germany, and France meant that, by 1884, the working class was the largest voting bloc in all three nations. Universal adult male suffrage was introduced in both the German Empire and the Third French Republic in 1871.

DOCUMENT 24-1

SIR EDWIN CHADWICK

From Inquiry Into the Sanitary Condition of the Poor

1842

Edwin Chadwick (1800–1880), a disciple of the radical philosopher Jeremy Bentham, spent his life in pursuit of social and sanitary reform. Bentham,

---

Edwin Chadwick, *Report . . . from the Poor Law Commissioners on an Inquiry into the Sanitary Conditions of the Labouring Population of Great Britain* (London: W. Clowes and Sons, 1842), 369–372.

Chadwick, and other radicals known as utilitarians shared many views with nineteenth-century liberals; both believed in human rationality and the concept of human progress, and both believed that poverty was chiefly the consequence of individual moral failings. They parted ways sharply, however, over the role of government. Liberals argued that it was an impediment to progress; utilitarians believed that government policy and intervention could speed the rate of progress.

After as careful an examination of the evidence collected as I have been enabled to make, I beg leave to recapitulate the chief conclusions which that evidence appears to me to establish.

First, as to the extent and operation of the evils which are the subject of this inquiry: —

That the various forms of epidemic, endemic, and other disease[1] caused, or aggravated, or propagated chiefly amongst the laboring classes by atmospheric impurities produced by decomposing animal and vegetable substances, by damp and filth, and close and overcrowded dwellings prevail amongst the population in every part of the kingdom, whether dwelling in separate houses, in rural villages, in small towns, in the larger towns — as they have been found to prevail in the lowest districts of the metropolis.

That such disease, wherever its attacks are frequent, is always found in connexion with the physical circumstances above specified, and that where those circumstances are removed by drainage, proper cleansing, better ventilation, and other means of diminishing atmospheric impurity, the frequency and intensity of such disease is abated; and where the removal of the noxious agencies appears to be complete, such disease almost entirely disappears.

The high prosperity in respect to employment and wages, and various and abundant food, have afforded to the laboring classes no exemptions from attacks of epidemic disease, which have been as frequent and as fatal in periods of commercial and manufacturing prosperity as in any others.

That the formation of all habits of cleanliness is obstructed by defective supplies of water.

---

[1] **epidemic, endemic, and other disease**: The laboring classes were wracked by cholera, typhus, typhoid fever, tuberculosis (known then as "consumption"), and numerous respiratory ailments primarily caused by air pollution and occupational hazards such as cotton dust ("Brown Lung").

That the annual loss of life from filth and bad ventilation are greater than the loss from death or wounds in any wars in which the country has been engaged in modern times.

That of the 43,000 cases of widowhood, and 112,000 cases of destitute orphanage relieved from the poor's rates in England and Wales alone, it appears that the greatest proportion of deaths of the heads of families occurred from the above specified and other removable causes; that their ages were under 45 years; that is to say, 13 years below the natural probabilities of life as shown by the experience of the whole population of Sweden.

That the public loss from the premature deaths of the heads of families is greater than can be represented by any enumeration of the pecuniary burdens consequent upon their sickness and death.

That, measuring the loss of working ability amongst large classes by the instances of gain, even from incomplete arrangements for the removal of noxious influences from places of work or from abodes, that this loss cannot be less than eight or ten years.

That the ravages of epidemics and other diseases do not diminish but tend to increase the pressure of population.

That in the districts where the mortality is greatest the births are not only sufficient to replace the numbers removed by death, but to add to the population.

That the younger population, bred up under noxious physical agencies, is inferior in physical organization and general health to a population preserved from the presence of such agencies.

That the population so exposed is less susceptible of moral influences, and the effects of education are more transient than with a healthy population.

That these adverse circumstances tend to produce an adult population short-lived, improvident, reckless, and intemperate, and with habitual avidity for sensual gratifications.

That these habits lead to the abandonment of all the conveniences and decencies of life, and especially lead to the overcrowding of their homes, which is destructive to the morality as well as the health of large classes of both sexes.

That defective town cleansing fosters habits of the most abject degradation and tends to the demoralization of large numbers of human beings, who subsist by means of what they find amidst the noxious filth accumulated in neglected streets and bye-places.

That the expenses of local public works are in general unequally and unfairly assessed, oppressively and uneconomically collected, by separate collections, wastefully expended in separate and inefficient operations by unskilled and practically irresponsible officers.

That the existing law for the protection of the public health and the constitutional machinery for reclaiming its execution, such as the Courts Leet,[2] have fallen into desuetude, and are in the state indicated by the prevalence of the evils they were intended to prevent.

Secondly. As to the means by which the present sanitary condition of the laboring classes may be improved: —

The primary and most important measures, and at the same time the most practicable, and within the recognized province of public administration, are drainage, the removal of all refuse of habitations, streets, and roads, and the improvement of the supplies of water.

That the chief obstacles to the immediate removal of decomposing refuse of towns and habitations have been the expense and annoyance of the hand labor and cartage requisite for the purpose.

That this expense may be reduced to one-twentieth or to one-thirtieth, or rendered inconsiderable, by the use of water and self-acting means of removal by improved and cheaper sewers and drains.

That refuse when thus held in suspension in water may be most cheaply and innoxiously conveyed to any distance out of towns, and also in the best form for productive use, and that the loss and injury by the pollution of natural streams may be avoided.

That for all these purposes, as well as for domestic use, better supplies of water are absolutely necessary.

That for successful and economical drainage the adoption of geological areas as the basis of operations is requisite.

That appropriate scientific arrangements for public drainage would afford important facilities for private land-drainage, which is important for the health as well as sustenance of the laboring classes.

That the expense of public drainage, of supplies of water laid on in houses, and of means of improved cleansing would be a pecuniary [monetary] gain, by diminishing the existing charges attendant on sickness and premature mortality.

---

[2] **Courts Leet**: Law courts dating back to medieval times, when the administration of justice was overseen by individual noblemen. Many early industrial towns, Manchester among them, lacked comprehensive municipal governments until the 1830s and afterward, and thus such antiquated institutions like Courts Leet confronted situations which their creators had never envisioned and for which they were, as Chadwick suggests, wholly inadequate.

That for the protection of the laboring classes and of the ratepayers against inefficiency and waste in all new structural arrangements for the protection of the public health, and to ensure public confidence that the expenditure will be beneficial, securities should be taken that all new local public works are devised and conducted by responsible officers qualified by the possession of the science and skill of civil engineers.

That the oppressiveness and injustice of levies for the whole immediate outlay on such works upon persons who have only short interests in the benefits may be avoided by care in spreading the expense over periods coincident with the benefits.

That by appropriate arrangements, 10 or 15 per cent. on the ordinary outlay for drainage might be saved, which on an estimate of the expense of the necessary structural alterations of one-third only of the existing tenements would be a saving of one million and a half sterling, besides the reduction of the future expenses of management.

That for the prevention of the disease occasioned by defective ventilation and other causes of impurity in places of work and other places where large numbers are assembled, and for the general promotion of the means necessary to prevent disease, that it would be good economy to appoint a district medical officer independent of private practice, and with the securities of special qualifications and responsibilities to initiate sanitary measures and reclaim the execution of the law.

That by the combinations of all these arrangements, it is probable that the full ensurable period of life indicated by the Swedish tables; that is, an increase of 13 years at least, may be extended to the whole of the laboring classes.

That the attainment of these and the other collateral advantages of reducing existing charges and expenditure are within the power of the legislature, and are dependent mainly on the securities taken for the application of practical science, skill, and economy in the direction of local public works.

And that the removal of noxious physical circumstances, and the promotion of civic, household, and personal cleanliness, are necessary to the improvement of the moral condition of the population; for that sound morality and refinement in manners and health are not long found co-existent with filthy habits amongst any class of the community.

READING AND DISCUSSION QUESTIONS

1. What, according to Chadwick, was the chief source of disease? Why?

2. What sorts of solutions does he offer to improve public health?

3. According to Chadwick, what is the relationship between sanitation and morality? Do you agree with his assessment? Why or why not?

DOCUMENT 24-2

ISABELLA BEETON

From Mrs. Beeton's Book of Household Management

1861

Isabella Beeton (1836–1865) was a British journalist whose earliest articles appeared in the English Woman's Domestic Magazine, *the first magazine targeted specifically at middle-class women. Mrs. Beeton's Book of Household Management contained more than 2,700 entries of recipes and practical instructions, from how to keep moths from attacking clothes to how to care for horses. A best seller that was continually reprinted, it was almost certainly the most widely consulted book on the subject in the decades following its appearance.*

It is the custom of "Society" to abuse its servants: *a façon de parler* ["a manner of speaking"], such as leads their lords and masters to talk of the weather, and, when rurally inclined, of the crops, — leads matronly ladies, and ladies just entering on their probation in that honored and honorable state, to talk of servants, and, as we are told, wax eloquent over the greatest plague in life while taking a quiet cup of tea. Young men at their clubs, also, we are told, like to abuse their "fellows," perhaps not without a certain pride and pleasure at the opportunity of intimating that they enjoy such appendages to their state. It is another conviction of "Society" that

Isabella Beeton, *Mrs. Beeton's Book of Household Management* (London, 1888 [first published in 1861]), 1453–1481.

the race of good servants has died out, at least in England, although they do order these things better in France; that there is neither honesty, conscientiousness, nor the careful and industrious habits which distinguished the servants of our grandmothers and great-grandmothers; that domestics no longer know their place; that the introduction of cheap silks and cottons, and, still more recently, those ambiguous "materials" and tweeds, have removed the landmarks between the mistress and her maid, between the master and his man.

Choice of Servants. — When the distinction really depends on things so insignificant, this is very probably the case; when the lady of fashion chooses her footman without any other consideration than his height, shape, and *tournure* of his calf, it is not surprising that she should find a domestic who has no attachment for the family, who considers the figure he cuts behind her carriage, and the late hours he is compelled to keep, a full compensation for the wages he exacts, for the food he wastes, and for the perquisites he can lay his hands on. Nor should the fast young man, who chooses his groom for his knowingness in the ways of the turf and in the tricks of low horse-dealers, be surprised if he is sometimes the victim of these learned ways. But these are the exceptional cases, which prove the existence of a better state of things. The great masses of society among us are not thus deserted; there are few families of respectability, from the shopkeeper in the next street to the nobleman whose mansion dignifies the next square, which do not contain among their dependents attached and useful servants; and where these are absent altogether, there are good reasons for it.

Masters and Mistresses. — It has been said that good masters and mistresses make good servants, and this to a great extent is true. There are certainly some men and women in the wide field of servitude whom it would be impossible to train into good servants, but the conduct of both master and mistress is seldom without its effect upon these dependents. They are not mere machines, and no one has a right to consider them in that light. The sensible master and the kind mistress know, that if servants depend on them for their means of living, in their turn they are dependent on their servants for very many of the comforts of life; and that, with a proper amount of care in choosing servants, and treating them like reasonable beings, and making slight excuses for the shortcomings of human nature, they will, save in some exceptional case, be tolerably well served, and, in most instances, surround themselves with attached domestics. . . .

The number of the male domestics in a family varies according to the wealth and position of the master, from the owner of the ducal mansion, with a retinue of attendants, at the head of which is the chamberlain and house-steward, to the occupier of the humbler house, where a single foot-man, or even the odd man-of-all-work, is the only male retainer. The majority of gentlemen's establishments probably comprise a servant out of livery, or butler, a footman, and coachman, or coachman and groom, where the horses exceed two or three. . . .

Politeness and civility to visitors is one of the things masters and mis-tresses have a right to expect, and should exact rigorously. When visitors present themselves, the servant charged with the duty of opening the door will open it promptly, and answer, without hesitation, if the family are "not at home," or "engaged"; which generally means the same thing, and might be oftener used with advantage to morals. On the contrary, if he has no such orders, he will answer affirmatively, open the door wide to admit them, and precede them to open the door of the drawing-room. If the family are not there, he will place chairs for them, open the blinds (if the room is too dark), and intimate civilly that he goes to inform his mistress. If the lady is in her drawing-room, he announces the name of the visitors, having previously acquainted himself with it. In this part of his duty it is necessary to be very careful to repeat the names correctly; mispronouncing names is very apt to give offence, and leads sometimes to other disagree-ables. The writer was once initiated into some of the secrets on the "other side" of a legal affair in which he took an interest, before he could correct a mistake made by the servant in announcing him. When the visitor is departing, the servant should be at hand, ready, when rung for, to open the door; he should open it with a respectful manner, and close it gently when the visitors are fairly beyond the threshold. When several visitors arrive together, he should take care not to mix up the different names together, where they belong to the same family, as Mr., Mrs., and Miss; if they are strangers, he should announce each as distinctly as possible.

Attendants on the Person. — "No man is a hero to his valet," saith the proverb; and the corollary may run, "No lady is a heroine to her maid." The infirmities of humanity are, perhaps, too numerous and too equally distributed to stand the severe microscopic tests which attendants on the person have opportunities of applying. The valet and waiting-maid are placed near the persons of the master and mistress, receiving orders only from them, dressing them, accompanying them in all their journeys, the confidants and agents of their most unguarded moments, of their most secret habits, and of course subject to their commands, — even to their caprices; they themselves being subject to erring judgment, aggravated by an imperfect education. All that can be expected from such servants is polite manners, modest demeanor, and a respectful reserve, which are indispensable. To these, good sense, good temper, some self-denial, and consideration for the feelings of others, whether above or below them in the social scale, will be useful qualifications. Their duty leads them to wait on those who are, from sheer wealth, station, and education, more polished, and consequently more susceptible of annoyance; and any vulgar familiarity of manner is opposed to all their notions of self-respect. Quiet unobtrusive manners, therefore, and a delicate reserve in speaking of their employers, either in praise or blame, is as essential in their absence, as good manners and respectful conduct in their presence.

Duties of the Lady's-Maid. — The duties of a lady's-maid are more numerous, and perhaps more onerous, than those of the valet; for while the latter is aided by the tailor, the hatter, the linen-draper, and the perfumer, the lady's-maid has to originate many parts of the mistress's dress herself: she should, indeed, be a tolerably expert milliner and dressmaker, a good hairdresser, and possess some chemical knowledge of the cosmetics with which the toilet-table is supplied, in order to use them with safety and effect. Her first duty in the morning, after having performed her own toilet, is to examine the clothes put off by her mistress the evening before, either to put them away, or to see that they are all in order to put on again. During the winter, and in wet weather, the dresses should be carefully examined, and the mud removed. Dresses of tweed, and other woollen materials, may be laid out on a table and brushed all over; but in general, even in woollen fabrics, the lightness of the tissues renders brushing unsuitable to dresses, and it is better to remove the dust from the folds by beating them lightly with a handkerchief or thin cloth. Silk dresses should never be brushed, but rubbed with a piece of merino, or other soft material, of a similar color, kept for the purpose. Summer dresses of barge, muslin, mohair, and other light materials, simply require shaking; but if the muslin be tumbled, it must be ironed afterwards. If the dresses require slight repair, it should be done at once: "a stitch in time saves nine."

A waiting-maid, who wishes to make herself useful, will study the fashion-books with attention, so as to be able to aid her mistress's judgment in dressing, according to the prevailing fashion, with such modifications as her style of countenance requires. She will also, if she has her mistress's interest at heart, employ her spare time in repairing and making up dresses which have served one purpose, to serve another also, or turning many things, unfitted for her mistress to use, for the younger branches of the family. The lady's-maid may thus render herself invaluable to her mistress, and increase her own happiness in so doing. The exigencies of fashion and luxury are such, that all ladies, except those of the very highest rank, will consider themselves fortunate in having about them a thoughtful person, capable of diverting their finery to a useful purpose.

The valet and lady's-maid, from their supposed influence with their master and mistress, are exposed to some temptations to which other servants are less subjected. They are probably in communication with the tradespeople who supply articles for the toilet; such as hatters, tailors, dressmakers, and perfumers. The conduct of waiting-maid and valet to these people should be civil but independent, making reasonable allowance for want of exact punctuality, if any such can be made: they should represent any inconvenience respectfully, and if an excuse seems unreasonable, put the matter fairly to master or mistress, leaving it to them to notice it further, if they think it necessary. No expectations of a personal character should influence them one way or the other. It would be acting unreasonably to any domestic to make them refuse such presents as tradespeople choose to give them; the utmost that can be expected is that they should not influence their judgment in the articles supplied — that they should represent them truly to master or mistress, without fear and without favor. Civility to all, servility to none, is a good maxim for every one. Deference to a master and mistress, and to their friends and visitors, is one of the implied terms of their engagement; and this deference must apply even to what may be considered their whims. A servant is not to be seated, or wear a hat in the house, in his master's or mistress's presence; nor offer any opinion, unless asked for it; nor even to say "good night," or "good morning," except in reply to that salutation.

Duties of the Housemaid. — "Cleanliness is next to godliness," saith the proverb, and "order" is in the next degree; the housemaid, then, may be said to be the handmaiden to two of the most prominent virtues. Her duties are very numerous, and many of the comforts of the family depend on their performance; but they are simple and easy to a person naturally clean and orderly, and desirous of giving satisfaction. In all families, whatever the habits of the master and mistress, servants will find it advantageous to rise early; their daily work will thus come easy to them. If they rise late, there is a struggle to overtake it, which throws an air of haste and hurry over the whole establishment. Where the master's time is regulated by early business or professional engagements, this will, of course, regulate the hours of the servants; but even where that is not the case, servants will find great personal convenience in rising early and getting through their work in an orderly and methodical manner. The housemaid who studies her own ease will certainly be at her work by six o'clock in the summer, and, probably, half-past six or seven in the winter months, having spent a reasonable time in her own chamber in dressing. Earlier than this would, probably, be an unnecessary waste of coals and candle in winter.

The first duty of the housemaid in winter is to open the shutters of all the lower rooms in the house, and take up the hearth-rugs of those rooms which she is going to "do" before breakfast. In some families, where there is only a cook and housemaid kept, and where the drawing-rooms are large, the cook has the care of the dining-room, and the housemaid that of the breakfast-room, library, and drawing-rooms. After the shutters are all opened, she sweeps the breakfast-room, sweeping the dust towards the fire-place, of course previously removing the fonder. She should then lay a cloth (generally made of coarse wrappering) over the carpet in front of the stove, and on this should place her housemaid's box, containing black-lead brushes, leathers, emery-paper, cloth, black lead, and all utensils necessary for cleaning a grate, with the cinder-pail on the other side.

She now sweeps up the ashes, and deposits them in her cinder-pail, which is a japanned tin pail, with a wire-sifter inside, and a closely-fitting top. In this pail the cinders are sifted, and reserved for use in the kitchen or under the copper, the ashes only being thrown away. The cinders disposed of, she proceeds to black-lead the grate, producing the black lead, the soft brush for laying it on, her blacking and polishing brushes, from the box which contains her tools. This housemaid's box should be kept well stocked. Having blackened, brushed, and polished every part, and made all clean and bright, she now proceeds to lay the fire.

Bright grates require unceasing attention to keep them in perfect order. A day should never pass without the housemaid rubbing with a dry leather the polished parts of a grate, as also the fender and fire-irons. A careful and attentive housemaid should have no occasion ever to use emery-paper for any part but the bars, which, of course, become blackened by the fire. (Some mistresses, to save labor, have a double set of bars, one set bright for the summer, and another black set to use when fires are in requisition.) When bright grates are once neglected, small rust-spots begin to show themselves, which a plain leather will not remove; the following method of cleaning them must then be resorted to: — First, thoroughly clean with emery-paper; then take a large smooth pebble from the road, sufficiently large to hold comfortably in the hand, with which rub the steel backwards and forwards one way, until the desired polish is obtained. It may appear at first to scratch, but continue rubbing, and the result will be success.

The several fires lighted, the housemaid proceeds with her dusting, and polishing the several pieces of furniture in the breakfast-parlor, leaving no corner unvisited. Before sweeping the carpet, it is a good practice to sprinkle it all over with tea-leaves, which not only lay all dust, but give a slightly fragrant smell to the room. It is now in order for the reception of the family; and where there is neither footman nor parlor-maid, she now proceeds to the dressing-room, and lights her mistress's fire, if she is in the habit of having one to dress by. Her mistress is called, hot water placed in the dressing-room for her use, her clothes — as far as they are under the house-maid's charge — put before the fire to air, hanging a fire-guard on the bars where there is one, while she proceeds to prepare the breakfast.

Breakfast served, the housemaid proceeds to the bed-chambers, throws up the sashes, if not already done, pulls up the blinds, throwing back curtains at the same time, and opens the beds, by removing the clothes, placing them over a horse, or, failing that, over the backs of chairs. She now proceeds to empty the slops. In doing this, everything is emptied into the slop-pail, leaving a little scalding-hot water for a minute in such vessels as require it; adding a drop of turpentine to the water, when that is not sufficient to cleanse them. The basin is emptied, well rinsed with clean water, and carefully wiped; the ewers emptied and washed; finally, the water-jugs themselves emptied out and rinsed, and wiped dry. As soon as this is done, she should remove and empty the pails, taking care that they also are well washed, scalded, and wiped as soon as they are empty.

Next follows bedmaking, at which the cook or kitchen-maid, where one is kept, usually assists; but, before beginning, velvet chairs, or other things injured by dust, should be removed to another room. In bedmaking, the fancy of its occupant should be consulted; some like beds sloping from the top towards the feet, swelling slightly in the middle; others, perfectly flat: a good housemaid will accommodate each bed to the taste of the sleeper, taking care to shake, beat, and turn it well in the process. Some persons prefer sleeping on the mattress; in which case a feather bed is usually beneath, resting on a second mattress, and a straw paillasse at the bottom. In this case, the mattresses should change places daily; the feather bed placed on the mattress shaken, beaten, taken up and opened several times, so as thoroughly to separate the feathers: if too large to be thus handled, the maid should shake and beat one end first, and then the other, smoothing it afterwards equally all over into the required shape, and place the mattress gently over it. Any feathers which escape in this process a tidy servant will put back through the seam of the tick; she will also be careful to sew up any stitch that gives way the moment it is discovered. The bedclothes are laid on, beginning with an under blanket and sheet, which are tucked under the mattress at the bottom. The bolster is then beaten and shaken, and put on, the top of the sheet rolled round it, and the sheet tucked in all round. The pillows and other bedclothes follow, and the counterpane over all, which should fall in graceful folds, and at equal distance from the ground all round. The curtains are drawn to the head and folded neatly across the bed, and the whole finished in a smooth and graceful manner. Where spring-mattresses are used, care should be taken that the top one is turned every day. The housemaid should now take up in a dustpan any pieces that may be on the carpet; she should dust the room, shut the door, and proceed to another room. When all the bedrooms are finished, she should dust the stairs, and polish the handrail of the banisters, and see that all ledges, window-sills, &c., are quite free from dust. It will be necessary for the housemaid to divide her work, so that she may not have too much to do on certain days, and not sufficient to fill up her time on other days. In the country, bedrooms should be swept and thoroughly cleaned once a week; and to be methodical and regular in her work, the housemaid should have certain days for doing certain rooms thoroughly. For instance, the drawing-room on Monday, two bedrooms on Tuesday, two on Wednesday, and so on, reserving a day for thoroughly cleaning the plate, bedroom candlesticks, &c. &c., which she will have to do where there is no parlor-maid or footman kept. By this means the work will be divided, and there will be no unnecessary bustling and hurrying, as is the case where the work is done any time, without rule or regulation.

READING AND DISCUSSION QUESTIONS

1. What do Beeton's instructions about the management and duties of household servants tell us about how life in modern urban societies has altered over the past century and a half?

2. What does Beeton infer are some of the most typical problems that exist between masters and servants?

3. What does this excerpt tell us about class divisions, and about Beeton's attitudes toward the "lower orders," from which servants came?

4. Britain's aristocracy had been managing servants for centuries at the time this guide was published. To whom do you think Beeton was imparting her instructions, regardless of the grandeur of the households she describes?

DOCUMENT 24-3

CLARA ZETKIN

Women's Work and the Trade Unions

1887

German socialist and feminist Clara Zetkin (1857–1933) was an influential politician and women's suffragist from 1878 until her forced exile by the Nazi regime shortly before her death. A friend of many prominent German radicals including Wilhelm Liebknecht, one of the founders of the German Social Democratic (i.e., Socialist) Party, Zetkin was part of the first generation of modern European feminists. Like their British, French, and American counterparts, late nineteenth-century German feminists, most of them, like Zetkin, from middle-class backgrounds, devoted the bulk of their energies to obtaining the vote. Zetkin founded the German social democratic women's movement and, for more than twenty-five years, edited the Social Democratic Party's women's newspaper Die Gleichheit (Equality).

It is not just the women workers who suffer because of the miserable payment of their labor. The male workers, too, suffer because of it. As a consequence of their low wages, the women are transformed from mere competitors into unfair competitors who push down the wages of men. Cheap women's labor eliminates the work of men and if the men want to continue to earn their daily bread, they must put up with low wages. Thus women's work is not only a cheap form of labor, it also cheapens the work of men and for that reason it is doubly appreciated by the capitalist, who craves profits. The economic advantages of the industrial activity of proletarian women only aid the tiny minority of the sacrosanct guild of coupon clippers and extortionists of profit.

Given the fact that many thousands of female workers are active in industry, it is vital for the trade unions to incorporate them into their movement. In individual industries where female labor plays an important role, any movement advocating better wages, shorter working hours, etc., would be doomed from the start because of the attitude of those women workers who are not organized. Battles which began propitiously enough, ended

Clara Zetkin, "Women's Work and the Trade Unions" in Philip S. Foner, ed., *Clara Zetkin, Selected Writings* (New York: International Publishers, 1984), 54–56.

up in failure because the employers were able to play off non-union female workers against those that are organized in unions. These non-union workers continued to work (or took up work) under any conditions, which transformed them from competitors in dirtywork to scabs [non-union strikebreakers].

Certainly one of the reasons for these poor wages for women is the circumstances that female workers are practically unorganized. They lack the strength which comes with unity. They lack the courage, the feeling of power, the spirit of resistance, and the ability to resist which is produced by the strength of an organization in which the individual fights for everybody and everybody fights for the individual. Furthermore, they lack the enlightenment and the training which an organization provides.

READING AND DISCUSSION QUESTIONS

1. Why, according to Zetkin, do women and men compete for jobs? What is the consequence of that competition? What is Zetkin's solution to the competition?

2. Why might Zetkin have advocated the peaceful organization of women into trade unions rather than striving for a communist revolution?

3. What do the author's arguments suggest about the nature and extent of working-class political power in late nineteenth-century Germany?

DOCUMENT 24-4

CHARLES DARWIN

From The Origin of Species:
On Natural Selection

1859

Charles Darwin (1809–1882) was the most prominent scientist in nineteenth-century Britain. His major works, On the Origin of Species by Means of

Charles Darwin, *The Origin of Species* (New York: Modern Library, n.d.), 367–368, 373–374.

Natural Selection *(1859) and* The Descent of Man *(1871), put forward the theory of natural selection and argued that humans were closely related to the great apes, respectively. Although they were immensely controversial upon publication (and remain, to this day, works of heated contention), they are the foundational texts of modern evolutionary science. In the following excerpt, drawn from a later edition of* The Origin of Species, *Darwin replies to his critics.*

I have now recapitulated the facts and considerations which have thoroughly convinced me that species have been modified, during a long course of descent. This has been effected chiefly through the natural selections of numerous successive, slight, favorable variations; aided in an important manner by the inherited effects of the use and disuse of parts; and in an unimportant manner, that is in relation to adaptive structures, whether past or present, by the direct action of external conditions, and by variations which seem to us in our ignorance to arise spontaneously. . . . But as my conclusions have lately been much misrepresented, and it has been stated that I attribute the modification of species exclusively to natural selection, I may be permitted to remark that in the first edition of this work, and subsequently, I placed in a most conspicuous position — namely, at the close of the Introduction — the following words: "I am convinced that natural selection has been the main but not the exclusive means of modification." This has been of no avail. Great is the power of steady misrepresentation; but the history of science shows that fortunately this power does not long endure.

It can hardly be supposed that a false theory would explain, in so satisfactory a manner as does the theory of natural selection, the several large classes of facts above specified. It has recently been objected that this is an unsafe method of arguing; but it is a method used in judging of the common events of life, and has often been used by the greatest natural philosophers. The undulatory theory of light[3] has thus been arrived at; and the belief in the revolution of the earth on its own axis was until lately supported by hardly any direct evidence. It is no valid objection that science as yet throws no light on the far higher problem of the essence or origin of life. Who can explain what is the essence of the attraction of gravity? No one now objects to following out the results consequent on this unknown

---

[3] **undulatory theory of light**: The theory that light, like sound, is diffused as a series of waves.

element of attraction; notwithstanding that [mathematician Gottfried Wilhelm] Leibnitz formerly accused [Isaac] Newton of introducing "occult qualities and miracles into philosophy."

I see no good reason why the views given in this volume should shock the religious feelings of any one. It is satisfactory, as showing how transient such impressions are, to remember that the greatest discovery ever made by man, namely, the law of the attraction of gravity, was also attacked by Leibnitz, "as subversive of natural, and inferentially of revealed, religion." A celebrated author and divine has written to me that "he has gradually learnt to see that it is just as noble a conception of the Deity to believe that He created a few original forms capable of self-development into other and needful forms, as to believe that He required a fresh act of creation to supply the voids caused by the action of His laws." . . .

. . . The chief cause of our natural unwillingness to admit that one species has given birth to clear and distinct species, is that we are always slow in admitting great changes of which we do not see the steps. The difficulty is the same as that felt by so many geologists, when [geologist Charles] Lyell first insisted that long lines of inland cliffs had been formed, and great valleys excavated, by the agencies which we see still at work. The mind cannot possibly grasp the full meaning of the term of even a million years; it cannot add up and perceive the full effects of many slight variations, accumulated during an almost infinite number of generations. . . .

Authors of the highest eminence seem to be fully satisfied with the view that each species has been independently created. To my mind it accords better with what we know of the laws impressed on matter by the Creator, that the production and extinction of the past and present inhabitants of the world should have been due to secondary causes, like those determining the birth and death of the individual. When I view all beings not as special creations, but as the lineal descendants of some few beings which lived long before the first bed of the Cambrian[4] system was deposited, they seem to me to become ennobled. Judging from the past, we may safely infer that not one living species will transmit its unaltered likeness to a distant futurity. And of the species now living very few will transmit progeny of any kind to a far distant futurity; for the manner in which all organic beings are grouped, shows that the greater number of species in each genus, and all the species in many genera, have left no descendants, but have become utterly extinct. We can so far take a prophetic glance into

---

[4]**Cambrian:** The geological epoch from about 543 to 490 million years ago, during which fossils of most of the major groups of animals first appear.

futurity as to foretell that it will be the common and widely-spread species, belonging to the larger and dominant groups within each class, which will ultimately prevail and procreate new and dominant species. As all the living forms of life are the lineal descendants of those which lived long before the Cambrian epoch, we may feel certain that the ordinary succession by generation has never once been broken, and that no cataclysm has desolated the whole world. Hence we may look with some confidence to a secure future of great length. And as natural selection works solely by and for the good of each being, all corporeal and mental endowments will tend to progress towards perfection.

It is interesting to contemplate a tangled bank, clothed with many plants of many kinds, with birds singing on the bushes, with various insects flitting about, and with worms crawling through the damp earth, and to reflect that these elaborately constructed forms, so different from each other, and dependent upon each other in so complex a manner, have all been produced by laws acting around us. . . . Thus, from the war of nature, from famine and death, the most exalted object which we are capable of conceiving, namely, the production of the higher animals, directly follows. There is grandeur in this view of life, with its several powers, having been originally breathed by the Creator into a few forms or into one; and that, whilst this planet has gone cycling on according to the fixed law of gravity, from so simple a beginning endless forms most beautiful and most wonderful have been and are being evolved.

READING AND DISCUSSION QUESTIONS

1. Why does Darwin argue that his theories of evolution and natural selection are not incompatible with belief in God?

2. With whom does Darwin align himself and his discoveries? What reasons would he have for doing so?

3. What are some of the reasons that Darwin may have faced an onslaught of criticism? Based on his reply, who do you suppose might have wished to discredit him?

DOCUMENT 24-5

HERBERT SPENCER

From Social Statistics: *Survival of the Fittest Applied to Human Kind*

1851

Like Darwin, Herbert Spencer (1820–1903) was an English intellectual, although his work concerned philosophy and social theory rather than science. Spencer was one of the earliest champions of what would later be called "Social Darwinism" — the idea that the very struggle for survival which characterized life in the natural world also applied to human societies. Indeed, Spencer coined the phrase "survival of the fittest," later adopted by Darwin (not the other way around!). The following excerpt comes from his first major work, Social Statistics *(1850), which attracted relatively little attention on publication, but contains many of the ideas which would make Spencer one of the most well-known and influential British intellectuals during the 1870s and 1880s.*

In common with its other assumptions of secondary offices, the assumption by a government of the office of Reliever-general to the poor, is necessarily forbidden by the principle that a government cannot rightly do anything more than protect. In demanding from a citizen contributions for the mitigation of distress — contributions not needed for the due administration of men's rights — the state is, as we have seen, reversing its function, and diminishing that liberty to exercise the faculties which it was instituted to maintain. Possibly . . . some will assert that by satisfying the wants of the pauper, a government is in reality extending his liberty to exercise his faculties. . . . But this statement of the case implies a confounding of two widely different things. To enforce the fundamental law — to take care that every man has freedom to do all that he wills, provided he infringes not the equal freedom of any other man — this is the special purpose for which the civil power exists. Now insuring to each the right to

---

Herbert Spencer, *Social Statistics*, in J. Salwyn Schapiro, ed., *Liberalism: Its Meaning and History* (New York: Van Nostrand Reinhold, 1958), 136–137.

pursue within the specified limits the objects of his desires without let or hindrance, is quite a separate thing from insuring him satisfaction. . . .

Pervading all nature we may see at work a stern discipline, which is a little cruel that it may be very kind. That state of universal warfare maintained throughout the lower creation, to the great perplexity of many worthy people, is at bottom the most merciful provision which the circumstances admit of. . . . The poverty of the incapable, the distresses that come upon the imprudent, the starvation of the idle, and those shoulderings aside of the weak by the strong, which leave so many "in shallows and in miseries," are the decrees of a large, farseeing benevolence. It seems hard that an unskilfulness which with all its efforts he cannot overcome, should entail hunger upon the artisan. It seems hard that a laborer incapacitated by sickness from competing with his stronger fellows, should have to bear the resulting privations. It seems hard that widows and orphans should be left to struggle for life or death. Nevertheless, when regarded not separately, but in connection with the interests of universal humanity, these harsh fatalities are seen to be full of the highest beneficence — the same beneficence which brings to early graves the children of diseased parents, and singles out the low-spirited, the intemperate, and the debilitated as the victims of an epidemic. . . .

READING AND DISCUSSION QUESTIONS

1. What, according to Spencer, is the "fundamental law"? Do you agree with it? Why or why not? Where else have you seen this "fundamental law"?

2. On what grounds could Spencer argue that the death of "the children of diseased parents" was in the "interests of universal humanity" and "full of the highest beneficence" for mankind?

COMPARATIVE QUESTIONS

1. How does Spencer's argument weigh against the tenets of classical liberalism as expressed in David Ricardo's "On Wages" (Document 23-1)?

2. In what ways does Beeton's *Book of Household Management* reflect the new nineteenth-century awareness of sanitation's relationship to health, made explicit in Chadwick's *Inquiry into the Sanitary Condition of the Poor*?

3. How might Edwin Chadwick respond to Spencer's Social Darwinism?

4. What do you think Darwin and Spencer would say in response to Zetkin's arguments, and why?

CHAPTER 25

The Age of Nationalism

1850–1914

B efore 1848, nationalism was a revolutionary ideology, often concerned with rebelling against deeply rooted, outmoded governments. In the second half of the nineteenth century, leaders such as France's Louis Napoleon Bonaparte and Germany's Otto von Bismarck used nationalist feeling to garner support for policies designed to build the power of the central government. Not all new governments fared well in the court of public opinion. In America, eleven southern states declared total freedom from a federal government that had been elected to stop the expansion of slavery. Between 1861 and 1865, Confederate and Union factions fought a bitter and bloody civil war. Toward the end of the century, the adoption of nationalism as the basis for personal identity led to horrifying violence against perceived outsiders, particularly Europe's Jewish population. The Dreyfus affair in France (1894–1906) spurred a Jewish movement — Zionism — to gain a nation for themselves and prevent future persecution.

DOCUMENT 25-1

LOUIS NAPOLEON BONAPARTE

Campaign Statement

1848

In 1830, the French rebelled against the last of the Bourbon kings, Charles X, and crowned Louis-Phillippe "King of the French People," rather than "King of France." In 1848, middle- and working-class discontent led to

---

Louis Napoleon Bonaparte, Campaign Statement, in James Harvey Robinson, ed., *Readings in European History* (Boston: Ginn, 1904), 2:562–563.

another revolution. The people proclaimed a Second Republic and elected a president instead of a king. The new leader, Louis Napoleon Bonaparte, was elected in large part because of the reputation of his uncle, Napoleon Bonaparte, who had briefly brought national glory to France. The authoritarian Louis suppressed the power of Parliament and proclaimed himself emperor in 1852, a move overwhelmingly approved by the French electorate. He was France's first president and, ultimately, its last monarch.

Those proofs of so honorable a confidence are, I am well aware, addressed to my name rather than to myself, who, as yet, have done nothing for my country; but the more the memory of the Emperor protects me and inspires your suffrages, the more I feel compelled to acquaint you with my sentiments and principles. There must be no equivocation between us.

I am moved by no ambition which dreams one day of empire and war, the next of the application of subversive theories. Brought up in free countries, disciplined in the school of misfortune, I shall ever remain faithful to the duties which your suffrages and the will of the Assembly impose upon me.

If elected president, I shall shrink from no danger, from no sacrifice, in the defense of society, which has been so outrageously assailed. I shall devote myself wholly and without reservation to the consolidation of the republic, so that it may be wise in its laws, honest in its aims, great and strong in its deeds. My greatest honor would be to hand on to my successor, after four years of office, the public power consolidated, its liberties intact, and a genuine progress assured. . . .

LOUIS NAPOLEON BONAPARTE.

READING AND DISCUSSION QUESTIONS

1. In his proclamation, on what does Louis Napoleon base his claim to rule France?

2. What goals does Louis Napoleon appear to have for his tenure as president of France? How does it change your understanding to know that he proclaimed himself emperor within four years?

DOCUMENT 25-2

ABRAHAM LINCOLN

The Gettysburg Address

1863

With the election of Abraham Lincoln to the U.S. presidency in 1860, eleven southern states left the Union to form the Confederate States of America — in large part because of Lincoln's commitment to ending the expansion of slavery. The ensuing Civil War sped the centralizing process already apparent in Europe, and federal power expanded dramatically. In his address President Lincoln dedicates the national cemetery for the soldiers killed at the Battle of Gettysburg, the largest battle ever waged in North America (fought July 1–3, 1862), and rallies a weary nation to continue the war.

Four score and seven years ago[1] our fathers brought forth on this continent, a new nation, conceived in Liberty, and dedicated to the proposition that all men are created equal.

Now we are engaged in a great civil war, testing whether that nation, or any nation so conceived and so dedicated, can long endure. We are met on a great battle-field of that war. We have come to dedicate a portion of that field, as a final resting place for those who here gave their lives that that nation might live. It is altogether fitting and proper that we should do this.

But, in a larger sense, we can not dedicate — we can not consecrate — we can not hallow — this ground. The brave men, living and dead, who struggled here, have consecrated it, far above our poor power to add or detract. The world will little note, nor long remember what we say here, but it can never forget what they did here. It is for us the living, rather, to be dedicated here to the unfinished work which they who fought here have thus far so nobly advanced. It is rather for us to be here dedicated to the great task remaining before us — that from these honored dead we take increased devotion to that cause for which they gave the last full measure

---

Abraham Lincoln, "The Gettysburg Address," November 19, 1863.

[1] **Four score and seven years ago**: A score is twenty, thus Lincoln means eighty-seven years ago: 1776.

of devotion — that we here highly resolve that these dead shall not have died in vain — that this nation, under God, shall have a new birth of freedom — and that government of the people, by the people, for the people, shall not perish from the earth.

READING AND DISCUSSION QUESTIONS

1. In what ways does Lincoln tie his policies to the past in this speech? In what ways does he look to the future?

2. What is the basis of Lincoln's argument for asserting federal power (abolishing slavery) and continuing the conflict with the Confederate forces?

DOCUMENT 25-3

OTTO VON BISMARCK

Speech Before the Reichstag: The Welfare State Is Born

1883

Otto von Bismarck (1815–1898), minister-president of Prussia and eventual chancellor of the German nation, was an aristocratic conservative who believed that those in power had an obligation to those they ruled. Caught between liberals who argued for few restrictions on economic behavior and socialists who wanted to strip the reins of power from the upper class, Bismarck outlawed the socialist party but implemented many of their reforms on his own terms. Under his leadership, Germany enacted a series of laws between 1883 and 1889 that created a comprehensive system of insurance and pensions to care for workers' needs, hoping to earn the loyalty of the working class in return.

Otto von Bismarck, "Speech Before the Reichstag," in J. Salwyn Shapiro, ed., *Liberalism: Its History and Meaning* (Princeton, N.J.: Princeton University Press, 1958), 174.

Deputy Richter[2] has called attention to the responsibility of the state for what it does, in the area now concerned. Well, gentlemen, I have a feeling that the state may also be responsible for its omissions. I am not of the opinion that "laisser faire, laisser aller,"[3] "pure Manchesterism[4] in politics," "as you make your bed, so you must lie," "every man for himself, and Devil take the hindmost," "to him that hath shall be given, and from him that hath not shall be taken away even that which he hath," have applicability in a state, especially a monarchical, paternalistic state; on the contrary, I believe that those who thus condemn the intervention of the state for the protection of the weaker are themselves suspect of wishing to exploit the strength they have, be it capitalistic, be it rhetorical, be it what it may, to gain a following, to oppress others, to build party dominance, and of becoming annoyed as soon as this understanding is disturbed by any influence of the government.

READING AND DISCUSSION QUESTIONS

1. How does Bismarck view the relationship between the state and those it governs? Does he seem to be in favor of democratic government?

2. Given that most political parties were his opponents, what view does Bismarck take of political organization in Germany?

---

[2] **Deputy Richter**: Eugen Richter, a socialist radical member of the German Reichstag (Parliament) and Bismarck's personal and political opponent. Richter thought the proposed legislation did not go far enough.

[3] **"laisser faire, laisser aller"**: In French, literally "let it go, let go." The phrase originated with a group of French economists in the eighteenth century who argued that the government's best policy toward agriculture was to leave it alone.

[4] **Manchesterism**: The "Manchester school" of economics, led by Richard Cobden and John Bright, argued for no state involvement in economic affairs. Cobden and Bright led the opposition to the Corn Laws, Britain's 1815 laws placing high import taxes on foreign grain, on these grounds (see Document 23-3).

DOCUMENT 25-4

ÉMILE ZOLA

"J'Accuse" the French Army: The Dreyfus Case

1898

Alfred Dreyfus was a Jewish French artillery officer arrested and convicted in 1894 for selling military secrets to the Germans. His case revealed the ambiguity of nineteenth-century nationalists toward Jewish citizens as well as the pressure the state's needs placed on its courts. Dreyfus' innocence was well established by the time Émile Zola, a famous novelist, wrote this letter, but his opponents — the Anti-Dreyfusards — argued that it was better that an innocent man be imprisoned than the government admit it had made a mistake and thereby undermine the nation. A sizable faction — the Dreyfusards — disagreed, and the argument split French politics for years.

Dreyfus knows several languages: a crime. No compromising papers were found in his possession: a crime. He sometimes visited his native country[5]: a crime. He is industrious and likes to find out about everything: a crime. He is calm: a crime. He is worried: a crime. . . .

I accuse Lieutenant-Colonel du Paty de Clam[6] of having been the diabolical, but I would fain believe the unwitting, artisan of the miscarriage of justice, and thereafter of having defended his unhallowed work for three years by the most clumsy and culpable machinations.

From Émile Zola, "J'Accuse" in Armand Charpentier, *The Dreyfus Case*, Lewis May, trans. (London: Geoffrey Bles, 1935), 142–144.

[5] **his native country**: Dreyfus was from Alsace (Alsatia in German), a French province at the time of his birth, but taken by Germany in 1871. For Dreyfus to visit his childhood home, he had to cross the new national border.

[6] **Lieutenant-Colonel du Paty de Clam**: Armand Mercier Paty de Clam was the French counterintelligence officer who conducted the first accusation against Dreyfus, and who remained convinced of Dreyfus' guilt long after the actual author of the document that began the case was revealed.

I accuse General Mercier[7] of having become, at all events through weakness, an accomplice in one of the greatest iniquities of the age.

I accuse General Billot[8] of having had in his hands sure proofs of the innocence of Dreyfus and of having hushed them up, of having incurred the guilt of crimes against humanity and justice, for political ends and to save the face of the General Staff.

I accuse General de Boisdeffre and General Gonse[9] of having been participators in the same crime, actuated, the one no doubt by clerical partisanship, the other, it may be, by that esprit de corps which would make the Army and the War Office the sacred Ark of the Covenant.

I accuse General de Pellieux and Major Ravary[10] of conducting a disgraceful inquiry, by which I mean an inquiry characterized by the most monstrous partiality, of which we have, in the report of the latter of these two men, an imperishable monument of stupid audacity.

I accuse the three handwriting experts, MM. Belhomme, Varinard, and Couard, of drawing up misleading and lying reports, unless, indeed, a medical examination should reveal them to be suffering from some pathological abnormality of sight and judgment.

I accuse the War Office of conducting an abominable campaign in the Press, and particularly in the newspapers l'Eclair and l'Echo de Paris, in order to mislead public opinion and to conceal their own misdeeds.

I accuse the first Court-Martial of acting contrary to law by condemning an accused man on the strength of a secret document; and I accuse the

---

[7] **General Mercier**: Mercier was the war minister who originated the case against Dreyfus and continued it to avoid political embarrassment after making public pronouncements of his certainty of Dreyfus' guilt.

[8] **General Billot**: Jean-Baptiste Billot was a French general and war minister during the later stages of the Dreyfus affair, 1896–98.

[9] **General de Boisdeffre and General Gonse**: General Gonse was the general to whom the counterintelligence division (called for secrecy purposes the Statistical Section) reported. Boisdeffre was the chief of staff of the French Army — its highest ranking soldier — at the time of the initial accusation, and according to Zola, a strong supporter of the Catholic clergy in France.

[10] **General de Pellieux and Major Ravary**: Pellieux was the general who investigated the accusations against Esterhazy — the man later proved to have committed the crime of which Dreyfus was accused — and found him innocent. Ravary oversaw the handwriting analysts, and reported on their findings, which turned out to be inaccurate.

second Court-Martial of having, in obedience to orders, concealed that illegality, and of committing in its turn the crime of knowingly acquitting a guilty man.

In bringing these charges, I am not unaware that I render myself liable to prosecution under Clauses 30 and 31 of the Act of the 29th of July, which deals with defamation of character in the public Press. But I do so of my own free will and with my eyes open.

As for those whom I accuse, I do not know them, I have never seen them. I entertain for them neither hatred nor ill-will. They are so far as I am concerned mere entities, spirits of social maleficence, and the action to which I have here committed myself is but a revolutionary means of hastening the explosion of Truth and Justice.

I have but one passion, and that is for light, and I plead in the name of that humanity which has so greatly suffered and has a right to happiness. My fiery protest is but the outcry of my soul. Let them drag me, then, into a Court of Justice and let the matter be thrashed out in broad daylight. I am ready.

READING AND DISCUSSION QUESTIONS

1. Based on this document, what is the relationship between the needs of the accused and the needs of the state in nineteenth-century France? How does Zola oppose this conception of justice?

2. Although the actions of the court that convicted Dreyfus were popular, were they compatible with the idea of government by the consent of the governed, which the French Third Republic claimed?

3. What motivations might Zola have had for making specific allegations against specific people, instead of charging a grand but vague conspiracy?

4. What is the role Dreyfus seems to play in "J'Accuse"? Does Zola seem to care about Dreyfus, or is he more a political symbol than an individual? What gives you that impression?

LEO PINSKER

From Auto-Emancipation: *A Russian Zionist Makes the Case for a Jewish Homeland*

1882

Nationalists in the second half of the nineteenth century were unsure how to categorize Europe's Jewish population. Anti-Semitism had a long history in Europe, but in an era worried about national identity, fear of Jews was based more on fears of disloyalty than religious motives. Leo Pinsker (1821–1891), a Jewish doctor born in Russian-ruled Poland, argued that the way to end these worries was not European tolerance but the creation of a nation-state (referred to as Zion) to which the Jews could emigrate. The Zionist movement led to the creation of the state of Israel in the mid-twentieth century.

> If I am not for myself, who will be for me?
> And if not now, when?
>
> — Hillel[11]

That hoary problem, subsumed under the Jewish question, today, as ever in the past, provokes discussion. Like the squaring of the circle it remains unsolved, but unlike it, continues to be the everburning question of the day. That is because the problem is not one of mere theoretical interest: it renews and revives in everyday life and presses ever more urgently for solution.

This is the kernel of the problem, as we see it: *the Jews comprise a distinctive element among the nations under which they dwell, and as such can neither assimilate nor be readily digested by any nation.*

Hence the solution lies in finding a means of so readjusting this exclusive element to the family of nations, that the basis of the Jewish question will be permanently removed. . . .

Leo Pinsker, *Auto-Emancipation: An Appeal to His People by a Russian Jew*, in Robert Chazan and Marc Lee Raphael, eds., *Modern Jewish History: A Source Reader* (New York: Schocken Books, 1974), 161, 163, 165–166, 169–171, 173–174.

[11] **Hillel**: Hillel the Elder was a Jewish scholar and leader active in the first century B.C.E., and one of the fathers of Jewish law.

A fear of the Jewish ghost has passed down the generations and the centuries. First a breeder of prejudice, later in the conjunction with other forces we are about to discuss, it culminated in Judeophobia.

Judeophobia, together with other symbols, superstitions, and idiosyncrasies, has acquired legitimacy among all the peoples of the earth with whom the Jews had intercourse. Judeophobia is a variety of demonopathy[12] with the distinction that it is not peculiar to particular races but is common to the whole of mankind, and that this ghost is not disembodied like other ghosts but partakes of flesh and blood, must endure pain inflicted by the fearful mob who imagines itself endangered.

Judeophobia is a psychic aberration. As a psychic aberration it is hereditary, and as a disease transmitted for two thousand years it is incurable. . . .

The Jews are aliens who can have no representatives, because they have no country. Because they have none, because their home has no boundaries within which they can be entrenched, their misery too is boundless. The *general law* does not apply to the Jews as true aliens, but there are everywhere *laws for the Jews*, and if the general law is to apply to them, a special and explicit bylaw is required to confirm it. Like the Negroes, like women, and unlike all free peoples, they must be *emancipated*. If, unlike the Negroes, they belong to an advanced race, and if, unlike women, they can produce not only women of distinction, but also distinguished men, even men of greatness, then it is very much the worse for them.

Since the Jew is nowhere at home, nowhere regarded as a native, he remains an alien everywhere. That he himself and his ancestors as well are born in the country does [not] alter this fact in the least.

When we are ill-used, robbed, plundered, and dishonored, we dare not defend ourselves, and, worse still, we take it almost as a matter of course. When our face is slapped, we soothe our burning cheek with cold water; and when a bloody wound has been inflicted, we apply a bandage. When we are turned out of the house which we ourselves built, we beg humbly for mercy, and when we fail to reach the heart of our oppressor we move on in search of another exile.

When an idle spectator on the road calls out to us: "You poor Jewish devils are certainly to be pitied," we are most deeply touched; and when a

---

[12] **demonopathy**: A mental disorder in which the victim believes he or she is possessed by a demon. Pinsker is comparing Judeophobia to mental illness, not to the belief in possession.

Jew is said to be an honor to his people, we are foolish enough to be proud of it. We have sunk so low that we become almost jubilant when, as in the West, a small fraction of our people is put on an equal footing with non-Jews. But he who must be *put* on a footing stands but weakly. If no notice is taken of our descent and we are treated like others born in the country, we express our gratitude by actually turning renegades. For the sake of the comfortable position we are granted, for the fleshpots which we may enjoy in peace, we persuade ourselves, and others, that we are no longer Jews, but full-blooded citizens. Idle delusion! Though you prove yourselves patriots a thousand times, you will still be reminded at every opportunity of your Semitic descent. This fateful *memento mori*[13] will not prevent you, however, from accepting the extended hospitality, until some fine morning you find yourself crossing the border and you are reminded by the mob that you are, after all, nothing but vagrants and parasites, without the protection of the law.

But even humane treatment does not prove that we are welcome. . . . Moreover, the belief in a Messiah, in the intervention of a higher power to bring about our political resurrection, and the religious assumption that we must bear patiently divine punishment, caused us to abandon every thought of our national liberation, unity, and independence. Consequently, we have renounced the idea of a nationhood and did so the more readily since we were preoccupied with our immediate needs. Thus we sank lower and lower. The people *without a country forgot their country*. Is it not high time to perceive the disgrace of it all?

Happily, matters stand somewhat differently now. The events of the last few years in *enlightened* Germany, in Romania, in Hungary, and especially in Russia, have effected what the far bloodiest persecutions of the Middle Ages could not. The national consciousness which until then had lain dormant in sterile martyrdom awoke the masses of the Russian and Romanian Jews and took form in an irresistible movement toward Palestine. Mistaken as this movement has proved to be by its results, it was, nevertheless, a right instinct to strike out for home. The severe trials which they have endured have now provoked a reaction quite different from the fatalistic submission to a divine condign punishment. Even the unenlightened masses of the Russian Jews have not entirely escaped the influences of the principles of modern culture. Without renouncing Judaism and

---

[13] *memento mori*: The Latin phrase supposedly spoken in the ear of someone granted a Roman triumph — a parade celebrating an accomplishment — that is usually translated as "remember, you are mortal."

their faith, they revolted against undeserved ill-treatment which could be inflicted with impunity only because the Russian Government regards the Jews as aliens. And the other European governments — why should they concern themselves with the citizens of a state in whose internal affairs they have no right to interfere?. . . .

If we would have a secure home, give up our endless life of wandering and rise to the dignity of a nation in our own eyes and in the eyes of the world, we must, above all, not dream of restoring ancient Judaea. We must not attach ourselves to the place where our political life was once violently interrupted and destroyed. The goal of our present endeavors must be not the "Holy Land," but a land of our own. We need nothing but a large tract of land for our poor brothers, which shall remain our property and from which no foreign power can expel us. There we shall take with us the most sacred possessions which we have saved from the shipwreck of our former country, the *God-idea* and the *Bible*. It is these alone which have made our old fatherland the Holy Land, and not Jerusalem or the Jordan. Perhaps the Holy Land will again become ours. If so, all the better, but *first of all*, we must determine — and this is the crucial point — what country is accessible to us, and at the same time adapted to offer the Jews of all lands who must leave their homes a secure and indisputed refuge, capable of productivization. . . .

READING AND DISCUSSION QUESTIONS

1. What are the characteristics that Pinsker believes distinguishes Jews from everyone else? What reaction would you expect his "Judeophobia" argument to draw today?

2. What does Pinsker's statement of the problem of anti-Semitism reveal about the nationalism of his era? In what ways might Europe's Jews be barred from the national community?

3. In what ways could the creation of a Jewish nation-state ease the discrimination Pinsker sees in Europe? What about those who may choose not to emigrate, but remain in their original countries?

4. What dangers does Pinsker see for his fellow Jews in the Zionist movement? What mistake does he see as having already been made?

COMPARATIVE QUESTIONS

1. Based on Zola's "J'Accuse" and Bismarck's speech to the Reichstag, what reasons might the individual have for accepting or resisting the power of the national government?

2. Based on the documents in this chapter, how did the definition of freedom and citizenship differ in each of the countries represented (France, Germany, the United States, and Russia)?

3. What positive aspects did the process of national consolidation have in the second half of the nineteenth century?

4. What similarities can you see between Lincoln's view of the nation and Bismarck's? How might the fact of Lincoln's election versus Bismarck's appointment by the German emperor Wilhelm I affect their understanding of nationalism?

5. Consulting Pinsker and Zola, what was the place in the new nation-state for those people whose identities were based on things other than membership in a national community?

CHAPTER 26

The West and the World

1815–1914

I n the nineteenth century, Europeans had powerful motives for expansion, including a self-appointed obligation to spread their "superior" Western culture and religion, as well as the industrialists' search for untapped markets and raw materials. Added to traditional motives was the unfortunate misinterpretation of Darwin's theories that suggested that societies as well as organisms had to compete for resources. While they fell short in their hunt for new markets, investors made fortunes off the raw materials they acquired as a result of imperialism. The push to spread European culture proved less fruitful, particularly in China, with its long-established customs. Ultimately, industrial innovation catapulted Europe into a position of global power. With the invention of the Maxim machine gun in 1884, European technology counterbalanced Asian and African manpower. In the imperial climate, native resistance never fully faded, and an undercurrent of fear persisted among the uninvited occupiers.

DOCUMENT 26-1

COMMISSIONER LIN
From a Letter to Queen Victoria
1839

China, the most populous country on Earth in the nineteenth century, was the prize in the search for markets for Western products. The Chinese imperial government's reluctance to allow Western access, combined with poverty and general disinterest in Western goods, restricted trade until the British

William H. McNeil and Mitsuko Iriye, eds., *Readings in World History, Vol. 9: Modern Asia and Africa* (New York: Oxford University Press, 1971), 111–118.

discovered they had a product that would sell in China — opium. Lin Zexu, the imperial commissioner for the southern province of Guangdong, attempted to suppress the opium trade, and published this open letter to the British queen in 1839. That same year, the British started the First Opium War (1839–1942) to ensure their continued right to sell opium in China.

We have heard that in your own country opium is prohibited with the utmost strictness and severity: this is a strong proof that you know full well how hurtful it is to mankind. Since then you do not permit it to injure your own country, you ought not to have the injurious drug transferred to another country, and above all others, how much less to the Inner Land! Of the products which China exports to your foreign countries, there is not one which is not beneficial to mankind in some shape or other. There are those which serve for food, those which are useful, and those which are calculated for re-sale; but all are beneficial. Has China (we should like to ask) ever yet sent forth a noxious article from its soil? Not to speak of our tea and rhubarb, things which your foreign countries could not exist a single day without, if we of the Central Land were to grudge you what is beneficial, and not to compassionate your wants, then wherewithal could you foreigners manage to exist? And further, as regards your woolens, camlets [goat or camel hair cloth], and longells [cloth of a specific weave], were it not that you get supplied with our native raw silk, you could not get these manufactured! If China were to grudge you those things which yield a profit, how could you foreigners scheme after any profit at all? Our other articles of food, such as sugar, ginger, cinnamon, &c., and our other articles for use, such as silk piece-goods, chinaware, &c., are all so many necessaries of life to you; how can we reckon up their number! On the other hand, the things that come from your foreign countries are only calculated to make presents of, or serve for mere amusement. It is quite the same to us if we have them, or if we have them not. If then these are of no material consequence to us of the Inner Land, what difficulty would there be in prohibiting and shutting our market against them? It is only that our heavenly dynasty most freely permits you to take off her tea, silk, and other commodities, and convey them for consumption everywhere, without the slightest stint or grudge, for no other reason, but that where a profit exists, we wish that it be diffused abroad for the benefit of all the earth!

Your honorable nation takes away the products of our Central Land, and not only do you thereby obtain food and support for yourselves, but moreover, by re-selling these products to other countries you reap a threefold profit. Now if you would only not sell opium, this threefold profit would be secured to you: how can you possibly consent to forgo it for a drug that is hurtful to men, and an unbridled craving after gain that seems to know no bounds! Let us suppose that foreigners came from another country, and brought opium into England, and seduced the people of your country to smoke it, would not you, the sovereign of the said country, look upon such a procedure with anger, and in your just indignation endeavor to get rid of it?

. . . [W]e have heard that in London the metropolis where you dwell, as also in Scotland, Ireland, and other such places, no opium whatever is produced. It is only in sundry parts of your colonial kingdom of Hindo-stan,[1] such as Bengal, Madras, Bombay, Patna, Malwa, Benares, Malacca, and other places where the very hills are covered with the opium plant, where tanks are made for the preparing of the drug; month by month, and year by year, the volume of the poison increases, its unclean stench ascends upwards, until heaven itself grows angry, and the very gods thereat get indignant! You, the queen of the said honorable nation, ought imme-diately to have the plant in those parts plucked up by the very root! Cause the land there to be hoed up afresh, sow in its stead the five grains, and if any man dare again to plant in these grounds a single poppy, visit his crime with the most severe punishment. . . .

Suppose the subject of another country were to come to England to trade, he would certainly be required to comply with the laws of England, then how much more does this apply to us of the celestial empire! Now it is a fixed statute of this empire, that any native Chinese who sells opium is pun-ishable with death, and even he who merely smokes it, must not less die. . . .

READING AND DISCUSSION QUESTIONS

1. What sort of tone does Lin assume in his letter to the English queen?

2. How does Lin classify China's policy on trade with Britain?

3. What benefits does Lin believe the British reap from their relationship with China, and how does he feel this should affect that relationship?

4. Based on what you have read here, what is the difference between the British relationship with China and with the Indian areas Lin mentions?

---

[1] **Hindostan**: British India, particularly the northwestern section, in today's India and Pakistan.

DOCUMENT 26-2

SIR HENRY MORTON STANLEY

From Autobiography: *European Imperialism in Africa*

1909

Henry Morton Stanley (1841–1904) was born John Rowlands in Great Britain but rose to fame as an American citizen in the employ of the king of the Belgians, Leopold II. In 1871, while working as a journalist for the New York Herald, *Stanley led an expedition to locate Dr. David Livingstone, a popular explorer and missionary who had gone missing in central Africa. Upon reading about Stanley's exploration of the Congo basin, Leopold II became interested in acquiring an empire in Africa, which in turn sparked the interest of other European countries fearful of being left behind in the race to colonize Africa. Stanley's expeditions were brutal even by the standards of other explorers, as this segment from his posthumous autobiography suggests.*

Some explorers say: "One must not run through a country, but give the people time to become acquainted with you, and let their worst fears subside."

Now on the expedition across Africa I had no time to give, either to myself or to them. The river bore my heavy canoes downward; my goods would never have endured the dawdling requirement by the system of teaching every tribe I met who I was. To save myself and my men from certain starvation, I had to rush on and on, right through. But on this expedition, the very necessity of making roads to haul my enormous six-ton wagons gave time for my reputation to travel ahead of me. My name, purpose, and liberal rewards for native help, naturally exaggerated, prepared a welcome for me, and transformed my enemies of the old time into workmen, friendly allies, strong porters, and firm friends. I was greatly forbearing also; but, when a fight was inevitable, through open violence, it was sharp and decisive. Consequently, the natives rapidly learned that though

Henry Morton Stanley, *Autobiography*, Dorothy Stanley, ed. (New York: Houghton Mifflin, 1909), 342–343.

everything was to be gained by friendship with me, wars brought nothing but ruin.

When a young white officer quits England for the first time, to lead blacks, he has got to learn to unlearn a great deal. We must have white men in Africa; but the raw white is a great nuisance there during the first year. In the second year, he begins to mend; during the third year, if his nature permits it, he has developed into a superior man, whose intelligence may be of transcendent utility for directing masses of inferior men.

My officers were possessed with the notion that my manner was "hard," because I had not many compliments for them. That is the kind of pap which we may offer women and boys. Besides, I thought they were superior natures, and required none of that encouragement, which the more childish blacks almost daily received.

READING AND DISCUSSION QUESTIONS

1. In what ways does Stanley seek to present himself as a "great" explorer? What factors does he see as decisive in his success?

2. What attitudes does Stanley display toward the natives he encounters? What are the benefits of "friendship" for his expedition?

3. How does Stanley seem to view the Europeans with whom he works? What does the final paragraph reveal about nineteenth-century attitudes toward masculinity?

DOCUMENT 26-3

The Boxers Declare Death to "Foreign Devils"

1900

Although China was never directly conquered or colonized by the West, the Chinese government was nearly powerless by the turn of the twentieth century. Various European states had extracted concessions and installed their

Louis Snyder, ed., *The Imperialism Reader: Documents and Readings on Modern Expansionism* (Princeton, N.J.: Van Nostrand, 1962), 322–323.

own administrations within foreign territory, laying claim to land and strip-
ping the Chinese government of control over foreigners in their territory. Dis-
enchanted with their weakened government, some Chinese groups reacted
independently. In 1900, followers of the Taoist religious secret society, the
Society of Harmonious Fists (Boxers), became convinced they had discovered
magical techniques to overcome Western technology and rose up against their
Christian oppressors. The normally squabbling colonial powers, including
the United States and Japan, united to suppress the Boxer Rebellion.

The gods assist the Boxers
The Patriotic Harmonious corps
It is because the "foreign Devils" disturb the "Middle Kingdom"
     [China]
Urging the people to join their religion,
To turn their backs on Heaven,
Venerate not the Gods and forget their ancestors.

Men violate the human obligations,
Women commit adultery,
"Foreign Devils" are not produced by mankind,
If you do not believe,
Look at them carefully.

The eyes of the "Foreign Devils" are bluish,
No rain falls,
The earth is getting dry,
This is because the churches stop Heaven,
The Gods are angry;
The Gods are vexed;
Both come down from the mountain to deliver the doctrine.

This is no hearsay,
The practices of boxing[2] will not be in vain;
Reciting incantations and pronouncing magic words,

---

[2] **practices of boxing**: The society trained in Chinese martial arts techniques, which
included intense physical and mental discipline and meditation techniques. They
essentially believed that their physical prowess would allow them to deflect bullets
fired at them. When trying to describe society members, Westerners compared the
Taoists' techniques to the art of boxing, to which they actually bore little resemblance.

Burn up yellow written prayers,
Light incense sticks
To invite the Gods and Genii [guardian spirits] of all the grottoes.

The Gods come out from grottoes,
The Genii come down from mountains,
Support the human bodies to practice the boxing.
When all the military accomplishments or tactics
Are fully learned,
It will not be difficult to exterminate the "Foreign Devils" then.

Push aside the railway tracks,
Pull out the telegraph poles,
Immediately after this destroy the steamers [steamboats].
The great France
Will grow cold and downhearted.
The English and Russians will certainly disperse.
Let the various "Foreign Devils" all be killed.
May the whole Elegant Empire of the Great Ching Dynasty[3] be ever
    prosperous.

READING AND DISCUSSION QUESTIONS

1.   What reasons do the Boxers cite for attacking foreigners?

2.   What are the Boxer's attitudes toward the culture of the West? What do
     their attitudes suggest about their vision of the ideal Chinese society?

3.   What reasons might the "Great Ching Dynasty" have for encouraging
     the Boxers in their rebellion? Why might the imperial government not
     be able to give its full support?

---

[3] **Great Ching Dynasty**: Also rendered as Qing, the Chinese imperial family between
1644 and 1912, who encouraged the Boxer uprising.

DOCUMENT 26-4

J. A. HOBSON
From Imperialism
1902

Not all Europeans were imperialists, although anti-imperialists were typically in the minority. One of the underlying assumptions of empire was that colonies would trade exclusively with their mother countries, a theory at odds with Adam Smith's eighteenth-century vision of free trade. In 1902, John Atkinson Hobson, an English economist, published a critique of the prevailing link between colonies, economies, and national security, questioning the benefits of imperialism for the colonizing countries. His work influenced the Communist leader Lenin's later critique of imperialism.

. . . Although the new Imperialism has been bad business for the nation, it has been good business for certain classes and certain trades within the nation. The vast expenditure on armaments, the costly wars, the grave risks and embarrassments of foreign policy, the stoppage of political and social reforms within Great Britain, though fraught with great injury to the nation, have served well the present business interests of certain industries and professions.

It is idle to meddle with politics unless we clearly recognize this central fact and understand what these sectional interests are which are the enemies of national safety and the commonwealth. We must put aside the merely sentimental diagnosis which explains wars or other national blunders by outbursts of patriotic animosity or errors of statecraft. Doubtless at every outbreak of war not only the man in the street but the man at the helm is often duped by the cunning with which aggressive motives and greedy purposes dress themselves in defensive clothing. There is, it may be safely asserted, no war within memory, however nakedly aggressive it may seem to the dispassionate historian, which has not been presented to the people who were called upon to fight as a necessary defensive

Louis L. Snyder, ed., *The Imperialism Reader: Documents and Readings on Modern Expansionism* (Princeton, N.J.: Van Nostrand, 1962), 322–323.

policy, in which the honor, perhaps the very existence, of the State was involved. . . .

What is the direct economic outcome of Imperialism? A great expenditure of public money upon ships, guns, military and naval equipment and stores, growing and productive of enormous profits when a war, or an alarm of war, occurs; new public loans and important fluctuations in the home and foreign Bourses [essentially a stock market]; more posts for soldiers and sailors and in the diplomatic and consular services; improvement of foreign investments by the substitution of the British flag for a foreign flag; acquisition of markets for certain classes of exports, and some protection and assistance for trades representing British houses in these manufactures; employment for engineers, missionaries, speculative miners, ranchers, and other emigrants.

Certain definite business and professional interests feeding upon imperialistic expenditure, or upon the results of that expenditure, are thus set up in opposition to the common good, and, instinctively feeling their way to one another, are found united in strong sympathy to support every new imperialist exploit. . . .

With them stand the great manufacturers for export trade, who gain a living by supplying the real or artificial wants of the new countries we annex or open up. . . . The proportion which such trade bears to the total industry of Great Britain is very small, but some of it is extremely influential and able to make a definite impression upon politics, through chambers of commerce, Parliamentary representatives, and semi-political, semi-commercial bodies like the Imperial South African Association or the China League.

The shipping trade has a very definite interest which makes for Imperialism. This is well illustrated by the policy of State subsidies now claimed by shipping firms as a retainer, and in order to encourage British shipping for purposes of imperial safety and defence.

The services are, of course, imperialist by conviction and by professional interest, and every increase of the army and navy enhances their numerical strength and the political power they exert. . . .

What is true of Great Britain is true likewise of France, Germany, the United States, and of all countries in which modern capitalism has placed large surplus savings in the hands of a plutocracy or of a thrifty middle class. A well-recognized distinction is drawn between creditor and debtor countries. Great Britain has been for some time by far the largest creditor country, and the policy by which the investing classes use the instrument of the State for private business purposes is most richly illustrated in the recent history of her wars and annexations.[4] But France, Germany, and the United States are advancing fast along the same path. . . .

Investors who have put their money in foreign lands, upon terms which take full account of risks connected with the political conditions of the country, desire to use the resources of their Government to minimize these risks, and so to enhance the capital value and the interest of their private investments. The investing and speculative classes in general also desire that Great Britain should take other foreign areas under her flag in order to secure new areas for profitable investment and speculation. . . .

READING AND DISCUSSION QUESTIONS

1. Based on this selection, what groups does Hobson see benefiting from imperialism? In what ways are the interests of these groups the same as or different from the interests of the nation as a whole?

2. What negative outcomes does Hobson believe result from imperial competition?

3. What is Hobson's attitude toward war, particularly regarding the relationship between the government and the citizens of the nation in wartime?

COMPARATIVE QUESTIONS

1. How did Chinese attitudes toward the West evolve between Commissioner Lin's letter and the Boxer Rebellion? What continuities do you discern between the two documents? What might account for changes?

---

[4]**recent history of . . . wars and annexations**: One such example was the British government's decision to buy the khedive of Egypt's stock shares in the Suez Canal company in 1875, about 40 percent of the company. This led to British control of the canal, and of Egypt when the khedive was unable to pay his debts. The most recent example would have been the expansion of the British Cape colony into the Boers' (European farmers of Dutch descent) Transvaal territories, resulting in the 1899–1902 Boer War. British companies gained access to gold and diamond mining as a result of the war.

2. Compare the documents produced by the two Westerners, Stanley and Hobson. Where do they seem to differ, and what similarities can you see? What differences in perspective might account for their different ideas on colonization?

3. Based on their documents, would Commissioner Lin agree with Hobson's views on the dangers of imperial trade?

4. Compare Stanley's attitude toward Africans and the Boxer view of the "Foreign Devils." What conclusions can you draw from this?

CHAPTER 27

The Great Break: War and Revolution

1914–1919

The outbreak of World War I was greeted with widespread European enthusiasm. For decades, Europe's Great Powers had been divided into alliance blocs in anticipation of a conflict. The currents of extreme nationalism and Social Darwinism that characterized the prewar era convinced many that war was not only inevitable, but desirable — a brief, decisive test of "survival of the fittest." In reality, the conflict was a long, brutal, industrial war in which the combatants had to mobilize all of their resources — people, raw materials, transportation infrastructure, and factories — for the goal of victory. In the trenches on the western front, the war stagnated into a contest of attrition. In the east, the collapse of the Russian Empire paved the way for the eventual Soviet state. In the end, the human and economic costs of the war were catastrophic. During the subsequent peacemaking process, U.S. President Woodrow Wilson sought to ensure that no such bloodbath would ever happen again, but leaders of the other victorious powers, France and Great Britain, did not fully endorse his plans.

DOCUMENT 27-1

A Franco-Russian Rapprochement

1892

Following its triumph in the Franco-German War (1870–1871), Germany annexed the French province of Alsace and most of neighboring Lorraine.

J. G. D'Arcy Paul and Denys P. Myers, trans., *The Secret Treaties of Austria-Hungary, 1879–1914, Vol. II* (Cambridge, Mass.: Harvard University Press, 1921), 215–217. William Henry Cooke and Edith Pierpont Stickney, eds., *Readings in European International Relations Since 1879* (Harper & Bros., 1931).

German Chancellor Otto von Bismarck (1815–1898) knew France would need a Great Power ally to regain its lost territory, and that Austria and Russia alone had the military means to assist. Through a series of preemptive treaties between Germany, Austria, and Russia, Bismarck kept the Powers out of France's diplomatic orbit. In 1890, Kaiser (Emperor) Wilhelm II forced Bismarck into retirement and allowed the defensive treaty between Germany and Russia to lapse. The following year, France and Russia opened negotiations that led to the following agreements.

(1) DRAFT OF MILITARY CONVENTION[1]

France and Russia, being animated by an equal desire to preserve peace, and having no other object than to meet the necessities of a defensive war, provoked by an attack of the forces of the Triple Alliance[2] against the one or the other of them, have agreed upon the following provisions:

1. If France is attacked by Germany, or by Italy supported by Germany, Russia shall employ all her available forces to attack Germany.

    If Russia is attacked by Germany, or by Austria supported by Germany, France shall employ all her available forces to fight Germany.
2. In case the forces of the Triple Alliance, or of one of the Powers composing it, should mobilize, France and Russia, at the first news of the event and without the necessity of any previous concert, shall mobilize immediately and simultaneously the whole of their forces and shall move them as close as possible to their frontiers.
3. The available forces to be employed against Germany shall be on the part of France, 1,300,000 men, on the part of Russia, 700,000 or 800,000 men.

    These forces shall engage to the full, with all speed, in order that Germany may have to fight at the same time on the East and on the West.
4. The General Staffs of the Armies of the two countries shall cooperate with each other at all times in the preparation and facilitation of the execution of the measures above foreseen.

---

[1] **Draft of Military Convention:** The formal alliance was not signed until January 1894.

[2] **Triple Alliance:** The Triple Alliance was the existing pact between Germany, Austria, and Italy. Its duration was five years, but it could be renewed, and in fact lasted from 1879, when first signed by Germany and Austria (Italy joined in 1882), to 1918.

They shall communicate to each other, while there is still peace, all information relative to the armies of the Triple Alliance which is or shall be within their knowledge.

Ways and means of corresponding in times of war shall be studied and arranged in advance.

5. France and Russia shall not conclude peace separately.

6. The present Convention shall have the same duration as the Triple Alliance.

7. All the clauses above enumerated shall be kept rigorously secret.[3] . . .

(2) GENERAL DE BOISDEFFRE'S[4] INTERVIEW WITH THE TSAR REGARDING THE MILITARY CONVENTION. "MOBILIZATION IS A DECLARATION OF WAR."

Saint Petersburg, August 18, 1892

This morning, Tuesday, I received from the Minister of War a letter dated August 17, in which . . . he made known to me that the Emperor [Russian Tsar Alexander III] had approved in principle the project [the draft of the Military Convention] as a whole. . . . The Emperor had evidently held that the basis of the entente [agreement] would have to be precisely and officially fixed before his audience.

We have now, awaiting the exchange of ratifications with ministries' signatures, an official basis for a definite convention, a basis that can be considered as absolutely sure and decisive when one knows the reserve and the prudence of the Russian Government and the firmness of the Emperor in his engagements.

At eleven o'clock, I was received by the Emperor. His Majesty declared to me immediately that he had read, re-read, and studied the project of the convention, that he gave it his full approbation, taking it as a whole, and that he thanked the French Government for accepting some changes of wording that he had requested.

His Majesty added that the convention contained, to his mind, some political articles which he desired to have examined by the Minister of Foreign Affairs; that there might be, as a result, some minor changes of wording to be made. Finally, His Majesty repeated that the project gave

---

[3] **rigorously secret**: Like all such treaties, its secrecy was not rigorously preserved. It was widely known by 1894 that France and Russia had an alliance, although its exact terms were not public.

[4] **General de Boisdeffre**: General Raoul François Charles le Mouton de Boisdeffre (1859–1919), a French officer, was then on a military mission to Russia.

him entire satisfaction and that everything seemed to him to be adjusted to the best interests of the two countries.

I did not believe it necessary to take up again the defense of the first text, since the new text had received the approval of the Government. I only said to the Emperor that the French Government had wished to testify once more through this concession to its confidence in him. The Emperor did not fail to tell me of his strong desire that we guard the secret absolutely. . . . The Emperor spoke of his desire for peace. I remarked to him that we were no less pacific than His Majesty. "I know it," he responded. "You have given proof of it for twenty-two years. I believe, moreover, that at this moment, peace is not threatened. The German Emperor has enough internal troubles, and England has as many. Moreover, with our convention, I estimate that our situation will be favorable. I surely desire to have at least two more years of peace, for it is necessary for us to complete our armament, our railways, and to recover from want and from the cholera. In fine, it is necessary to hope that peace will be maintained for a long time yet, and let us wish for it."

The Emperor then spoke of mobilization under Article 2. I ventured to remark that mobilization was the declaration of war; that to mobilize was to oblige one's neighbor to do so also; that the mobilization entailed the execution of strategic transportation and of concentration. Without that, to allow the mobilization of a million men on one's frontier without doing the same simultaneously was to deny to one's self all possibility of stirring later. It would be like the situation an individual would be in if he had a pistol in his pocket and would allow his neighbor to point a gun at his forehead without drawing his own. "That is the way I understand it," the Emperor responded. . . .

READING AND DISCUSSION QUESTIONS

1. Based on Boisdeffre's report, what was the protocol for creating a formal alliance? Who contributed, and who else would have known of the "secret agreement"?

2. Why might Russia have been interested in an alliance with France?

3. Why did "mobilization mean war"?

DOCUMENT 27-2

SIR EDWARD GREY

The British Rationale for Entering World War I
1914

By 1894, the five continental powers were aligned in two alliance blocs: Germany, Austria, and Italy in one, France and Russia in the other. In 1904, compelled by German naval ambitions and imperial security concerns in Africa and India, the British military drew up plans for assisting France if Germany launched a war of aggression. The British, however, never signed a formal treaty with either France or Russia and were not obliged to enter the war when it broke out in August 1914. On August 3, 1914, the British Foreign Secretary, Sir Edward Grey (1862–1933), informed the House of Commons of the reasons that impelled the British government to take up arms against Germany.

In the present crisis, it has not been possible to secure the peace of Europe; because there has been little time, and there has been a disposition — at any rate in some quarters on which I will not dwell — to force things rapidly to an issue, at any rate, to the great risk of peace, and, as we now know, the result of that is that the policy of peace, as far as the Great Powers generally are concerned, is in danger. I do not want to dwell on that, and to comment on it, and to say where the blame seems to us to lie, which powers were most in favor of peace, which were most disposed to risk or endanger peace, because I would like the House to approach this crisis in which we are now, from the point of view of British interests, British honor, and British obligations, free from all passion, as to why peace has not been preserved. . . .

We have great and vital interests in the independence — and integrity in the least part — of Belgium. If Belgium[5] is compelled to submit to allow her neutrality to be violated, of course the situation is clear. Even if by agreement she admitted the violation of her neutrality, it is clear she could only do so under duress. The smaller states in that region of Europe ask

---

Hansard Parliamentary Debates, 5th Series, Vol. 65, Cols. 1809–1827.

[5] **Belgium**: Britain was signatory to an 1839 treaty by which it, Prussia, and France guaranteed the territorial integrity of Belgium, which was to be independent and perpetually neutral.

but one thing. Their one desire is that they should be left alone and in-dependent. The one thing they fear is, I think, not so much that their integrity but that their independence should be interfered with. If in this war which is before Europe the neutrality of one of those countries is vio-lated, if the troops of one of the combatants violate its neutrality and no action be taken to resist it, at the end of the war, whatever the integrity may be, the independence will be gone.

No, Sir, if it be the case that there has been anything in the nature of an ultimatum to Belgium, asking her to compromise or violate her neu-trality, whatever may have been offered to her in return, her independence is gone if that holds. If her independence goes, the independence of Hol-land will follow. I ask the House from the point of view of British interests, to consider what may be at stake. If France is beaten in a struggle of life or death, beaten to her knees, loses her position as a great power, becomes subordinate to the will and power of one greater than herself — conse-quences which I do not anticipate, because I am sure that France has the power to defend herself with all the energy and ability and patriotism which she has shown so often — still, if that were to happen, and if Bel-gium fell under the same dominating influence, and then Holland, and then Denmark, then would not Mr. Gladstone's[6] words come true, that just opposite to us there would be a common interest against the unmea-sured aggrandizement of any power? . . .

We are going to suffer, I am afraid, terribly in this war whether we are in it or whether we stand aside. . . .

. . . I do not believe for a moment, that at the end of this war, even if we stood aside and remained aside, we should be in a position, a material position to use our force decisively to undo what had happened in the course of the war, to prevent the whole of the west of Europe opposite to us — if that has been the result of the war — falling under the domination of a single power, and I am quite sure that our moral position would be such as to have lost us all respect. . . .

READING AND DISCUSSION QUESTIONS

1. Why did Grey dwell so heavily on Belgium's independence? Why did Belgium matter to the British?

---

[6]**Mr. Gladstone:** William E. Gladstone (1809–1898), Liberal politician, statesman, and four-time British prime minister.

2. What inferences can you draw from Grey's speech about Britain's strategic interests in Europe?

3. What outcomes did Grey foresee if Britain were to stand aside in the conflict?

DOCUMENT 27-3

HELENA SWANWICK

The War in Its Effect Upon Women

1916

The years immediately preceding World War I had witnessed a massive and sometimes violent campaign for women's suffrage in Britain. Helena Swanwick, a German-born academic and journalist, was one of the prominent participants in that campaign, editing the suffragist newspaper Common Cause *from 1909 to 1914. When war broke out, Swanwick split with much of the suffragist leadership which supported Britain's participation. Throughout the conflict, she advocated a negotiated peace and the establishment of an international organization to maintain it. As a feminist and a socialist, she regarded the war as an opportunity for women to improve their socioeconomic as well as their political status.*

How has the war affected women? How will it affect them? Women, as half the human race, are compelled to take their share of evil and good with men, the other half. The destruction of property, the increase of taxation, the rise of prices, the devastation of beautiful things in nature and art — these are felt by men as well as by women. Some losses doubtless appeal to one or the other sex with peculiar poignancy, but it would be difficult to say whose sufferings are the greater, though there can be no doubt at all that men get an exhilaration out of war which is denied to most women. When they see pictures of soldiers encamped in the ruins of what was once a home, amidst the dead bodies of gentle milch [sic] cows, most women

Helena Swanwick, "The War in Its Effect Upon Women," in Marilyn Shevin-Coetzee and Frans Coetzee, eds., *World War I and European Society* (Lexington, Mass.: D. C. Heath, 1995), 160–164, 166.

would be thinking too insistently of the babies who must die for need of milk to entertain the exhilaration which no doubt may be felt at "the good work of our guns." When they read of miles upon miles of kindly earth made barren, the hearts of men may be wrung to think of wasted toil, but to women the thought suggests a simile full of an even deeper pathos; they will think of the millions of young lives destroyed, each one having cost the travail and care of a mother, and of the millions of young bodies made barren by the premature death of those who should have been their mates. The millions of widowed maidens in the coming generation will have to turn their thoughts away from one particular joy and fulfilment of life. While men in war give what is, at the present stage of the world's development, the peculiar service of men, let them not forget that in rendering that very service they are depriving a corresponding number of women of the opportunity of rendering what must, at all stages of the world's development, be the peculiar service of women. After the war, men will go on doing what has been regarded as men's work; women, deprived of their own, will also have to do much of what has been regarded as men's work. These things are going to affect women profoundly, and one hopes that the reconstruction of society is going to be met by the whole people — men and women — with a sympathetic understanding of each other's circumstances. When what are known as men's questions are discussed, it is generally assumed that the settlement of them depends upon men only; when what are known as women's questions are discussed, there is never any suggestion that they can be settled by women independently of men. Of course they cannot. But, then, neither can "men's questions" be rightly settled so. In fact, life would be far more truly envisaged if we dropped the silly phrases "men's and women's questions"; for, indeed, there are no such matters, and all human questions affect all humanity.

Now, for the right consideration of human questions, it is necessary for humans to understand each other. This catastrophic war will do one good thing if it opens our eyes to real live women as they are, as we know them in workaday life, but as the politician and the journalist seem not to have known them. When war broke out, a Labour newspaper, in the midst of the news of men's activities, found space to say that women would feel the pinch, because their supply of attar of roses would be curtailed. It struck some women like a blow in the face. When a great naval engagement took place, the front page of a progressive daily was taken up with portraits of the officers and men who had won distinction, and the back page with portraits of simpering mannequins in extravagantly fashionable hats; not frank advertisement, mind you, but exploitation of women under the guise of news supposed to be peculiarly interesting to the feeble-minded creatures.

When a snapshot was published of the first women ticket collectors in England, the legend underneath the picture ran "Super-women"! It took the life and death of Edith Cavell[7] to open the eyes of the Prime Minister to the fact that there were thousands of women giving life and service to their country. "A year ago we did not know it," he said, in the House of Commons. Is that indeed so? Surely in our private capacities as ordinary citizens, we knew not only of the women whose portraits are in the picture papers (mostly pretty ladies of the music hall or of society), but also of the toiling millions upon whose courage and ability and endurance and goodness of heart the great human family rests. Only the politicians did not know, because their thoughts were too much engrossed with faction fights to think humanly; only the journalists would not write of them, because there was more money in writing the columns which are demanded by the advertisers of feminine luxuries. Anyone who has conducted a woman's paper knows the steady commercial pressure for that sort of "copy." . . .

THE NEED FOR PRODUCTION

It is often forgotten that for full prosperity a country needs to be producing as much wealth as possible, consistently with the health, freedom, and happiness of its people. To arrive at this desired result, it is quite clear that as many people as possible should be employed productively, and it is one of the unhappy results of our economic anarchy that employers have found it profitable to have a large reserve class of unemployed and that wage-earners have been driven to try and diminish their own numbers and to restrict their own output. To keep women out of the "labour market" (by artificial restrictions, such as the refusal to work with them, or the refusal to allow them to be trained, or the refusal to adapt conditions to their health requirements) is in truth anti-social. But it is easy to see how such antisocial restrictions have been forced upon the workers, and it is futile to blame them. A way must be found out of industrial war before we can hope that industry will be carried on thriftily. Men and women must take counsel together and let the experience of the war teach them how to solve economic problems by co-operation rather than conflict. Women have been increasingly conscious of the satisfaction to be got from economic independence, of the sweetness of earned bread, of the dreary depression of subjection. They have felt the bitterness of being "kept out"; they are feeling the exhilaration of being "brought in." They are ripe for instruction and organization in working for the good of the whole. . . .

---

[7] **Edith Cavell**: A British nurse working in Belgium, Cavell was executed by the Germans for providing aid to Belgian insurgents.

READJUSTMENT OF EMPLOYMENT

Most people were astonished in 1914 at the rapidity with which industry and social conditions adapted themselves to the state of war, and there are those who argue that, because the fears of very widespread and continued misery at the outbreak of the war were not justified, we need not have any anxiety about any widespread and continued misery at the establishment of peace. Certainly depression or panic are worse than useless, and a serene and cheerful heart will help to carry the nation beyond difficulties. But comfortable people must beware of seeming to bear the sorrows of others with cheerfulness, and a lack of preparation for easily foreseen contingencies will not be forgiven by those who suffer from carelessness or procrastination. We know quite well what some, at least, of our problems are going to be, and the fool's paradise would lead straight to revolution.

It would be wise to remember that the dislocation of industry at the outbreak of the war was easily met; first, because the people thrown out by the cessation of one sort of work were easily absorbed by the increase of another sort; second, because there was ample capital and credit in hand; third, because the State was prepared to shoulder many risks and to guarantee stability; fourth, because there was an untapped reservoir of women's labor to take the place of men's. The problems after the war will be different, greater, and more lasting . . . Because it will obviously be impossible for all to find work quickly (not to speak of the right kind of work), there is almost certain to be an outcry for the restriction of work in various directions, and one of the first cries (if we may judge from the past) will be to women: "Back to the Home!" This cry will be raised whether the women have a home or not. . . . We must understand the unimpeachable right of the man who has lost his work and risked his life for his country, to find decent employment, decent wages and conditions, on his return to civil life. We must also understand the enlargement and enhancement of life which women feel when they are able to live by their own productive work, and we must realize that to deprive women of the right to live by their work is to send them back to a moral imprisonment (to say nothing of physical and intellectual starvation), of which they have become now for the first time fully conscious. And we must realize the exceeding danger that conscienceless employers may regard women's labor as preferable, owing to its cheapness and its docility, and that women, if unsympathetically treated by their male relatives and fellow workers, may be tempted to continue to be cheap and docile in the hands of those who have no desire except that of exploiting them and the community. The kind of man who likes "to keep women in their place" may find he has made slaves who will be used by his enemies against him. Men need have no fear of free women; it is the slaves and the parasites who are a deadly danger.

The demand for equal wage for equal work has been hotly pressed by men since the war began, and it is all to the good so far as it goes. But most men are still far from realizing the solidarity of their interests with those of women in all departments of life, and are still too placidly accepting the fact that women are sweated over work which is not the same as that of men. They don't realize yet that starved womanhood means starved manhood, and they don't enough appreciate the rousing and infectious character of a generous attitude on the part of men, who, in fighting the women's battles unselfishly and from a love of right, would stimulate the women to corresponding generosity. There are no comrades more staunch and loyal than women, where men have engaged their truth and courage. But men must treat them as comrades; they must no longer think only of how they can "eliminate female labor"; they must take the women into their trade unions and other organizations, and they must understand that the complexities of a woman's life are not of her invention or choosing, but are due to her function as mother of men. The sexual side of a woman's life gravely affects the economic side, and we can never afford to overlook this. As mothers and home-makers women are doing work of the highest national importance and economic value, but this value is one which returns to the nation as a whole and only in small and very uncertain part to the women themselves. . . . Unless men are prepared to socialize the responsibilities of parenthood, one does not see how women's labor is ever to be organized for the welfare of the whole, nor does one see how women are to perform their priceless functions of motherhood as well as possible if they are to be penalized for them in the future as they have been in the past. . . .

ENFRANCHISEMENT AND EMANCIPATION

The course and conduct of the war, throwing upon women greater and greater responsibilities, bringing home to them how intimately their own lives and all they hold dear and sacred are affected by the government of the country, will tend greatly to strengthen and enlarge their claim for a share in the government. The growth of what was known as "militancy," in the last few years of the British suffrage movement, was the disastrous result of the long denial of justice, the acrid fruit of government which had become coercion, because it was no longer by consent.[8] Now that, for two

---

[8] **"militancy," in the last few years . . . consent**: The "militant" suffragists, led by Emmaline Pankhurst, had, during the years preceding the war's outbreak, conducted a campaign of domestic terrorism to publicize their cause.

years past, the women of Great Britain have made common cause with their men in this time of stress, the heat of the internal conflict has died down, and one hears on all sides that prominent anti-suffragists have become ardent suffragists, while others have declared their resolve at any rate never again to *oppose* the enfranchisement of women. The battle of argument was won long ago, but we are not, as a people, much given to theory; custom has a very strong hold over us. The shock of war has loosened that hold, and now almost every one who used to oppose, when asked whether women should be given votes, would reply: "Why not? They have earned them!" I cannot admit that representation is a thing that people should be called upon to "earn," nor that, if essential contribution to the nation is to count as "earning," the women have not earned the vote for just as long as the men. . . .

What the war has put in a fresh light, so that even the dullest can see, is that if the State may claim women's lives and those of their sons and husbands and lovers, if it may absorb all private and individual life, as at present, then indeed the condition of those who have no voice in the State is a condition of slavery, and Englishmen don't feel quite happy at the thought that their women are still slaves, while their Government is saying they are waging a war of liberation. Many women had long ago become acutely aware of their ignominious position, but the jolt of the war has made many more aware of it. . . .

READING AND DISCUSSION QUESTIONS

1. Having studied Swanwick's essay, how would you answer the two questions she poses at its beginning? "How has the war affected women? How will it affect them?"

2. Swanwick notes that the war brought about a major increase in the number of women in the workforce. What does she foresee happening to those women when the war ends?

3. Why, according to Swanwick, do employers prefer to hire women?

4. Why does she charge, in the final paragraph, that "women are still slaves"?

DOCUMENT 27-4

VLADIMIR I. LENIN
On Russian Autocracy
1903

Whereas Britain, France, Germany, and Italy had evolved into constitutional regimes with mass electorates by the 1890s, Russia remained staunchly autocractic. The tsar's power was in theory as absolute as it had been in Peter the Great's time. There was no national legislature and citizens who engaged in political activities, like the revolutionary socialist Vladimir Lenin (1870–1924), ran the risk of imprisonment or worse. Russia's economy posed an especially daunting problem for the revolutionaries. Marx had argued that industrial capitalism was a necessary prerequisite to communist revolution and, as of 1900, Russian industry was still in its infancy.

The history of the revolutionary movement is so little known among us that the name "Narodnaya Volya"[9] is used to denote any idea of a militant centralized organization which declares determined war upon tsarism. . . . [N]o revolutionary trend, if it seriously thinks of struggle, can dispense with such an organization. The mistake the Narodnaya Volya committed was not in striving to enlist *all* the discontented in the organization and to direct this organization to resolute struggle against autocracy; on the contrary, that was its great historical merit. The mistake was in relying on a theory which in substance was not a revolutionary theory at all, and the Narodnaya Volya members either did not know how, or were unable, to link their movement inseparably with the class struggle in the developing capitalist society. Only a gross failure to understand Marxism . . . could prompt the opinion that the rise of a mass, spontaneous working-class movement *relieves* us of the duty of creating as good an organization of revolutionaries as the Zemlya i Volya[10]

Vladimir I. Lenin, "What Is to Be Done?" in Robert C. Tucker, ed. and trans., *The Lenin Anthology* (New York: W. W. Norton, 1975), 85–89.

[9] **"Narodnaya Volya"**: "The People's Will," a pioneering populist revolutionary movement of the late nineteenth century.

[10] **Zemlya i Volya**: "Land and Freedom," the most militant of the populist revolutionary groups that arose out of Narodnaya Volya prior to Tsar Alexander II's assassination by revolutionaries in 1881.

had, or, indeed, an incomparably better one. On the contrary, this movement *imposes* the duty upon us; for the spontaneous struggle of the proletariat will not become its genuine "class struggle" until this struggle is led by a strong organization of revolutionaries.

We have always protested, and will, of course, continue to protest against *confining* the political struggle to conspiracy. But this does not, of course, mean that we deny the need for a strong revolutionary organization. . . . In *form* such a strong revolutionary organization in an autocratic country may also be described as a "conspiratorial" organization, because the French word *conspiration* is the equivalent of the Russian word *zagovor* ("conspiracy"), and such an organization must have the utmost secrecy. Secrecy is such a necessary condition for this kind of organization that all the other conditions (number and selection of members, functions, etc.) must be made to conform to it. It would be extremely naive indeed, therefore, to fear the charge that we Social-Democrats desire to create a conspiratorial organization. . . .

The objection may be raised that such a powerful and strictly secret organization, which concentrates in its hands all the threads of secret activities, an organization which of necessity is centralized, may too easily rush into a premature attack, may thoughtlessly intensify the movement before the growth of political discontent, the intensity of the ferment and anger of the working class, etc., have made such an attack possible and necessary. Our reply to this is: Speaking abstractly, it cannot be denied, of course, that a militant organization *may* thoughtlessly engage in battle, which *may* end in defeat entirely avoidable under other conditions. But we cannot confine ourselves to abstract reasoning on such a question, because every battle bears within itself the abstract possibility of defeat, and there is no way of *reducing* this possibility except by organized preparation for battle. If, however, we proceed from the concrete conditions at present obtaining in Russia, we must come to the positive conclusion that a strong revolutionary organization is absolutely necessary precisely for the purpose of giving stability to the movement and of *safeguarding* it against the possibility of making thoughtless attacks. Precisely at the present time, when no such organization yet exists, and when the revolutionary movement is rapidly and spontaneously growing, we *already observe* two opposite extremes (which, as it is to be expected, "meet"). These are: the utterly unsound Economism [concentrating on gaining economic improvements for the workers] and the preaching of moderation, and the equally unsound "excitative terror" which strives "artificially to call forth symptoms of the end of the movement, which is developing and strengthening itself, when this movement is as yet nearer to the start than the end. . . ."[11]

Only a centralized, militant organization that consistently carries out a Social-Democratic policy, that satisfies, so to speak, all revolutionary instincts and strivings, can safeguard the movement against making thoughtless attacks and prepare attacks that hold out the promise of success.

A further objection may be raised, that the views on organization here expounded contradict the "democratic principle." . . .

. . . For the present, we shall examine more closely the "principle" that the Economists advance. Everyone will probably agree that "the broad democratic principle" presupposes the two following conditions: first, full publicity, and secondly, election to all offices. It would be absurd to speak of democracy without publicity, moreover, without a publicity that is not limited to the membership of the organization. We call the German Socialist Party a democratic organization because all its activities are carried out publicly; even its party congresses are held in public. But no one would call an organization democratic that is hidden from every one but its members by a veil of secrecy. What is the use, then, of advancing "the *broad* democratic principle" when the fundamental condition for this principle *cannot be fulfilled* by a secret organization? "The broad principle" proves itself simply to be a resounding but hollow phrase. Moreover, it reveals a total lack of understanding of the urgent tasks of the moment in regard to organization. Everyone knows how great the lack of secrecy is among the "broad" masses of our revolutionaries. We have heard the bitter complaints of B — v[12] on this score and his absolutely just demand for a "strict selection of members". Yet, persons who boast a keen "sense of realities" *urge*, in a situation like this, not the strictest secrecy and the strictest (consequently, more restricted) selection of members, but "the *broad* democratic principle"! This is what you call being wide of the mark.

Nor is the situation any better with regard to the second attribute of democracy, the principle of election. In politically free countries [Lenin cites Germany], this condition is taken for granted. . . .

Try to fit this picture into the frame of our autocracy! Is it conceivable in Russia for all "who accept the principles of the Party programme and

---

[11] **"excitative terror"** . . . : Lenin was quoting the populist revolutionary Vera Zasulich (1849–1919).

[12] **B — v**: Probably Alexander Bogdanov (1873–1928), Russian physician, philosopher, economist, science fiction writer, and radical politician.

render the Party all possible support" to control every action of the revolutionary working in secret? Is it possible for all to elect one of these revolutionaries to any particular office, when, in the very interests of the work, the revolutionary *must* conceal his identity from nine out of ten of these "all"? Reflect somewhat over the real meaning of the high-sounding phrases [about democracy] . . . and you will realize that "broad democracy" in Party organization, amidst the gloom of the autocracy and the domination of gendarmerie [Russian secret police], is nothing more than a *useless and harmful toy.* It is a useless toy because, in point of fact, no revolutionary organization has ever practiced, or could practice, *broad* democracy, however much it may have desired to do so. It is a harmful toy because any attempt to practice "the broad democratic principle" will simply facilitate the work of the police in carrying out large-scale raids, will perpetuate the prevailing primitiveness, and will divert the thoughts of the practical workers from the serious and pressing task of training themselves to become professional revolutionaries to that of drawing up detailed "paper" rules for election systems. Only abroad, where very often people with no opportunity for conducting really active work gather, could this "playing at democracy" develop here and there, especially in small groups. . . .

READING AND DISCUSSION QUESTIONS

1. For what reasons, does Lenin argue, are the public political activities of socialist parties in countries like Germany simply impossible in Russia?

2. What does Lenin advocate in place of public political activity?

3. What does Lenin's argument that "the spontaneous struggle of the proletariat will not become its genuine 'class struggle' until this struggle is led by a strong organization of revolutionaries" suggest both about his opinion of the proletariat's revolutionary instincts and his belief that Russia could be led toward communism by the "vanguard of the proletariat"? *Who* would form the "vanguard of the proletariat"?

4. Based on what Lenin outlines as unhelpful models of revolution, how do you imagine the structure of his ideal revolutionary organization?

DOCUMENT 27-5

WOODROW WILSON
The Fourteen Points
1918

From the war's outbreak through early 1917, the United States kept aloof from the fray, with President Woodrow Wilson (1856–1924) entreating the American people to be neutral "in spirit as well as in deed." In fact, the nation was heavily invested in the Allied (British, French, and Russian) war effort, and most Americans sympathized with the Allies. Wilson regarded himself and the country as arbiters in the bitter struggle. Even prior to the U.S. declaration of war against Germany in April, he outlined his vision of the postwar international order in "fourteen points" in a January 1918 speech to Congress.

1. Open covenants of peace, openly arrived at. Diplomacy shall proceed always frankly and in the public view.
2. Absolute freedom of navigation upon the seas, outside territorial waters.
3. The removal, so far as possible, of all economic barriers and the establishment of an equality of trade conditions.
4. Adequate guarantees given and taken that national armaments will be reduced.
5. A free, open-minded, and absolutely impartial adjustment of all colonial claims. In determining all such questions of sovereignty the interests of the populations concerned must have equal weight with the equitable claims of the Government whose title is to be determined.
6. The evacuation of all Russian territory.
7. Belgium must be evacuated and restored. Without this healing act the whole structure and validity of international law is forever impaired.
8. All French territory should be freed and the invaded portions restored; and the wrong done to France by Prussia in 1871 in the matter of Alsace-Lorraine should be righted.

From Charles F. Horne, ed., *The Great Events of the Great War* (National Alumni, 1920), 6:3–6.

9. A readjustment of the frontiers of Italy should be effected along clearly recognizable lines of nationality.

10. The [...] of Austria-Hungary, whose place among the nations we wish to see safeguarded and assured, should be accorded the freest opportunity of autonomous development.

11. Rumania, Serbia, and Montenegro should be evacuated; occupied territories restored; Serbia accorded free and secure access to the sea; and international guarantees of the political and economic independence and territorial integrity of the several Balkan states should be entered into.

12. Nationalities which are now under Turkish rule should be assured an unmolested opportunity of autonomous development, and the Dardanelles should be permanently opened as a free passage to the ships and commerce of all nations.

13. An independent Polish state should be erected which should be assured a free and secure access to the sea.

14. A general association of nations must be formed, for the purpose of affording mutual guarantees of political independence and territorial integrity to great and small states alike.

READING AND DISCUSSION QUESTIONS

1. How does Wilson want to treat Germany?

2. On what underlining principles did Wilson base points six through thirteen?

3. What do you think prompted Wilson's demand for "absolute freedom of the seas"?

4. A "general association of nations . . . for the purpose of affording mutual guarantees of political independence and territorial integrity" was indeed formed after World War I (the League of Nations), and its successor (the United Nations) exists to this day. To what extent do you think Wilson's vision that these entities would provide "mutual guarantees of political independence and territorial integrity" has been realized in the more than nine decades since he delivered his speech?

A Defeated Germany Contemplates the Peace Treaty

1919

Unlike the Congress of Vienna (1814–1815), in which defeated France participated, the Treaty of Versailles was written without German input. Indeed, the German government was only presented with the completed treaty and told that it faced the choice of signing it or having the Allied armies resume their advance. By June 1919, the German army had been entirely demobilized. Moreover, the Allied naval blockade, which contributed approximately 750,000 civilian deaths by starvation and disease during its duration, remained in place until Germany signed the treaty on June 28, 1919. The following document captures the reception of Germany's several political parties (the National Assembly of the Germany Republic) to the treaty.

Bauer,[13] [Social Democratic Party, acting chancellor]: Ladies and gentlemen!

The Reich president has entrusted me with the formation of a new cabinet, to replace the Scheidemann[14] government which has resigned. . . . The resignation of the cabinet resulted from its inability to reach an undivided position regarding the peace treaty that has been presented to us. . . . For each of us who were members of the former government it was a bitterly difficult matter to take a position between feelings of indignation and cold rage. And not less difficult was the decision to join this new government whose first and most pressing task it is to conclude this unjust peace. . . . We are here because of our sense of responsibility, aware that it is our damnable duty to try to salvage what can be salvaged. . . .

"Deutsche Parlamentsdebatten" in Benjamin Sax and Dieter Kuntz, eds. and trans., *The Making of Modern Germany* (Lexington, Mass.: D. C. Heath, 1992), 45–47.

[13] **Bauer**: Gustav Adolf Bauer (1870–1944), German chancellor, August 1919–March 1920.

[14] **Scheidemann**: German journalist and politician Philipp Scheidemann (1865–1939), who led a short-lived government from February to June of 1919.

No matter how each one of us feels about the question of acceptance or rejection, we are all united about one thing: in strong criticism of this peace treaty (*"Very true!"*) to which we are being forced to affix our signatures! When this draft was first presented to us, it was greeted with a unanimous protest of indignation and rejection from our people. We defied disappointment and hoped for the indignation of the entire world. . . .

Rejection did not mean averting the treaty. (*"Very true!" from the Social Democrats.*) A no vote would only have meant a short delay of the yes vote. (*"Very true!"*) Our ability to resist has been broken; we do not have the capability to avert [signing]. . . . In the name of the national government, ladies and gentlemen, I ask you in view of the circumstances and pending ratification by the National Assembly,[15] to sign the peace treaty laid before you! . . .

. . . The government of the German Republic pledges to fulfill the imposed conditions of the peace. The government, however, wishes during this solemn occasion to express its views quite clearly. . . . The imposed conditions exceed the limits of Germany's ability to comply. . . .

. . . Moreover, we emphatically declare that we cannot accept Article 231 of the peace treaty, which demands that Germany accept responsibility for singly initiating the war. (*Applause.*)

Gröber,[16] *delegate of the Center Party:* Honored Assembly! The Center Party delegation of the National Assembly wishes to acknowledge the government's declaration. We accept this program and will support this government and accept [cabinet] participation. . . . We say we are prepared to accept the responsibility of fulfilling its terms as far as is humanly possible, but we do not recognize a responsibility for carrying out conditions that are impossible or intolerable. However, although these are oppressive and hardly fulfillable conditions and will have a detrimental effect on the German people, we must also take other facts into account.

First, the peace will shortly bring hundreds of thousands of prisoners back to German families. . . . Second, the peace will end starvation. . . . Third, only the peace will give us the possibility of economically rebuilding Germany. . . . Fourth, the peace also allows us to maintain our German unity. . . .

---

[15] **pending ratification . . . Assembly**: It was a vote by individual delegates and, as the socialists were in a majority, the treaty was accepted even though, as Bauer states, they hated it too. The vote was 237 to 138 for *conditional* acceptance.

[16] *Gröber*: Conrad Gröber (1872–1948), Catholic archbishop and politician.

Schiffer,[17] *delegate of the DDP* [German Democratic Party]: Contrary to the first two speakers, I wish to declare to this esteemed assembly, that the great majority of my political friends have decided to withhold their approval of the peace treaty laid before us. . . .

Count von Posadowsky,[18] *delegate of the DNVP* [German National People's Party]: Our Fatherland finds itself in the most difficult hour of its history. The enemy stands before our gates, and in the country there are disconcerting signs of internal breakup. . . . We in our party are aware of the ramifications for our people which a rejection of the peace treaty will entail. (*"Very true!" from the right.*) The resultant harm, however, will only be temporary, but if we accept this treaty we will abandon countless generations of our people to misery. . . . For us, acceptance of the treaty is impossible for many reasons. . . . In addition to making Germany defenseless, there is also the matter of theft of our territory. . . .

Haase,[19] *delegate of the USPD* [Independent Social Democratic Party]: We know that the peace treaty will bring incredible burdens for our people. . . . Nonetheless, we have no choice but to accept the treaty. Not only will rejection increase the harm, it will moreover mean sure ruin. (*Agreement from the Independent Social Democrats.*) Our people are in this desperate situation only because of the wicked warmongers and war extenders. . . .

Kahl,[20] *delegate of the DVP* [German People's Party]: Gentlemen! The German People's Party unanimously rejects this peace. . . . We reject it because to accept it would mean the destruction of the German state. . . . We reject because we cannot justify the separation of precious segments of German earth, such as the eastern provinces, from the Motherland. . . . Yes, if only we had swords in our hands! (*Laughter from the Social Democrats.*) Then we would easily find a response! (*"Very true" from the right.*) . . .

---

[17] *Schiffer*: Eugen Schiffer (1860–1954), German politician.
[18] *Count von Posadowsky*: Arthur Adolf Graf von Posadowsky-Wehner (1845–1932), German politician.
[19] *Hasse*: Hugo Haase (1863–1919), German jurist, politician, and pacifist.
[20] *Kahl*: Wilhelm Kahl (1849–1932), German academic and politician.

READING AND DISCUSSION QUESTIONS

1. Why were all of the speakers unhappy with the Treaty of Versailles?

2. Which spokesmen do you think represented left-leaning (socialist) parties and which represented right-leaning (conservative and nationalist) parties? Why?

3. On what grounds did Bauer, Gröber, and Haase advocate accepting the treaty?

4. On what grounds did Schiffer, Posadowsky, and Kahl advocate its rejection?

COMPARATIVE QUESTIONS

1. After the conflict's end, Edward Grey is supposed to have remarked that "Europe slid into war" in 1914. Judging by the Franco-Russian alliance, the belief that "mobilization meant war," and Grey's own speech justifying British involvement, what do you think he meant by that remark? Why?

2. How did World War I open opportunities for both women and radical revolutionaries, as gleaned from Swanwick and Lenin's statements?

3. What does the German legislature's universal condemnation of the Treaty of Versailles suggest about the degree to which Woodrow Wilson's views influenced its content? What might account for the inclusion of Article 231?

4. Compare and contrast Swanwick's views regarding women's place in the workforce during World War I with those of Clara Zetkin (Document 24-3) regarding prewar industrial society. What had changed? How?

CHAPTER 28

The Age of Anxiety

ca. 1900–1940

A number of developments in the twentieth century began to suggest that reason and science had limits when it came to understanding and controlling the world. Even before the slaughter of the Great War demonstrated that advanced technological achievement did not translate into superior morality, philosophers like Nietzsche and Freud began to question the role of reason in morality and behavior. Their intellectual uncertainty was soon mirrored by economic troubles. The Treaty of Versailles, which essentially dictated the terms of peace and lay the moral and economic responsibilities of World War I at the feet of the Germans, left the future of Western Europe under a cloud of uncertainty. The Great Depression in the United States that followed (1929–1939) forced many Europeans to reconsider their beliefs about economics, politics, and social relationships.

DOCUMENT 28-1

FRIEDRICH NIETZSCHE

From The Gay Science: *God Is Dead, the Victim of Science*

1882

Friedrich Wilhelm Nietzsche (1844–1900) was a tormented philosopher who deserted academic life in 1879 to wander Europe, writing books that criticized most aspects of European, particularly German, society. He

---

Friedrich Nietzsche, "The Madman," in Eugen Weber, ed. and trans., *Movements, Currents, Trends: Aspects of European Thought in the Nineteenth and Twentieth Centuries* (Lexington, Mass.: D. C. Heath, 1992), 454–455.

rejected nationalism, socialism, liberalism, and Christianity as promoting a weak herd morality and argued that the "overman" (ubermensch) should emerge to create his own morality, based on his will (choice) rather than external commandments. This excerpt from his 1882 work Die Frölische Wissenschaft (The Gay Science) is ironic given that Nietzsche collapsed seven years after its publication and spent the rest of his life in an insane asylum.

Have you not heard of that madman who lit a lantern in the bright morning hours, ran to the market place, and cried incessantly, "I seek God! I seek God!" As many of those who do not believe in God were standing around just then, he provoked much laughter. Why, did he get lost? said one. Did he lose his way like a child? said another. Or is he hiding? Is he afraid of us? Has he gone on a voyage? or emigrated? Thus they yelled and laughed. The madman jumped into their midst and pierced them with his glances.

"Whither is God?" he cried. "I shall tell you. *We have killed him* — you and I. All of us are his murderers. But how have we done this? How were we able to drink up the sea? Who gave us the sponge to wipe away the entire horizon? What did we do when we unchained this earth from its sun? Whither is it moving now? Away from all suns? Are we not plunging continually? Backward, sideward, forward, in all directions? Is there any up or down left? Are we not straying as through an infinite nothing? Do we not feel the breath of empty space? Has it not become colder? Is not night and more night coming on all the while? Must not lanterns be lit in the morning? Do we not hear anything yet of the noise of the grave-diggers who are burying God? Do we not smell anything yet of God's decomposition? Gods too decompose. God is dead. God remains dead. And we have killed him. How shall we, the murderers of all murderers, comfort ourselves? What was holiest and most powerful of all that the world has yet owned has bled to death under our knives. Who will wipe this blood off us? What water is there for us to clean ourselves? What festivals of atonement, what sacred games shall we have to invent? Is not the greatness of this deed too great for us? Must not we ourselves become gods simply to seem worthy of it? There has never been a greater deed; and whoever will be born after us — for the sake of this deed he will be part of a higher history than all history hitherto."

Here the madman fell silent and looked again at his listeners; and they too were silent and stared at him in astonishment. At last he threw his lantern on the ground, and it broke and went out. "I come too early," he said then; "my time has not come yet. This tremendous event is still on its way, still wandering — it has not yet reached the ears of man. Lightning and thunder require time, the light of the stars requires time, deeds require time even after they are done, before they can be seen and heard. This deed is still more distant from them than the most distant stars — *and yet they have done it themselves.*"

It has been related further that on that same day the madman entered divers churches and there sang his *requiem aeternam deo.*[1] Led out and called to account, he is said to have replied each time, "What are the churches now if they are not the tombs and sepulchers of God?" . . .

READING AND DISCUSSION QUESTIONS

1. From Nietzsche's perspective of wanting others to abide by their own moralities what benefits can you see to the death of God?

2. What in the passage indicates that the death of God may not be an entirely positive event in the author's mind?

3. What could Nietzsche's madman mean when he accuses his listeners — and himself — of murdering God?

4. What does the reaction of the crowd in the marketplace reveal about attitudes toward religion at the time, at least in some circles?

DOCUMENT 28-2

SIGMUND FREUD

From The Interpretation of Dreams

1900

Sigmund Freud (1856–1939), a Viennese psychoanalyst, stunned the European intellectual world when he published The Interpretation of Dreams, *in which he argued that the body controls the mind. European scientific and*

A. A. Brill, trans. and ed., *The Basic Writings of Sigmund Freud* (New York: Random House, 1938), 540–549.

[1] *requiem aeternam deo*: A funeral song for the "eternal god."

moral thought at the time still reflected the Enlightenment belief in the
power of reason, and in the ability of humans to choose their own course.
Freud later argued that the mind was shaped more by events it did not
remember (the unconscious) than by those it did, undermining European
faith in the mind to actively and purposefully direct the world around them.

Thus far, we have developed our psychology on our own responsibility; it
is now time to turn and look at the doctrines prevailing in modern psychology, and to examine the relation of these to our theories. The problem
of the unconscious in psychology is, according to the forcible statement of
Lipps,[2] less a psychological problem than the problem of psychology. As
long as psychology disposed of this problem by the verbal explanation that
the psychic is the conscious, and that unconscious psychic occurrences
are an obvious contradiction, there was no possibility of a physician's
observations of abnormal mental states being turned to any psychological
account. The physician and the philosopher can meet only when both
acknowledge that unconscious psychic processes is the appropriate and
justified expression for all established fact. The physician cannot but
reject, with a shrug of his shoulders, the assertion that consciousness is the
indispensable quality of the psychic; if his respect for the utterances of the
philosophers is still great enough, he may perhaps assume that he and they
do not deal with the same thing and do not pursue the same science. For
a single intelligent observation of the psychic life of a neurotic, a single
analysis of a dream, must force upon him the unshakable conviction that
the most complicated and the most accurate operations of thought, to
which the name of psychic occurrences can surely not be refused, may
take place without arousing consciousness. The physician, it is true, does
not learn of these unconscious processes until they have produced an
effect on consciousness which admits of communication or observation.
But this effect on consciousness may show a psychic character which dif-
fers completely from the unconscious process, so that internal perception
cannot possibly recognize in the first a substitute for the second. The
physician must reserve himself the right to penetrate, by a Process of
deduction, from the effect on consciousness to the unconscious psychic
process; he learns in this way that the effect on consciousness is only a
remote psychic product of the unconscious process, and that the latter has

---

[2] **Lipps**: Thedor Lipps (1851–1914), a German psychologist, and author of an influential book on thought, the 1883 *Basic Facts of Mental Life*.

not become conscious as such, and has, moreover, existed and operated without in any way betraying itself to consciousness. . . .

A return from the over-estimation of the property of consciousness is the indispensable preliminary to any genuine insight into the course of psychic events. As Lipps has said, the unconscious must be accepted as the general basis of the psychic life. The unconscious is the larger circle which includes the smaller circle of the conscious; everything conscious has a preliminary unconscious stage, whereas the unconscious can stop at this stage, and yet claim to be considered a full psychic function. The unconscious is the true psychic reality; *in its inner nature it is just as much unknown to us as the reality of the external world, and it is just as imperfectly communicated to us by the data of consciousness as is the external world by the reports of our sense-organs.*

We get rid of a series of dream-problems which have claimed much attention from earlier writers on the subject when the old antithesis between conscious life and dream-life is discarded, and the unconscious psychic assigned to its proper place. Thus, many of the achievements which are a matter for wonder in a dream are now no longer to be attributed to dreaming, but to unconscious thinking, which is active also during the day. If the dream seems to make play with a symbolical representation of the body, as Scherner[3] has said, we know that this is the work of certain unconscious phantasies, which are probably under the sway of sexual impulses and find expression not only in dreams, but also in hysterical phobias and other symptoms. If the dream continues and completes mental work begun during the day, and even brings valuable new ideas to light, we have only to strip off the dream-disguise from this, as the contribution of the dream-work, and a mark of the assistance of dark powers in the depths of the psyche. . . . The intellectual achievement as such belongs to the same psychic forces as are responsible for all such achievements during the day. We are probably much too inclined to over-estimate the conscious character even of intellectual and artistic production. From the reports of certain writers who have been highly productive, such as Goethe[4] and Helmholtz,[5] we learn, rather, that the most essential and original part

---

[3] **Scherner**: Karl Albert Scherner, a psychologist who published an 1861 work on dream theory, *The Life of Dreams.*
[4] **Goethe**: Johann Wolfgang von Goethe (1749–1832), a German author of the classical and romantic schools, most famous for his version of Faust's deal with the devil.
[5] **Helmholtz**: Hermann Ludwig Ferdinand von Helmholtz (1821–1894), a German doctor who wrote extensively on perception and theory of science.

of their creations came to them in the form of inspirations, and offered itself to their awareness in an almost completed state. In other cases, where there is a concerted effort of all the psychic forces, there is nothing strange in the fact that conscious activity, too, lends its aid. But it is the much-abused privilege of conscious activity to hide from us all other activities wherever it participates.

It hardly seems worth while to take up the historical significance of dreams as a separate theme. Where, for instance, a leader has been impelled by a dream to engage in a bold undertaking, the success of which has had the effect of changing history, a new problem arises only so long as the dream is regarded as a mysterious power and contrasted with other more familiar psychic forces. The problem disappears as soon as we regard the dream as a form of expression for impulses to which a resistance was attached during the day, whilst at night they were able to draw reinforcement from deep-lying sources of excitation. But the great respect with which the ancient peoples regarded dreams is based on a just piece of psychological divination. It is a homage paid to the unsubdued and indestructible element in the human soul, to the demonic power which furnishes the dream-wish, and which we have found again in our unconscious. . . .

What role is now left, in our representation of things, to the phenomenon of consciousness, once so all-powerful and over-shadowing all else? None other than that of a sense-organ for the perception of psychic qualities. . . .

It is only on a dissection of hysterical mental processes that the manifold nature of the problems of consciousness becomes apparent. One then receives the impression that the transition from the preconscious to the conscious cathexis[6] is associated with a censorship similar to that between Ucs [unconscious] and Pcs [preconscious]. This censorship, too, begins to act only when a certain quantitative limit is reached, so that thought-formations which are not very intense escape it. All possible cases of detention from consciousness and of penetration into consciousness under certain restrictions are included within the range of psychoneurotic phenomena; all point to the intimate and twofold connection between the censorship and consciousness. I shall conclude these psychological considerations with the record of two such occurrences.

---

[6] **cathexis**: For Freud, this term represented the libido's energy, the driving force in most human behavior.

On the occasion of a consultation a few years ago, the patient was an intelligent-looking girl with a simple, unaffected manner. She was strangely attired; for whereas a woman's dress is usually carefully thought out to the last pleat, one of her stockings was hanging down and two of the buttons of her blouse were undone. She complained of pains in one of her legs, and exposed her calf without being asked to do so. Her chief complaint, however, was as follows: She had a feeling in her body as though something were sticking into it which moved to and fro and shook her through and through. This sometimes seemed to make her whole body stiff. On hearing this, my colleague in consultation looked at me: the trouble was quite obvious to him. To both of us it seemed peculiar that this suggested nothing to the patient's mother, though she herself must repeatedly have been in the situation described by her child. As for the girl, she had no idea of the import of her words, or she would never have allowed them to pass her lips. Here the censorship had been hoodwinked so successfully that under the mask of an innocent complaint a phantasy was admitted to consciousness which otherwise would have remained in the preconscious. . . .

If I were asked what is the theoretical value of the study of dreams, I should reply that it lies in the additions to psychological knowledge and the beginnings of an understanding of the neuroses which we thereby obtain. Who can foresee the importance a thorough knowledge of the structure and functions of the psychic apparatus may attain, when even our present state of knowledge permits of successful therapeutic intervention in the curable forms of psychoneuroses? But, it may be asked, what of the practical value of this study in regard to a knowledge of the psyche and discovery of the hidden peculiarities of individual character? Have not the unconscious impulses revealed by dreams the value of real forces in the psychic life? Is the ethical significance of the suppressed wishes to be lightly disregarded, since, just as they now create dreams, they may some day create other things?

I do not feel justified in answering these questions. I have not followed up this aspect of the problem of dreams. In any case, however, I believe that the Roman Emperor was in the wrong in ordering one of his subjects to be executed because the latter had dreamt that he had killed the Emperor. He should first of all have endeavored to discover the significance of the man's dreams; most probably it was not what it seemed to be. And even if a dream of a different content had actually had this treasonable meaning, it would still have been well to recall the words of Plato —

that the virtuous man contents himself with dreaming of that which the wicked man does in actual life. I am therefore of the opinion that dreams should be acquitted of evil. Whether any reality is to be attributed to the unconscious wishes, I cannot say. Reality must, of course, be denied to all transitory and intermediate thoughts. If we had before us the unconscious wishes, brought to their final and truest expression, we should still do well to remember that psychic reality is a special form of existence which must not be confounded with material reality. It seems, therefore, unnecessary that people should refuse to accept the responsibility for the immorality of their dreams. With an appreciation of the mode of functioning of the psychic apparatus, and an insight into the relations between conscious and unconscious, all that is ethically offensive in our dream-life and the life of phantasy for the most part disappears.

"What a dream has told us of our relations to the present (reality) we will then seek also in our consciousness and we must not be surprised if we discover that the monster we saw under the magnifying-glass of the analysis is a tiny little infusorian [single-cell organism]" (H. Sachs[7]).

For all practical purposes in judging human character, a man's actions and conscious expressions of thought are in most cases sufficient. Actions, above all, deserve to be placed in the front rank; for many impulses which penetrate into consciousness are neutralized by real forces in the psychic life before they find issue in action; indeed, the reason why they frequently do not encounter any psychic obstacle on their path is because the unconscious is certain of their meeting with resistances later. In any case, it is highly instructive to learn something of the intensively tilled soil from which our virtues proudly emerge. For the complexity of human character, dynamically moved in all directions, very rarely accommodates itself to the arbitrament of a simple alternative, as our antiquated moral philosophy would have it.

And what of the value of dreams in regard to our knowledge of the future? That, of course, is quite out of the question. One would like to substitute the words: in regard to our knowledge of the past. For in every sense a dream has its origin in the past. The ancient belief that dreams reveal the future is not indeed entirely devoid of the truth. By representing a wish as fulfilled the dream certainly leads us into the future; but this future, which the dreamer accepts as his present, has been shaped in the likeness of the past by the indestructible wish.

---

[7] **H. Sachs:** Hanns Sachs (1881–1947), a Viennese psychologist and student of Freud's who later wrote an admiring biography of his teacher.

READING AND DISCUSSION QUESTIONS

1. How might someone who believed in the absolute responsibility of individuals for their actions, particularly their moral actions, respond to Freud's theories?

2. Freud argues what forms the basis of human behavior? What does he present as evidence of this pathway to expression?

3. Assume for a moment that Freud is correct, that the unconscious influences behavior more than the conscious; what then does that say about how he proves his case?

4. How might Freud's theory be received by someone who believes in the power of science to reveal the nature of the world, and ultimately to control it? Knowing what we now know about the division of the brain by function (at least to a degree), how might you respond? Does our scientific understanding help or harm Freud's argument?

DOCUMENT 28-3

JOHN MAYNARD KEYNES

From The Economic Consequences of the Peace: *An Analysis of the Versailles Treaty*

1920

Of the observers at Versailles, British economist John Maynard Keynes was one of the most prescient. Upset that the peace between Germany and the Allied Powers had been decided on political rather than economic grounds, Keynes publicly criticized the leaders who had negotiated the treaty. He warned that it would destroy the European economy, a prediction that seemed to come true in 1923, with the German economic collapse, and again in 1929 with the U.S. stock market crash and ensuing Great Depression. Keynes's criticism of the treaty that ended World War I was unusual coming from an Allied nation; most of the Allies thought their economies would benefit from the agreement.

John Maynard Keynes, *The Economic Consequences of the Peace* (New York: Harcourt, Brace and Howe, 1920), 226–227, 296–297.

The Treaty includes no provisions for the economic rehabilitation of Europe, — nothing to make the defeated Central Empires[8] into good neighbors, nothing to stabilize the new States of Europe,[9] nothing to reclaim Russia; nor does it promote in any way a compact of economic solidarity amongst the Allies themselves; no agreement was reached at Paris for restoring the disordered finances of France and Italy, or to adjust the systems of the Old World and the New.

The Council of Four[10] paid no attention to these issues, being preoccupied with others, — Clemenceau to crush the economic life of his enemy, Lloyd George to do a deal and bring home something which would pass muster for a week, the President to do nothing that was not just and right. It is an extraordinary fact that the fundamental economic problems of a Europe starving and disintegrating before their eyes, was the one question in which it was impossible to arouse the interest of the Four. Reparation was their main excursion into the economic field, and they settled it as a problem of theology, of politics, of electoral chicane, from every point of view except that of the economic future of the States whose destiny they were handling.

. . . For the immediate future events are taking charge, and the near destiny of Europe is no longer in the hands of any man. The events of the coming year will not be shaped by the deliberate acts of statesmen, but by the hidden currents, flowing continually beneath the surface of political history, of which no one can predict the outcome. In one way only can we influence these hidden currents, — by setting in motion those forces of instruction and imagination which change opinion. The assertion of truth, the unveiling of illusion, the dissipation of hate, the enlargement and instruction of men's hearts and minds, must be the means.

In this autumn of 1919, in which I write, we are at the dead season of our fortunes. The reaction from the exertions, the fears, and the sufferings of the past five years is at its height. Our power of feeling or caring beyond the immediate questions of our own material well-being is temporarily

---

[8] **Central Empires**: Germany, Austria-Hungary, and the Ottoman Empire — the losing alliance in the Great War.

[9] **new States of Europe**: The Treaty of Versailles dismembered the Austro-Hungarian and German Empires in the process creating newly independent states, including Czechoslovakia, Hungary, Yugoslavia, Lithuania, Latvia, and Estonia.

[10] **Council of Four**: The leaders of the Allied nations at Versailles: Woodrow Wilson of the United States, Georges Clemenceau of France, David Lloyd George of Great Britain, and Vittorio Orlando of Italy.

eclipsed. The greatest events outside our own direct experience and the most dreadful anticipations cannot move us.

We have been moved already beyond endurance, and need rest. Never in the lifetime of men now living has the universal element in the soul of man burnt so dimly.

READING AND DISCUSSION QUESTIONS

1. What motivations does Keynes believe shaped the treaty that emerged from the Versailles negotiations? Whose motivations were they? What does he think should have influenced it instead?

2. In what ways does Keynes think Europeans have lost control of their lives? What, if any, ideas does he seem to offer to help them recover that control?

3. What about Keynes's document suggests that reason is not the driving force in international relations?

4. As Keynes portrays them, how have the citizens of the warring countries responded to the peace?

DOCUMENT 28-4

SIR PERCY MALCOLM STEWART

From First and Second Reports of the Commissioner for the Special Areas: *Parliament Addresses the Great Depression in Britain*

1934

Great Britain's response to the depression was dictated by classical economic theory: when tax revenues drop, government spending should drop as well. Proponents of this view argued that in instances of financial instability, no

"First and Second Reports of the Commissioner for the Special Areas [England and Wales]," in W. C. Langsam, ed., *Documents and Readings in the History of Europe Since 1918*, rev. and enlarged ed. (Philadelphia: Lippincott, 1951), 303–304, 306.

government intervention was necessary, and that the economy would right itself after a time. When this righting took longer than expected, Parliament, under pressure, commissioned a study of which areas of the country were the hardest hit, and what steps could be taken to revitalize them. Despite the compelling findings, the government did little in response.

25. The Special Areas[11] are in their present unfortunate position owing to the decline of the main industries, coal mining, ship building and iron and steel, which attracted such large numbers of workers to them during the nineteenth century under more prosperous conditions. It seems unlikely that these industries will again employ the numbers engaged in them even up to ten years ago. During the period of prosperity large communities with full equipment of railways, roads, houses, schools, and other municipal and social services were created. Many millions of pounds were spent in building up these services. A large proportion of the inhabitants have been associated with the Areas for several generations; they are bound to the Areas by ties of home and family and religion, by local patriotism and, especially in Wales, by a fervent national spirit and, sometimes, a distinctive language. It is natural, therefore, that wherever one goes in these Areas one should be met by the demand that something should be done to attract fresh industries to the Area. This is the general request, and I regard it as at once the most important and the most difficult of my duties to try to satisfy it. I have given more time and personal attention to this side of my work than to any other, but it must be frankly admitted that up to the present the results have been negligible. Many of the negotiations I have initiated with this end in view were necessarily confidential, and it would only prejudice the present slender chances of success if I were to give a full account of them. The following paragraphs will, however, indicate the main lines on which I have been working.

26. In the first place I approached a number of the larger and more prosperous firms in the country in the hope that I might persuade them to open new branches of their industry in one or other of the Special Areas. Without exception they were sympathetic to my rep-

---

[11] **The Special Areas:** Specifically, the areas in South Wales supported by coal mining and areas such as Sheffield and Lancashire in northern England that were formerly centers of manufacturing and industry.

resentations, but except in one case they had good reasons which made it impossible for them to accede to my request. . . .

29. Some hundreds of new factories have been established in recent years in the Midlands and South, but very few in the Special Areas. Why is this so? The main reasons appear to fall in the following categories: —

    (1) Inaccessibility to markets. This applies particularly to Cumberland.[12] . . .

    (2) High rates.[13] These probably have a deterrent effect on employers out of proportion to their real significance. . . .

    (3) Fear of industrial unrest. This fear is very general and is bred from past disputes mainly in the coal-mining industry. It prevails particularly with regard to South Wales, but the facts scarcely warrant the attitude adopted. Statistics apart from those of coal-mining do not justify the fear which undoubtedly exists in the minds of many employers. . . .

    (4) The fact that the areas are, and for some years have been, suffering from industrial depression. This factor, coupled with the common application to them of the term "depressed" or "distressed" areas, has itself a deterrent effect. While it is true that "trade brings trade," the converse unfortunately is equally true. Unemployment undermines business confidence and reduces purchasing power. A vicious circle is thus set up. . . .

    (5) Difficulty in obtaining finance to start new industries. . . .

255. . . . Probably the most serious human problem of the Special Areas is that presented by unemployment among young men between 18 and 21. . . .

256. Many of these young persons have done practically no work; they have been brought up in a home where the father has been continuously out of work, and they have little or no conception that a man's ordinary occupation should be such as will provide the means of subsistence for himself and for his family. They have seen their own families and their friends kept for years by the State, and they have come to accept this as a normal condition of life. It is hardly

---

[12] **Cumberland:** Cumberland is one of the two English counties that border Scotland — the other is Northumberland — and one of the industrial areas hardest hit by unemployment in Great Britain.

[13] **High rates:** Shipping rates, meaning that freight was more expensive to ship.

surprising in the circumstances that young persons with this background and upbringing should be ready victims of all manner of demoralizing influences. In short, these young persons present in my view the most tragic aspect of the problem of the Special Areas and one fraught with great danger to the State.

READING AND DISCUSSION QUESTIONS

1. What factors make the Special Areas particularly unsuited for new business?

2. From the perspective of the workers mentioned in the report, what control do residents of the Special Areas seem to have over their lives in hard times? How do they react to this?

3. In what ways is the report concerned with workers, and in what ways with employers?

4. What reasons might members of Parliament who were generally opposed to taking action to relieve unemployment have had for commissioning this report?

COMPARATIVE QUESTIONS

1. What similarities can you discern between Freud and Nietzsche's understanding of human nature?

2. In what ways do Keynes's forebodings about the Treaty of Versailles seem to have been borne out by the report on the Special Areas?

3. If the nineteenth century's science was defined by certainty, in what ways do these documents undermine that certainty? Do any of these authors see this loss of certainty as a good thing? Why or why not?

4. How might the Social Darwinists, particularly Herbert Spencer (Document 24-5) respond to the report of the commissioner for the Special Areas? In what ways might the depression support or undercut Spencer's ideology?

CHAPTER 29

Dictatorships and the Second World War

1919–1945

The period of anxiety and depression that followed the Great War led many to question whether democracy and capitalism could meet the challenges of modern society. In this context, two radical totalitarian governments came to power. In the Soviet Union after 1928, Joseph Stalin led his nation through a brutal and repressive "second revolution." In 1933, Germany's new chancellor and Nazi Party leader Adolf Hitler began plans to create a German Nazi empire based on the ideology of Aryan supremacy. Hampered by their own worries, other nations, including Great Britain, seemed powerless to stop Stalin or Hitler. By 1939, Hitler had provoked the Second World War, and Great Britain, led by Winston Churchill, was forced to respond militarily. As the war intensified, the Nazis determined to exterminate all European Jews, a goal which they very nearly achieved.

DOCUMENT 29-1

VLADIMIR TCHERNAVIN
From I Speak for the Silent: *Stalinist Interrogation Techniques Revealed*

1930

To maintain his power and Communist rule in the Soviet Union, Joseph Stalin instituted a massive security apparatus that pervaded most aspects

Vladimir Tchernavin, *I Speak for the Silent* (Newton Center, Mass.: Charles T. Branford, 1935), 116–120.

of Soviet life. Vladimir Tchernavin was a scientist in the northwestern port city of Murmansk, working to transform the Soviet Union from an agrarian to an industrial state. Such an ambitious project was bound to have its share of failures, but in the climate of paranoia that pervaded Stalinist society, such failures were attributed to sabotage, and sabotage was brutally punished.

It was my second day in prison — my second cross-examination. I was called before the tea ration was given out and had only time to eat an apple.

"How do you do?" the examining officer asked, scanning me attentively to see if I showed signs of a sleepless night.

"All right."

"It isn't so good in your cell. You are in 22?"

"A cell like any other."

"Well, did you do any thinking? Are you going to tell the truth today?"

"Yesterday I told only the truth."

He laughed. "What will it be today — not the truth?"

Then he returned to the subject of the cell.

"I tried to choose a better cell for you, but we are so crowded. I hope we will come to an understanding and that I will not be forced to change the regime I have ordered for you. The third category is the mildest: exercise in the yard, permission to receive food parcels from outside, a newspaper and books. The first two categories are much stricter. Remember, however, that it depends entirely on me; any minute you may be deprived of everything and transferred to solitary confinement. Or rather, this depends not on me but on your own behavior, your sincerity. The more frank your testimony, the better will be the conditions of your imprisonment. . . ."

He spoke slowly, looking me straight in the eye, emphasizing his words with evident pleasure and relish, watching for their effect.

"Did you know Scherbakoff? He was a strong man, but I broke him and forced him to confess."

With great difficulty I controlled myself before replying.

"I don't doubt for a minute that you use torture, and if you believe that this assists in discovering the truth and speeding up the investigation, and since Soviet laws permit its use, I would suggest that you don't give up mediaeval methods: a little fire is a wonderful measure. Try it! I am not afraid of you. Even with that you can't get anything out of me."

"Well, we will see about that later. Now let's get down to business. Let's talk about your acquaintances. Did you know V. K. Tolstoy, the wrecker, executed in connection with the case of the '48'?"[1]

"Yes, I knew him. How could I not know him when he was the director of the fishing industry in the north?" I replied in frank astonishment. "We both worked in it for more than twenty years."

"And did you (know) him well?"

"Very well."

"How long did you know him?"

"From childhood."

His manner changed completely; he hurriedly picked up a statement sheet and placed it in front of me. "Write down your confession."

"What confession?"

"That you knew Tolstoy, that you were in friendly relation with him from such and such a time. I see that we will come to an understanding with you; your frankness will be appreciated. Write."

He evidently was in a hurry, did not quite know what he was saying, afraid that I might reverse my statements.

I took the sheet and wrote down what I had said.

"Excellent. Let's continue."

Then followed a barrage of questions about Tolstoy, about Scherbakoff and other people that I had known. He did not find me quite so tractable and we launched into a battle of wits that kept up hour after hour. He questioned me with insistence and in great detail, trying without success to make me give dates.

"You'll not succeed in outwitting me," he snapped sharply. "I advise you not to try. I am going home to dinner now and you will stay here till evening. This examination will continue — not for a day or two, but for months and, if necessary, for years. Your strength is not equal to mine. I will force you to tell us what we need."

After threatening me still further he handed me some sheets of paper.

"You are going to state in writing your opinion regarding the building of a fertilization factory in Murmansk, its equipment and work in the future. I'll soon be back; when I return, your comments on these questions must be completed."

---

[1] **the case of the '48'**: Tchernavin refers to the accusation and subsequent execution of forty-eight prominent Russian scientists accused of sabotaging the food supply in 1930.

He put on his overcoat and left. His assistant took his place, and I busied myself with my writing. It was three or four hours before he returned, already evening.

Although I had eaten almost nothing for three days, I was still in good fighting form. He questioned me about the buying of a ship from abroad, trying to make me say that here was "wrecking," because the price had been exorbitant and the ship itself had proved unsatisfactory. It was most confusing and his questions farfetched. We talked and we argued, but I would not give the answers he wanted.

He began on another tack. . . .

"All right," he said. "And what is your attitude regarding the subject of the fish supply in the Sea of Barents in connection with the construction of trawlers as provided for by the Five-Year Plan?"

Now he had broached a subject with which I could have a direct connection. The evening was already changing into night, but I was still sitting in the same chair. I was becoming unconscious of time: was it my second day in prison or my tenth? In spite of the depressing weariness, mental and physical, which was taking hold of me, I told him that I thought the fresh fish supply should be minutely and thoroughly investigated. I tried to make him see the hazards of the fishing industry in Murmansk and the enormous equipment that would be necessary to meet the proposals of the Five-Year Plan.

"And thus you confess that you doubted the practicability of the Five-Year Plan?" he said with a smile of smug satisfaction.

What could one say? I believed, as did everybody, that the plan was absurd, that it could not be fulfilled. For exactly such statements — no, for only a suspicion of having such thoughts — forty-eight men had been shot. . . .

READING AND DISCUSSION QUESTIONS

1. From the perspective of the state, what purposes would be served by arresting and torturing Vladimir Tchernavin?

2. What incentives could Tchernavin have for resisting, and what might convince him to comply with the interrogator?

3. Based on your reading of this account, what relationship did truth and guilt have in the Stalinist justice system?

DOCUMENT 29-2

ADOLF HITLER

From Mein Kampf: *The Art of Propaganda*

1924

While in prison for a failed 1923 coup attempt, Hitler dictated his autobiography, Mein Kampf (My Struggle), *excerpted here, detailing his views on politics and society. Based on his interpretation of the end of the Great War, Hitler argued that Germany had been defeated not by Allied armies, but by the failure of German propaganda to counter Allied propaganda effectively, something he proposed to change when he came to power. At the time,* Mein Kampf *was not popular, but it proved prophetic: one of Hitler's first acts as chancellor was to establish the Ministry for Enlightenment and Propaganda in March 1933.*

The psyche of the great masses is not receptive to anything that is half-hearted and weak. . . .

To whom should propaganda be addressed? To the scientifically trained intelligentsia or to the less educated masses?

It must be addressed always and exclusively to the masses. . . .

All propaganda must be popular and its intellectual level must be adjusted to the most limited intelligence among those it is addressed to. Consequently, the greater the mass it is intended to reach, the lower its purely intellectual level will have to be. . . .

The art of propaganda lies in understanding the emotional ideas of the great masses and finding, through a psychologically correct form, the way to the attention and thence to the heart of the broad masses. The fact that our bright boys do not understand this merely shows how mentally lazy and conceited they are.

Once we understand how necessary it is for propaganda to be adjusted to the broad mass, the following rule results:

It is a mistake to make propaganda many-sided, like scientific instruction, for instance. The receptivity of the great masses is very limited, their

Adolf Hitler, *Mein Kampf*, trans. Ralph Mannheim (Boston: Houghton-Mifflin, 1943), 42, 179–185.

intelligence is small, but their power of forgetting is enormous. In consequence of these facts, all effective propaganda must be limited to a very few points and must harp on these in slogans until the last member of the public understands what you want him to understand by your slogan. As soon as you sacrifice this slogan and try to be many-sided, the effect will piddle away, for the crowd can neither digest nor retain the material offered. In this way, the result is weakened and in the end entirely cancelled out. . . .

The broad mass of a nation does not consist of diplomats, or even professors of political law, or even individuals capable of forming a rational opinion; it consists of plain mortals, wavering and inclined to doubt and uncertainty. As soon as our own propaganda admits so much as a glimmer of right on the other side, the foundation for doubt in our own right has been laid. . . .

The people in their overwhelming majority are so feminine by nature and attitude that sober reasoning determines their thoughts and actions far less than emotion and feeling. . . . But the most brilliant propagandist technique will yield no success unless one fundamental principle is borne in mind constantly and with unflagging attention. It must confine itself to a few points and repeat them over and over. Here, as so often in this world, persistence is the first and most important requirement for success. . . .

The purpose of propaganda is not to provide interesting distraction for blase young gentlemen, but to convince, and what I mean is to convince the masses. But the masses are slow-moving, and they always require a certain time before they are ready even to notice a thing, and only after the simplest ideas are repeated thousands of times will the masses finally remember them. . . .

[During World War I] at first the claims of the [enemy] propaganda were so impudent that people thought it insane; later, it got on people's nerves; and in the end, it was believed. . . .

READING AND DISCUSSION QUESTIONS

1. What are Hitler's main suggestions for the propagandist who wants to be successful? How does it affect your evaluation of the passage to know that it took him almost ten more years to gain power?

2. What does Hitler's conception of who matters in society reveal about his attitudes toward both the powerful and the average members of society?

The Nuremberg Laws: The Centerpiece of Nazi Racial Legislation

1935

Part of Hitler's vision for Germany was based on a pseudoscientific racist division of the world that was not uncommon at the time. He believed that "Jewishness" was both biological and religious. Two years after the Nazi party took power in Germany, the first legal restrictions on German Jews were announced at a Nazi rally in Nuremburg. Hitler presented the Nuremburg Laws as a means to curb popular violence against Jews, allowing him to present himself as a defender of law and order.

ARTICLE 5

1. A Jew is anyone who descended from at least three grandparents who were racially full Jews. Article 2, par. 2, second sentence will apply.
2. A Jew is also one who descended from two full Jewish parents, if: (a) he belonged to the Jewish religious community at the time this law was issued, or who joined the community later; (b) he was married to a Jewish person, at the time the law was issued, or married one subsequently; (c) he is the offspring from a marriage with a Jew, in the sense of Section 1, which was contracted after the Law for the Protection of German Blood and German Honor became effective . . . ; (d) he is the offspring of an extramarital relationship, with a Jew, according to Section 1, and will be born out of wedlock after July 31, 1936. . . .

LAW FOR THE PROTECTION OF GERMAN BLOOD AND GERMAN HONOR OF 15 SEPTEMBER 1935

Thoroughly convinced by the knowledge that the purity of German blood is essential for the further existence of the German people and animated by the inflexible will to safe-guard the German nation for the entire future,

U.S. Chief of Counsel for the Prosecution of Axis Criminality, *Nazi Conspiracy and Aggression* (Washington, D.C.: U.S. Government Printing Office, 1946), vol. 4, doc. no. 1417-PS, 8–10; vol. 4, doc. no. 2000-PS, 636–638.

the Reichstag[2] has resolved upon the following law unanimously, which is
~~nulgated herewith:

~~ ..~n 1
1. Marriages between Jews and nationals of German or kindred blood are
   forbidden. Marriages concluded in defiance of this law are void, even
   if, for the purpose of evading this law, they are concluded abroad. . . .

Section 2
Relation[s] outside marriage between Jews and nationals of German or
kindred blood are forbidden.

Section 3
Jews will not be permitted to employ female nationals of German or kindred blood in their household.

Section 4
1. Jews are forbidden to hoist the Reich and national flag and to present
   the colors of the Reich. . . .

Section 5
1. A person who acts contrary to the prohibition of section 1 will be punished with hard labor.
2. A person who acts contrary to the prohibition of section 2 will be punished with imprisonment or with hard labor.
3. A person who acts contrary to the provisions of sections 3 or 4 will be
   punished with imprisonment up to a year and with a fine or with one
   of these penalties. . . .

READING AND DISCUSSION QUESTIONS

1. From these laws, what can you conclude about Nazi attitudes toward
   women and marriage?
2. What do these laws suggest about the basis of personal and national
   identity in the Nazi mind-set?

---

[2] **Reichstag:** The Reichstag was the German legislative assembly, a holdover from Bismarck's Second Empire (1871–1919) that had little real power after it granted Hitler
"temporary" dictatorial powers in March 1933.

3. Based on the document, what economic impact could these laws have
    had on the Jewish community in Germany? Why might the Nazis have
    wanted that impact?

D. :UMENT 29-4

WINSTON CHURCHILL

Speech Before the House of Commons

June 18, 1940

*Once the Second World War began in 1939, much of central and western
Europe quickly fell to the German* blitzkrieg *strategy. After sending troops to
aid the French against the Germans in 1940, the British Army lost most of
its tanks, trucks, and other heavy equipment while evacuating from Dunkirk
following a decisive Nazi victory. Germany held the deep-water ports along
the English Channel crucial for an invasion, and had the most feared air
force in Europe. Facing these grim prospects, Churchill addressed the House
of Commons to rally a nation unenthusiastic about another war.*

The military events which have happened during the past fortnight have
not come to me with any sense of surprise. Indeed, I indicated a fortnight
ago as clearly as I could to the House that the worst possibilities were open,
and I made it perfectly clear then that whatever happened in France
would make no difference to the resolve of Britain and the British Empire
to fight on, "if necessary for years, if necessary alone." During the last few
days we have successfully brought off the great majority of the troops we
had on the lines of communication in France — a very large number,
scores of thousands — and seven-eighths of the troops we have sent to
France since the beginning of the war, that is to say, about 350,000 out of
400,000 men, are safely back in this country. Others are still fighting with
the French, and fighting with considerable success in their local encounters with the enemy. We have also brought back a great mass of stores,

Winston Churchill, "June 18, 1940, Speech Before House of Commons," in Walter
Arnstein, ed., *The Past Speaks*, 2d ed. (Lexington, Mass.: D. C. Heath, 1993), 2:376–
378.

rifles, and munitions of all kinds which had been accumulated in France during the last nine months.

We have, therefore, in this island to-day a very large and powerful military force. . . .

This brings me, naturally, to the great question of invasion from the air and of the impending struggle between the British and German air forces. It seems quite clear that no invasion on a scale beyond the capacity of our land forces to crush speedily is likely to take place from the air until our air force has been definitely overpowered. In the meantime, there may be raids by parachute troops and attempted descents of airborne soldiers. We should be able to give those gentry a warm reception both in the air and if they reach the ground in any condition to continue the dispute. But the great question is, can we break Hitler's air weapon? Now, of course, it is a very great pity that we have not got an air force at least equal to that of the most powerful enemy within striking distance of these shores. But we have a very powerful air force which has proved itself far superior in quality, both in men and in many types of machine, to what we have met so far in the numerous fierce air battles which have been fought. In France, where we were at a considerable disadvantage and lost many machines on the ground, we were accustomed to inflict losses of as much as two to two and a half to one. In the fighting over Dunkirk, which was a sort of no man's land, we undoubtedly beat the German air force, and this gave us the mastery locally in the air, and we inflicted losses of three or four to one. . . .

There remains the danger of bombing attacks, which will certainly be made very soon upon us by the bomber forces of the enemy. It is true that the German bomber force is superior in numbers to ours, but we have a very large bomber force also which we shall use to strike at military targets in Germany without intermission. I do not at all underrate the severity of the ordeal which lies before us, but I believe our countrymen will show themselves capable of standing up to it. . . .

What General Weygand[3] called the "Battle of France" is over. I expect that the battle of Britain is about to begin. Upon this battle depends the survival of Christian civilization. Upon it depends our own British life and the long continuity of our institutions and our empire. The whole fury and might of the enemy must very soon be turned on us. Hitler knows that he will have to break us in this island or lose the war. If we can stand up to

---

[3] **General Weygand**: General Maxime Weygand took command of all French forces on May 17, 1940, and held that post until the French surrender, after which he collaborated with the German occupation.

him all Europe may be free, and the life of the world may move forward into broad, sunlit uplands, but if we fail then the whole world, including the United States, and all that we have known and cared for, will sink into the abyss of a new dark age made more sinister, and perhaps more prolonged, by the lights of a perverted science. Let us therefore brace ourselves to our duty and so bear ourselves that if the British Commonwealth and Empire lasts for a thousand years men will still say, "This was their finest hour."

READING AND DISCUSSION QUESTIONS

1. What reasons would Churchill have for mentioning the United States specifically in the last paragraph? For what audiences might this speech be intended?

2. What could this speech reveal about Churchill's attitude toward the British citizenry, and the concept of democratic rule in general?

3. What are the advantages and disadvantages Churchill sees facing the British war effort? How convincing do you find his assessment of the situation, and why?

DOCUMENT 29-5

TRAIAN POPOVICI

From Mein Bekenntnis: *The Ghettoization of the Jews*

1941

Nazi policy toward Europe's Jews moved toward extermination after 1941, though the shift in policy took some time to work out in practice. After forcing public identification of Jewish citizens, often by requiring them to wear yellow stars, the next step was to segregate them, which made deportation to

Traian Popovici, "Mein Bekenntnis (My Declaration)," in Richard Levy, ed. and trans., *Antisemitism in the Modern World* (Lexington, Mass.: D.C. Heath, 1991), 243–244.

the death camps easier. Romania was a German ally, and could be expected to reap the same economic benefit Germany did from plundering those scheduled for death. Popovici, the mayor of the capital city of Czernowitz, nevertheless urged his government to resist Nazi pressure, eventually saving close to twenty thousand lives through his efforts.

On the morning of October 11 . . . I looked out the window. It was snowing and — I could not believe my eyes: on the street in front of my window long columns of people were hurrying by. Old people supported by children, women with infants in their arms, invalids dragging their maimed bodies along, all with their luggage in wagons or on their backs, with hastily packed suitcases, bedding, bundles, clothes; they all made silent pilgrimage into the city's valley of death, the ghetto. . . .

Great activity in the city hall. . . . The "abandoned" wealth of the Jews was to be inventoried and their dwellings sealed. Romanianization departments were to be formed and with police assistants to be distributed throughout the city neighborhoods.

It first dawned on me then that the procedure had been a long time in the planning. I hurried to military headquarters where General Jonescu informed me of events. He let me see the promulgated ordinances. . . . I paged through the instructions in haste and read the regulations for the functioning of the ghetto. The bakeries were to be under city hall control, as were the [food] markets. Then I hurried again to the city hall in order to see to the measures necessary for the uninterrupted provisioning of bread, food, and especially milk for the children. For the time being, this was the role that providence allotted to me, thanks to the military cabinet.

Only those who know the topography of the city can measure how slight was the space for the ghetto to which the Jewish population was confined and in which, under pain of death, they had to be by six o'clock.

In this part of the city, even with the greatest crowding, ten thousand people could be housed at most. Fifty thousand had to be brought in, not counting the Christian population already living there. Then, and even today, I compare the ghetto to a cattle pen.

The accommodation possibilities were minimal. Even if the available rooms were to receive thirty or more people, a great number would have to seek shelter from the snow and rain in corridors, attics, cellars, and similar sorts of places. I would rather not speak of the demands of hygiene. Pure drinking water was lacking; the available public fountains did not suffice. I noted that the city already suffered from a water shortage since two of the three pumping stations had been destroyed. The strong odors of sweat, urine, and human waste, of mold and mildew, distinguished the quarter from the rest of the city. . . . It was a miracle that epidemics that would endanger the whole city did not break out. With surprising speed the ghetto was nearly hermetically sealed with barbed wire. At the main exits, wooden gates were erected and military guards posted. I do not know whether it was intentional, but the effect was clear: the despised were being intimidated. . . .

Although . . . the regulation concerning the ghetto categorically stated that no one could enter without the authorization of the governor, no one observed this rule. As early as the second day after the erection of the ghetto, there began a pilgrimage consisting of ladies of all social strata and intellectual jobbers, well known to the Czernowitz public. Persons of "influence" from all strata and professions — hyenas all — caught the scent of cadaverous souls among the unfortunates. Under the pretext that they were in the good graces of the governor, the military cabinet, or the mayor, they began the high-level pillaging of all that was left to the unfortunates. Their gold coins, jewelry, precious stones, furs, and valuable foodstuffs (tea, coffee, chocolate, cocoa) were supposedly to be used to bribe others or to compensate [the interlopers] for putting in a good word to save someone from deportation. Trading in influence was in full bloom. Another category of hyena was the so-called friend who volunteered to protect all these goods from theft or to deliver them to family members and acquaintances elsewhere in the country. Individuals never previously seen in the city of Czernowitz streamed in from all corners of the country in order to draw profit from a human tragedy. If the deportation with all its premeditation was in itself monstrous, then the exploitation of despair surpassed even this. . . .

READING AND DISCUSSION QUESTIONS

1. What issues did the ghettoization of Czernowitz's Jewish population raise, for Jews and non-Jews alike?

2. Traian Popovici obviously opposed the policies he carried out. What options did he have in the face of the Nazi orders?

3. Whom does Popovici see as the worst offenders during the ghettoization, and why?

4. What are some reasons why Popovici may not have heard of the segregation until it was well under way?

COMPARATIVE QUESTIONS

1. What similarities can you see between German and Soviet attitudes toward their citizens, and how might this contrast with the British attitude expressed by Churchill?

2. After reading Hitler's definition of effective propaganda, apply it to Churchill's speech. Where does it seem Churchill agrees with Hitler's principles, and where does it seem he departs from them?

3. Based on your reading of the first and last documents, which dictatorship, Stalin's or Hitler's, took greater steps to transform their societies, and on what do you base your evaluation?

CHAPTER 30

Cold War Conflicts and Social Transformations

1945–1985

T he alliance that destroyed Nazi Germany crumbled shortly after its
victory. Within five years, the Soviet Union and the United States
had organized alliances aimed at thwarting the other's perceived attempts
to dominate Europe. The development of nuclear weapons lent a new
urgency to simultaneous desire for nuclear dominance and fear of nuclear
destruction. The Soviets feared another attack from the West, and the West
distrusted the Soviets, who had promised but never held free elections in
Poland. Ironically, despite the ever-present threat of nuclear war between
1949 and 1991, these years were among the most peaceful Europe ever experienced. American aid gave the Western European economies the means
to recover, and in the shadow of the two superpowers, Europe developed a
concern for universal human rights, including those for women.

DOCUMENT 30-1

GEORGE C. MARSHALL

An American Plan to Rebuild a Shattered Europe

June 5, 1947

*In 1945, American policymakers wanted to avoid repeating the mistake of
withdrawing into neutrality as they had in 1919. George Marshall was the
highest ranking American officer in the Second World War and served as
secretary of state for the Truman administration. When communist parties*

"The Address of Secretary Marshall at Harvard," *The New York Times*, Friday, June 6,
1947.

began to win elections in France and Italy, Marshall, in a speech to Harvard University's graduating class, proposed spending billions to rebuild Europe and hopefully prevent another war, this time fought with atomic weapons. While the allied Western nations embraced the Marshall plan, the Stalin-headed Soviet Union rejected its terms, believing the Soviet Union would be stripped of its control of the Eastern bloc.

I need not tell you, gentlemen, that the world situation is very serious. That must be apparent to all intelligent people. I think one difficulty is that the problem is one of such enormous complexity that the very mass of facts presented to the public by press and radio make it exceedingly difficult for the man in the street to reach a clear appraisement of the situation. Furthermore, the people of this country are distant from the troubled areas of the earth and it is hard for them to comprehend the plight and consequent reactions of the long-suffering peoples, and the effect of those reactions on their governments in connection with our efforts to promote peace in the world.

In considering the requirements for the rehabilitation of Europe the physical loss of life, the visible destruction of cities, factories, mines and railroads was correctly estimated, but it has become obvious during recent months that this visible destruction was probably less serious than the dislocation of the entire fabric of European economy. For the past ten years conditions have been highly abnormal.

The feverish preparation for war and the more feverish maintenance of the war effort engulfed all aspects of national economies. Machinery has fallen into disrepair or is entirely obsolete. Under the arbitrary and destructive Nazi rule, virtually every possible enterprise was geared into the German war machine. Long-standing commercial ties, private institutions, banks, insurance companies and shipping companies disappeared, through loss of capital, absorption through nationalization or by simple destruction.

In many countries, confidence in the local currency has been severely shaken. The breakdown of the business structure of Europe during the war was complete. Recovery has been seriously retarded by the fact that two years after the close of hostilities a peace settlement with Germany and Austria has not been agreed upon. But even given a more prompt solution of these difficult problems, the rehabilitation of the economic structure of Europe quite evidently will require a much longer time and greater effort than had been foreseen.

There is a phase of this matter which is both interesting and serious. The farmer has always produced the foodstuffs to exchange with the city dweller for the other necessities of life. This division of labor is the basis of modern civilization. At the present time it is threatened with breakdown. The town and city industries are not producing adequate goods to exchange with the food-producing farmer. Raw materials and fuel are in short supply. Machinery is lacking or worn out.

The farmer or the peasant cannot find the goods for sale which he desires to purchase. So the sale of his farm produce for money which he cannot use seems to him an unprofitable transaction. He, therefore, has withdrawn many fields from crop cultivation and is using them for grazing. He feeds more grain to stock and finds for himself and his family an ample supply of food, however short he may be on clothing and the other ordinary gadgets of civilization. Meanwhile, people in the cities are short of food and fuel. So the governments are forced to use their foreign money and credits to procure these necessities abroad. This process exhausts funds which are urgently needed for reconstruction. Thus a very serious situation is rapidly developing which bodes no good for the world. The modern system of the division of labor upon which the exchange of products is based is in danger of breaking down.

The truth of the matter is that Europe's requirements for the next three or four years of foreign food and other essential products — principally from America — are so much greater than her present ability to pay that she must have substantial additional help, or face economic, social and political deterioration of a very grave character.

The remedy lies in breaking the vicious circle and restoring the confidence of the European people in the economic future of their own countries and of Europe as a whole. The manufacturer and the farmer throughout wide areas must be able and willing to exchange their products for currencies, the continuing value of which is not open to question.

Aside from the demoralizing effect on the world at large and the possibilities of disturbances arising as a result of the desperation of the people concerned, the consequences to the economy of the United States should be apparent to all. It is logical that the United States should do whatever it is able to do to assist in the return of normal economic health in the world, without which there can be no political stability and no assured peace.

Our policy is directed not against any country or doctrine but against hunger, poverty, desperation and chaos. Its purpose should be the revival of a working economy in the world so as to permit the emergence of political and social conditions in which free institutions can exist. Such assistance,

I am convinced, must not be on a piecemeal basis as various crises develop. Any assistance that this Government may render in the future should provide a cure rather than a mere palliative.

Any government that is willing to assist in the task of recovery will find full cooperation, I am sure, on the part of the United States Government. Any government which maneuvers to block the recovery of other countries cannot expect help from us. Furthermore, governments, political parties or groups which seek to perpetuate human misery in order to profit therefrom politically or otherwise will encounter the opposition of the United States.

It is already evident that, before the United States Government can proceed much further in its efforts to alleviate the situation and help start the European world on its way to recovery, there must be some agreement among the countries of Europe as to the requirements of the situation and the part those countries themselves will take in order to give proper effect to whatever action might be undertaken by this Government. It would be neither fitting nor efficacious for this Government to undertake to draw up unilaterally a program designed to place Europe on its feet economically. This is the business of the Europeans. The initiative, I think, must come from Europe. The role of this country should consist of friendly aid in the drafting of a European program and of later support of such a program so far as it may be practical for us to do so. The program should be a joint one, agreed to by a number of, if not all, European nations.

An essential part of any successful action on the part of the United States is an understanding on the part of the people of America of the character of the problem and the remedies to be applied. Political passion and prejudice should have no part. With foresight, and a willingness on the part of our people to face up to the vast responsibility which history has clearly placed upon our country, the difficulties I have outlined can and will be overcome.

READING AND DISCUSSION QUESTIONS

1. According to Marshall, what problems does Europe face? What solutions does he propose?

2. In what ways might this document mean that Europe no longer dominated the world's economy? In what ways is it still critical?

3. In what ways does Marshall's plan incorporate the Soviets? What impact could their decision not to participate have had on the Eastern European economy?

4. How much American self-interest is involved in the program Marshall proposes? What concrete benefits, beyond not having another war, can you see in this plan?

ALEXANDER SOLZHENITSYN

From One Day in the Life of Ivan Denisovich: *The Stalinist Gulag*

1962

After Joseph Stalin died in 1953, the Soviet Union backed away from many of his policies. The next Soviet leader, Nikita Khrushchev (r. 1953–1964), denounced the gulag — the terror and labor camps Stalin had created — and considerably relaxed censorship. In this new period of increased critical freedom, Alexander Solzhenitsyn was permitted to publish an account of his life in the camps, to which he had been sentenced in 1945 for criticizing Stalin's conduct of the war. His continued criticism of the Soviet regime led to his deportation to the West in 1974. From his exile, Solzhenitsyn condemned both the repression of the Soviets and the materialism of the capitalist world.

At that very moment the door bolt rattled to break the calm that now reigned in the barracks. From the corridor ran two of the prisoners. . . .

"Second count," they shouted.

On their heels came a guard.

"All out to the other half." . . .

"Damn them," said Shukhov. Mildly, because he hadn't gone to sleep yet.

Tsezar raised a hand and gave him two biscuits, two lumps of sugar, and a slice of sausage.

"Thank you, Tsezar Markovich," said Shukhov, leaning over the edge of his bunk. . . .

Alexander Solzhenitsyn, *One Day in the Life of Ivan Denisovich*, trans. Max Hayward and Ronald Hingley (New York: Praeger, 1963), 206–210.

Then he waited a little till more men had been sent out — he wouldn't have to stand barefoot so long in the corridor. But the guard scowled at him and shouted: "Come on, you there in the corner." . . .

"Do you want to be carried out, you shits?" the barracks commander shouted.

They shoved them all into the other half of the barracks . . . Shukhov stood against the wall near the bucket. The floor was moist underfoot. An icy draft crept in from the porch.

They had them all out now, and once again the guard and the orderly did their round, looking for any who might be dozing in dark corners. There'd be trouble if they counted short. . . .

Shukhov managed to squeeze in eighteenth. He ran back to his bunk. . . .

All right. Feet back into the sleeve of his jacket. Blanket on top. Then the coat. . . .

Now for that slice of sausage. Into the mouth. Getting your teeth into it. Your teeth. The meaty taste. And the meaty juice, the real stuff. Down it goes, into your belly.

Gone. . . .

Shukhov went to sleep fully content. He'd had many strokes of luck that day: they hadn't put him in the cells; they hadn't sent his squad to the settlement; he'd swiped a bowl of kasha [porridge] at dinner. . . .

READING AND DISCUSSION QUESTIONS

1. What motivations does Solzhenitsyn ascribe to the inhabitants of the gulags? Do they seem particularly criminal to you? Why or why not?

2. In what ways could this passage contradict the official Soviet image of the USSR as a "worker's paradise"?

3. What motivations might the Soviet leadership have had for allowing this publication?

GENERALS LESLIE GROVES AND
THOMAS F. FARRELL

Witnesses to the Birth of the Atomic Age

July 18, 1945

All major nations involved in World War II, including Japan, had active programs to develop an atomic bomb. Fears of apocalyptic destruction from the air dated from the early twentieth century, but by 1945 the United States had created the means to achieve and deploy it. On August 6 and 9, 1945, the Japanese cities of Hiroshima and Nagasaki witnessed the horrors of nuclear destruction in two U.S. strikes. In the aftermath, fears of nuclear obliteration intensified in both the West and the East, especially after Soviet detonation of its own atomic bomb in 1949.

18 JULY 1945
TOP SECRET
MEMORANDUM FOR THE SECRETARY OF WAR.
SUBJECT: THE TEST.

1. This is not a concise, formal military report but an attempt to recite what I would have told you if you had been here on my return from New Mexico.

2. At 0530, 16 July 1945, in a remote section of the Alamogordo Air Base, New Mexico, the first full scale test was made of the implosion type atomic fission bomb. For the first time in history there was a nuclear explosion. And what an explosion! It resulted from the atomic fission of about 13½ pounds of plutonium which was compressed by the detonation of a surrounding sphere of some 5000 pounds of high explosives. The bomb was not dropped from an airplane but was exploded on a platform on top of a 100-foot high steel tower.

3. The test was successful beyond the most optimistic expectations of anyone. . . . There were tremendous blast effects. For a brief period there was a lighting effect within a radius of 20 miles equal to several suns in midday; a huge ball of fire was formed which lasted for several

Martin Sherwin, *A World Destroyed* (New York: Vintage Books, 1976), 308–312.

seconds. This ball mushroomed and rose to a height of over ten thousand feet before it dimmed. The light from the explosion was seen clearly at Albuquerque, Santa Fe, Silver City, El Paso and other points generally to about 180 miles away. The sound was heard to the same distance in a few instances but generally to about 100 miles. Only a few windows were broken although one was some 125 miles away. A massive cloud was formed which surged and billowed upward with tremendous power, reaching the substratosphere at an elevation of 41,000 feet, 36,000 feet above the ground, in about five minutes. . . . Huge concentrations of highly radioactive materials resulted from the fission and were contained in this cloud.

4. A crater from which all vegetation had vanished, with a diameter of 1200 feet and a slight slope toward the center, was formed. In the center was a shallow bowl 130 feet in diameter and 6 feet in depth. The material within the crater was deeply pulverized dirt. The material within the outer circle is greenish and can be distinctly seen from as much as 5 miles away. The steel from the tower was evaporated. 1500 feet away there was a four-inch iron pipe 16 feet high set in concrete and strongly guyed. It disappeared completely. . . .

11. Brigadier General Thomas F. Farrell was at the control shelter located 10,000 yards south of the point of explosion. His impressions are given below:

"The scene inside the shelter was dramatic beyond words. In and around the shelter were some twenty-odd people concerned with last minute arrangements prior to firing the shot. Included were: Dr. Oppenheimer,[1] the Director who had borne the great scientific burden of developing the weapon from the raw materials made in Tennessee and Washington, and a dozen of his key scientists. . . .

"For some hectic two hours preceding the blast, General Groves stayed with the Director, walking with him and steadying his tense excitement. Every time the Director would be about to explode because of some untoward happening, General Groves would take him off and walk with him in the rain, counselling with him and reassuring him that everything would be all right. . . .

---

[1] **Dr. Oppenheimer**: J. Robert Oppenheimer, the civilian head of the project (Groves was the military head) who later came to oppose the development and deployment of nuclear weapons. He was stripped of his security clearance and blacklisted in 1954 for his loose communist affiliations in the 1930s.

"Just after General Groves left, announcements began to be broadcast of the interval remaining before the blast. They were sent by radio to the other groups participating in and observing the test. As the time interval grew smaller and changed from minutes to seconds, the tension increased by leaps and bounds. Everyone in that room knew the awful potentialities of the thing that they thought was about to happen. The scientists felt that their figuring must be right and that the bomb had to go off but there was in everyone's mind a strong measure of doubt. The feeling of many could be expressed by 'Lord, I believe; help Thou mine unbelief.' We were reaching into the unknown and we did not know what might come of it. It can be safely said that most of those present — Christian, Jew and Atheist — were praying and praying harder than they had ever prayed before. If the shot were successful, it was a justification of the several years of intensive effort of tens of thousands of people — statesmen, scientists, subatomic universe. . . .

"In that brief instant in the remote New Mexico desert the tremendous effort of the brains and brawn of all these people came suddenly and startlingly to the fullest fruition. Dr. Oppenheimer, on whom had rested a very heavy burden, grew tenser as the last seconds ticked off. He scarcely breathed. He held on to a post to steady himself. For the last few seconds, he stared directly ahead and then when the announcer shouted 'Now!' and there came this tremendous burst of light followed shortly thereafter by the deep growling roar of the explosion, his face relaxed into an expression of tremendous relief. Several of the observers standing back of the shelter to watch the lighting effects were knocked flat by the blast.

"The tension in the room let up and all started congratulating each other. Everyone sensed 'This is it!' No matter what might happen now all knew that the impossible scientific job had been done. Atomic fission would no longer be hidden in the cloisters of the theoretical physicists' dreams. It was almost full grown at birth. It was a great new force to be used for good or for evil. There was a feeling in that shelter that those concerned with its nativity should dedicate their lives to the mission that it would always be used for good and never for evil. . . .

"The effects could well be called unprecedented, magnificent, beautiful, stupendous and terrifying. No man-made phenomenon of such tremendous power had ever occurred before. The lighting effects beggared description. The whole country was lighted by a searing light with the intensity many times that of the midday sun. It was golden, purple, violet, gray and blue. It lighted every peak, crevasse and ridge of the nearby mountain range with a clarity and beauty that cannot be described but must be seen to be imagined. It was that beauty the great poets dream about but describe most poorly and inadequately. Thirty seconds after the explosion came first, the air blast pressing hard against the people and things, to be followed almost immediately by the strong, sustained, awesome roar which warned of doomsday and made us feel that we puny things were blasphemous to dare tamper with the forces heretofore reserved to The Almighty. Words are inadequate tools for the job of acquainting those not present with the physical, mental and psychological effects. It had to be witnessed to be realized. . . ."

READING AND DISCUSSION QUESTIONS

1. Given the destructiveness of the atomic bomb, what motivations did the scientists and soldiers have for celebrating the successful test?

2. In what technical features of the bomb does General Groves seem interested?

3. What hints of unease over the power of atomic weapons can you find in the document? Does General Groves seem to share General Farrell's sentiment?

DOCUMENT 30-4

The Helsinki Final Act: Human Rights and Fundamental Freedoms Enunciated

1975

Of the numerous efforts to get the American and Soviet alliances to coexist, none were more successful than the Helsinki Accords, negotiated in the capital of neutral Finland in the summer of 1975. The accords preserved existing territorial boundaries, a major Soviet concern, but guaranteed the same international sanction to the internal expression of dissent, something the Americans valued more than the Soviets. On a broader level, the accords

John Fry, *The Helsinki Process: Negotiating Security and Cooperation in Europe* (Washington, D.C.: National Defense University Press, 1993), 186–187.

represented the height of the postwar concern with resolving the political issues many believed had provoked World War II.

VII. RESPECT FOR HUMAN RIGHTS AND FUNDAMENTAL FREEDOMS, INCLUDING THE FREEDOM OF THOUGHT, CONSCIENCE, RELIGION OR BELIEF

The participating States will respect human rights and fundamental freedoms, including the freedom of thought, conscience, religion or belief, for all without distinction as to race, sex, language, or religion.

They will promote and encourage the effective exercise of civil, political, economic, social, cultural, and other rights and freedoms all of which derive from the inherent dignity of the human person and are essential for his free and full development.

Within this framework the participating States will recognize and respect the freedom of the individual to profess and practice, alone or in community with others, religion or belief acting in accordance with the dictates of his own conscience.

The participating States on whose territory national minorities exist will respect the right of persons belonging to such minorities to equality before the law, will afford them the full opportunity for the actual enjoyment of human rights and fundamental freedoms and will, in this manner, protect their legitimate interests in this sphere.

The participating States recognize the universal significance of human rights and fundamental freedoms, respect for which is an essential factor for the peace, justice and well-being necessary to ensure the development of friendly relations and cooperation among themselves as among all States.

They will constantly respect these rights and freedoms in their mutual relations and will endeavor jointly and separately, including in cooperation with the United Nations,[2] to promote universal and effective respect for them. They confirm the right of the individual to know and act upon his rights and duties in this field.

In the field of human rights and fundamental freedoms, the participating States will act in conformity with the purposes and principles of the

---

[2] **United Nations**: The international security agency formed in San Francisco in 1945 as an attempt to prevent future conflicts, based on the post–World War I League of Nations but with a Permanent Security Council that could (and still can) authorize military action.

Charter of the United Nations[3] and with the Universal Declaration of Human Rights. They will also fulfill their obligations as set forth in the international declarations and agreements in this field, including, inter alia, the International Covenants on Human Rights,[4] by which they may be bound.

VIII. EQUAL RIGHTS AND SELF-DETERMINATION OF PEOPLES

The participating States will respect the equal rights of peoples and their right to self-determination, acting at all times in conformity with the purposes and principles of the Charter of the United Nations and with the relevant norms of international law, including those relating to territorial integrity of States.

By virtue of the principle of equal rights and self-determination of peoples, all peoples always have the right, in full freedom, to determine, when and as they wish, their internal and external political status, without external interference, and to pursue as they wish their political, economic, social, and cultural development.

The participating States reaffirm the universal significance of respect for and effective exercise of equal rights and self-determination of peoples for the development of friendly relations among themselves as among all States; they also recall the importance of the elimination of any form of violation of this principle.

READING AND DISCUSSION QUESTIONS

1. What fundamental rights does the declaration affirm are essential to the inhabitants of modern states?

2. What sort of relationship does the document envision between the citizen and the state?

3. What might the guaranteed human rights accomplish in the daily lives of the citizens of the signatory nations?

---

[3] **Charter of the United Nations**: The founding document of the United Nations, dedicated mainly to collective security and equal rights.
[4] **International Covenants on Human Rights**: Refers to the 1948 UN Declaration of Universal Human Rights and the 1966 International Covenant on Civil and Political Rights, which essentially placed the ideals of the Declaration of the Rights of Man and of the Citizen (Document 21-3) into international law.

DOCUMENT 30-5

SIMONE DE BEAUVOIR

From The Second Sex: *Existential Feminism*

1949

In twentieth-century Europe, women achieved many goals of the nineteenth century's feminists, notably the rights to vote and to own property. Simone de Beauvoir (1908–1986) — a French writer and companion of the existentialist philosopher Jean-Paul Sartre — was part of the generation of women who wanted full inclusion in society, but realized that suffrage and proprietary equality did not always translate to social equality. De Beauvoir's writing took up the complex issues of attitudes and values, and was particularly concerned with the persistence of traditional attitudes long after the circumstances that had created them had evolved.

According to French law, obedience is no longer included among the duties of a wife, and each woman citizen has the right to vote; but these civil liberties remain theoretical as long as they are unaccompanied by economic freedom. A woman supported by a man — wife or courtesan — is not emancipated from the male because she has a ballot in her hand; if custom imposes less constraint upon her than formerly, the negative freedom implied has not profoundly modified her situation; she remains bound in her condition of vassalage. It is through gainful employment that woman has traversed most of the distance that separated her from the male; and nothing else can guarantee her liberty in practice. Once she ceases to be a parasite, the system based on her dependence crumbles; between her and the universe there is no longer any need for a masculine mediator.

The curse that is upon woman as vassal consists, as we have seen, in the fact that she is not permitted to do anything; so she persists in the vain pursuit of her true being through narcissism, love, or religion. . . .

It is quite understandable, also, that the milliner's apprentice, the shopgirl, the secretary, will not care to renounce the advantages of masculine support. I have already pointed out that the existence of a privileged

Simone de Beauvoir, *The Second Sex*, H. M. Parshley, ed. and trans. (New York: Alfred A. Knopf, 1952), 679, 681, 696–697, 715.

caste [social status], which she can join by merely surrendering her body, is an almost irresistible temptation to the young woman; she is fated for gallantry by the fact that her wages are minimal while the standard of living expected of her by society is very high. If she is content to get along on her wages, she is only a pariah: ill lodged, ill dressed, she will be denied all amusement and even love. Virtuous people preach asceticism to her, and, indeed, her dietary regime is often as austere as that of a Carmelite [nun]. Unfortunately, not everyone can take God as a lover; she has to please men if she is to succeed in her life as a woman. She will therefore accept assistance, and this is what her employer cynically counts on in giving her starvation wages. This aid will sometimes allow her to improve her situation and achieve a real independence; in other cases, however, she will give up her work and become a kept woman. She often retains both sources of income and each serves more or less as an escape from the other; but she is really in double servitude: to job and to protector. For the married woman her wages represent only pin money as a rule; for the girl who "makes something on the side" it is the masculine contribution that seems extra; but neither of them gains complete independence through her own efforts.

There are, however, a fairly large number of privileged women who find in their professions a means of economic and social autonomy. These come to mind when one considers woman's possibilities and her future. This is the reason why it is especially interesting to make a close study of their situation, even though they constitute as yet only a minority; they continue to be a subject of debate between feminists and antifeminists. The latter assert that the emancipated women of today succeed in doing nothing of importance in the world and that furthermore they have difficulty in achieving their own inner equilibrium. The former exaggerate the results obtained by professional women and are blind to their inner confusion. . . .

There is one feminine function that is actually almost impossible to perform in complete liberty. It is maternity. In England and America and some other countries a woman can at least decline maternity at will, thanks to contraceptive techniques.[5] We have seen that in France she is

_____

[5] **contraceptive techniques:** French women did not gain legal access to contraceptives until 1967, whereas Americans gained full access in 1936. Abortion was illegal in both countries in 1949, becoming legal in the United States in 1973 and in France in 1975.

often driven to painful and costly abortion or she frequently finds herself responsible for an unwanted child that can ruin her professional life. If this is a heavy charge, it is because inversely, custom does not allow a woman to procreate when she pleases. The unwed mother is a scandal to the community, and [an] illegitimate birth is a stain on the child; only rarely is it possible to become a mother without accepting the chains of marriage or losing caste. If the idea of artificial insemination interests many women, it is not because they wish to avoid intercourse with a male, it is because they hope that freedom of maternity is going to be accepted by society at last. It must be said in addition that in spite of convenient day nurseries and kindergartens, having a child is enough to paralyze a woman's activity entirely; she can go on working only if she abandons it to relatives, friends, or servants. She is forced to choose between sterility, which is often felt as a painful frustration, and burdens hardly compatible with a career.

Thus the independent woman of today is torn between her professional interests and the problems of her sexual life; it is difficult for her to strike a balance between the two; if she does, it is at the price of concessions, sacrifices, acrobatics, which require her to be in a constant state of tension. . . .

The free woman is just being born; when she has won possession of herself perhaps Rimbaud's[6] prophecy will be fulfilled: "There shall be poets! When women's unmeasured bondage shall be broken, when she shall live for and through herself, man — hitherto detestable — having let her go, she, too, will be poet! Woman will find the unknown! Will her ideational worlds be different from ours? She will come upon strange, unfathomable, repellent, delightful things; we shall take them, we shall comprehend them." It is not sure that her "ideational worlds" will be different from those of men, since it will be through attaining the same situation as theirs that she will find emancipation; to say in what degree she will remain different, in what degree these differences will retain their importance — this would be to hazard bold predictions indeed. What is certain is that hitherto woman's possibilities have been suppressed and lost to humanity, and that it is high time she be permitted to take her chances in her own interest and in the interest of all.

---

[6] **Rimbaud**: Arthur Rimbaud, a radical French poet who died in the late nineteenth century.

READING AND DISCUSSION QUESTIONS

1. Based on this excerpt, what does "equality" mean to Simone de Beauvior?

2. What problems does de Beauvoir see for women attempting to achieve her definition of equality?

3. What reasons could women have for not wanting to achieve the sort of liberation de Beauvoir promotes?

4. Based on your reading, what would de Beauvoir like to see change?

COMPARATIVE QUESTIONS

1. What similarities in outlook can you discern between George Marshall and Leslie Groves? How might the two differ in pursuit of their goals?

2. How does the society that produced *One Day in the Life of Ivan Denisovich* contrast with the ideals illustrated in the Helsinki Conference's declaration? In the age of atomic armament, have the Helsinki Final Act countries upheld "the inherent dignity of the human person . . . his free and full development"? Explain why or why not.

3. Based on her document, what critiques of the Helsinki declaration might Simone de Beauvior make?

4. In what ways does George Marshall's plan anticipate the Helsinki declaration? What differences can you see between the two documents?

5. How did ideas about feminism and women's rights change from the time that Mary Wollstonecraft wrote her *Vindication of the Rights of Women* (Document 21-4) and when de Beauvoir wrote *The Second Sex*? What continuities in thinking can you discern?

CHAPTER 31

Revolution, Rebuilding, and New Challenges

1985 to the Present

B y the mid-1980s, the Cold War was thawing. Between 1979 and 1989, the Soviet Union fought a long, bloody, and ultimately fruitless war against anti-communist rebels in Afghanistan and confronted economic troubles and worker dissatisfaction at home. Communist Party Secretary Mikhail Gorbachev, in collusion with U.S. President Reagan, negotiated a Soviet withdrawal from Afghanistan so he could focus on dire domestic problems. As the Soviet Union weakened, its European factions clamored for independence, which they achieved by the end of the decade. Although the fall of the Berlin wall in 1989 and the collapse of the Soviet Union in 1991 were celebrated at the time, there were undesirable and unforeseen consequences to the upheaval. The collapse of Yugoslavia led to a brutal war over the ethnic makeup of the Balkans, and the Muslim radicals who had fought the Soviets in Afghanistan turned their focus on the West as a potential enemy.

DOCUMENT 31-1

SOLIDARITY UNION

Twenty-One Demands: A Call for Workers' Rights and Freedom in a Socialist State

1980

Soviet control of Eastern Europe did not go uncontested. Soviet troops intervened in Hungary in 1956 and crushed a 1968 reform movement in

"The Twenty-One Demands," in Lawrence Weschler, *The Passion of Poland* (New York: Pantheon, 1984), 206–208.

Czechoslovakia. Polish resistance in the 1980s emerged from the anti-communist shipbuilder's union Solidarność (Solidarity), in the port city of Gdansk. Shipyard workers looking for a better life hung the Twenty-One Demands at the entrance to a shipyard on a pair of wooden boards, since all media outlets were state-controlled. Labor unions and strikes were illegal in the Soviet empire, but Solidarity, headed by worker Lech Walesa, successfully directed a group of ex-communist ally parties in broad resistance to the Soviets. In 1989, negotiations between Solidarity and the Community Party that led to semi-free Polish elections.

1. Acceptance of Free Trade Unions independent of both the Party and employers, in accordance with the International Labor Organization's Convention number 87 on the freedom to form unions, which was ratified by the Polish government.

2. A guarantee of the right to strike and guarantees of security for strikers and their supporters.

3. Compliance with the freedoms of press and publishing guaranteed in the Polish constitution. A halt to repression of independent publications and access to the mass media for representatives of all faiths.

4. (a) Reinstatement to their former positions for: people fired for defending workers' rights, in particular those participating in the strikes of 1970 and 1976; students dismissed from school for their convictions.

   (b) The release of all political prisoners. . . .

   (c) A halt to repression for one's convictions.

5. The broadcasting on the mass media of information about the establishment of the Interfactory Strike Committee (MKS) and publication of the list of demands.

6. The undertaking of real measures to get the country out of its present crisis by:

   (a) providing comprehensive, public information about the socio-economic situation;

   (b) making it possible for people from every social class and stratum of society to participate in open discussions concerning the reform program.

7. Compensation of all workers taking part in the strike for its duration with holiday pay from the Central Council of Trade Unions.[1]

---

[1] **Central Council of Trade Unions**: The official Soviet union organization, state-run and officially responsible for preventing the sorts of situations of which the workers complained in Gdansk.

8. Raise the base pay of every worker 2,000 zlotys[2] per month to compensate for price rises to date.

9. Guaranteed automatic pay raises indexed to price inflation and to decline in real income.

10. Meeting the requirements of the domestic market for food products: only surplus goods to be exported.

11. The rationing of meat and meat products through food coupons (until the market is stabilized).

12. Abolition of "commercial prices" and hard currency sales in so-called "internal export" shops.[3]

13. A system of merit selection for management positions on the basis of qualifications rather than [Communist] Party membership. Abolition of the privileged status of MO[4] SB[5] and the party apparatus through: equalizing all family subsidies; eliminating special stores, etc.

14. Reduction of retirement age for women to 50 and for men to 55. Anyone who has worked in the PRL [Polish People's Republic] for 30 years, for women, or 35 years for men, without regard to age, should be entitled to retirement benefits.

15. Bringing pensions and retirement benefits of the "old portfolio" to the level of those paid currently.

16. Improvement in the working conditions of the Health Service, which would assure full medical care to working people.

17. Provision for sufficient openings in daycare nurseries and preschools for the children of working people.

18. Establishment of three-year paid maternity leaves for the raising of children.

19. Reduce the waiting time for apartments.

20. Raise per diem [allowance for work-related travel] from 40 zlotys to 100 zlotys and provide cost-of-living increases.

---

[2] **zlotys**: The basic unit of Polish currency, not convertible into Western currency at the time. It was losing value due to rising inflation.

[3] **"internal export" shops**: State-run shops where people with Western currency could buy consumer goods not available to workers paid in zlotys (the government had introduced a special type of currency), as part of the Communist government's efforts to keep its economy afloat.

[4] **MO**: The *Milicja Obywatelska*, People's Militia, the main Polish police force.

[5] **SB**: *Służba Bezpieczeństwa*, literally "Security Service," the Communist secret police, roughly analogous to the Russian KGB.

21. Saturdays to be days off from work. Those who work on round-the-clock jobs or three-shift systems should have the lack of free Saturdays compensated by increased holiday leaves or through other paid holidays off from work.

READING AND DISCUSSION QUESTIONS

1. What sort of problems do Solidarity's leaders see with their workplace?

2. What does the document reveal about the relationship between the current Polish governance and the reality of everyday life in Soviet-occupied Europe? What do the workers consider the standard of care?

3. Although these demands were made against a communist state, in what ways do the authors accept the premise that the state has a responsibility to its citizens?

DOCUMENT 31-2

MIKHAIL GORBACHEV

From Perestroika: New Thinking for Our
Country and the World

1987

Soviet leadership in the late 1970s increasingly refused to adapt their ideology to real-world conditions, to disastrous effect. Years of focus on military production and heavy industry had created a shortage of consumer goods, a situation that led the West German chancellor to liken the Soviet Union to an abysmally poor African country, but with rockets. When Mikhail Gorbachev rose to become head of the Communist Party in 1985, he worked to reform the Soviet economy and the apparatus by which the party controlled information. These changes were referred to, respectively, as "perestroika" — restructuring — and "glasnost" — openness.

Mikhail Gorbachev, *Perestroika: New Thinking for Our Country and the World* (New York: Harper & Row, 1987).

Perestroika is an urgent necessity arising from the profound processes of development in our socialist society. This society is ripe for change. It has long been yearning for it. Any delay in beginning perestroika could have led to an exacerbated internal situation in the near future, which, to put it bluntly, would have been fraught with serious social, economic and political crises. . . .

. . . In the latter half of the seventies — something happened that was at first sight inexplicable. The country began to lose momentum. Economic failures became more frequent. Difficulties began to accumulate and deteriorate, and unresolved problems to multiply. Elements of what we call stagnation and other phenomena alien to socialism began to appear in the life of society. A kind of "braking mechanism" affecting social and economic development formed. And all this happened at a time when scientific and technological revolution opened up new prospects for economic and social progress. . . .

An absurd situation was developing. The Soviet Union, the world's biggest producer of steel, raw materials, fuel and energy, has shortfalls in them due to wasteful or inefficient use. One of the biggest producers of grain for food, it nevertheless has to buy millions of tons of grain a year for fodder. We have the largest number of doctors and hospital beds per thousand of the population and, at the same time, there are glaring shortcomings in our health services. Our rockets can find Halley's comet and fly to Venus with amazing accuracy, but side by side with these scientific and technological triumphs is an obvious lack of efficiency in using scientific achievements for economic needs, and many Soviet household appliances are of poor quality.

This, unfortunately, is not all. A gradual erosion of the ideological and moral values of our people began.

It was obvious to everyone that the growth rates were sharply dropping and that the entire mechanism of quality control was not working properly; there was a lack of receptivity to the advances in science and technology; the improvement in living standards was slowing down and there were difficulties in the supply of foodstuffs, housing, consumer goods and services.

On the ideological plane as well, the braking mechanism brought about ever greater resistance to the attempts to constructively scrutinize the problems that were emerging and to the new ideas. Propaganda of success — real or imagined — was gaining the upper hand. Eulogizing and servility were encouraged; the needs and opinions of ordinary working people, of the public at large, were ignored. . . .

The presentation of a "problem-free" reality backfired: a breach had formed between word and deed, which bred public passivity and disbelief in the slogans being proclaimed. It was only natural that this situation re-sulted in a credibility gap: everything that was proclaimed from the rostrums and printed in newspapers and textbooks was put in question. Decay began in public morals; the great feeling of solidarity with each other that was forged during the heroic times of the Revolution [1917], the first five-year plans,[6] the Great Patriotic War[7] and postwar rehabilitation was weakening; alcoholism, drug addiction and crime were growing; and the penetration of the stereotypes of mass culture alien to us, which bred vulgarity and low tastes and brought about ideological barrenness increased. . . .

An unbiased and honest approach led us to the only logical conclu-sion that the country was verging on crisis. . . .

I would like to emphasize here that this analysis began a long time before the April Plenary Meeting[8] and that therefore its conclusions were well thought out. It was not something out of the blue, but a balanced judgment. It would be a mistake to think that a month after the Central Committee Plenary Meeting in March 1985, which elected me General Secretary, there suddenly appeared a group of people who understood everything and knew everything, and that these people gave clearcut answers to all questions. Such miracles do not exist.

The need for change was brewing not only in the material sphere of life but also in public consciousness. People who had practical experience, a sense of justice and commitment to the ideals of Bolshevism[9] criticized the established practice of doing things and noted with anxiety the symp-toms of moral degradation and erosion of revolutionary ideals and socialist values. . . .

Perestroika is closely connected with socialism as a system. That side of the matter is being widely discussed, especially abroad, and our talk about perestroika won't be entirely clear if we don't touch upon that aspect.

Does perestroika mean that we are giving up socialism or at least some of its foundations? Some ask this question with hope, others with misgiving.

There are people in the West who would like to tell us that socialism is in a deep crisis and has brought our society to a dead end. That's how

---

[6]**five-year plans**: Stalin's attempts to transform the rural, agrarian Soviet Union into an industrial state. The first plan began in 1928, the second in 1932 (a year early), and succeeded at tremendous human cost.

[7]**Great Patriotic War**: The Soviet name for World War II, in which the Soviets lost at least twenty million people.

[8]**April Plenary Meeting**: The regular meeting of the Communist Party's officials.

[9]**Bolshevism**: Vladimir Lenin's — the first Soviet leader — interpretation of Marx's ideas, named after the Bolshevik faction of the pre-revolutionary Social Democratic Party.

they interpret our critical analysis of the situation at the end of the seventies and beginning of the eighties. We have only one way out, they say: to adopt capitalist methods of economic management and social patterns, to drift toward capitalism.

They tell us that nothing will come of perestroika within the framework of our system. They say we should change this system and borrow from the experience of another socio-political system. To this they add that, if the Soviet Union takes this path and gives up its socialist choice, close links with the West will supposedly become possible. They go so far as to claim that the October 1917 Revolution was a mistake which almost completely cut off our country from world social progress.

To put an end to all the rumors and speculations that abound in the West about this, I would like to point out once again that we are conducting all our reforms in accordance with the socialist choice. We are looking within socialism, rather than outside it, for the answers to all the questions that arise. We assess our successes and errors alike by socialist standards. Those who hope that we shall move away from the socialist path will be greatly disappointed. Every part of our program of perestroika — and the program as a whole, for that matter — is fully based on the principle of more socialism and more democracy. . . .

We will proceed toward better socialism rather than away from it. We are saying this honestly, without trying to fool our own people or the world. Any hopes that we will begin to build a different, nonsocialist society and go over to the other camp are unrealistic and futile. Those in the West who expect us to give up socialism will be disappointed. It is high time they understood this, and, even more importantly, proceeded from that understanding in practical relations with the Soviet Union. . . .

We want more socialism and, therefore, more democracy. . . .

READING AND DISCUSSION QUESTIONS

1. What attitudes does Gorbachev seem to hold toward the West, particularly Western culture, as gleaned from this document?

2. In what ways might this document be seen as a refutation of the policies of former Soviet leaders? In what ways does it seek to continue them?

3. Based on this document, what is Mikhail Gorbachev's relationship with Western free-market ideology?

4. To whom does Gorbachev ascribe the blame for the Soviet Union's recent economic failures? What solutions does he propose?

DOCUMENT 31-3

KOFI ANNAN

The Fall of Srebrenica: An Assessment

1999

The nation of Yugoslavia had been cobbled together out of several ethnic groups in 1919, and the 1980 death of Josip Tito, dictator since 1945, catalyzed the process of the country's disintegration. In the 1990s, ethnic Serbs attempted to create a greater Serbia, free of other ethnic groups, by driving them out or through acts of genocide. Although the various civil and international conflicts of the Bosnian War (1992–1995) were precisely the sorts of circumstances that the United Nations had been designed to mediate, the collective security body was unable to bring the war to a halt or protect the victims of Serbian attacks. The brutality of these attacks was most evident against the Bosniac (Bosnian Muslims) in Srebrenica.

XI. THE FALL OF SREBRENICA: AN ASSESSMENT

467. The tragedy that took place following the fall of Srebrenica is shocking for two reasons. It is shocking, first and foremost, for the magnitude of the crimes committed. Not since the horrors of World War II had Europe witnessed massacres on this scale. The mortal remains of close to 2,500 men and boys have been found on the surface, in mass grave sites and in secondary burial sites. Several thousand more men are still missing, and there is every reason to believe that additional burial sites, many of which have been probed but not exhumed, will reveal the bodies of thousands more men and boys. The great majority of those who were killed were not killed in combat: the exhumed bodies of the victims show large numbers had their hands bound, or were blindfolded, or were shot in the back or the back of the head. Numerous eyewitness accounts, now well corroborated by forensic evidence, attest to scenes of mass slaughter of unarmed victims.

468. The fall of Srebrenica is also shocking because the enclave's[10] inhabitants believed that the authority of the United Nations Secu-

---

"Report of the Secretary-General Pursuant to General Assembly Resolution 53/35," 467–506.

[10] **the enclaves:** The United Nations set up six supposedly safe areas in which Bosnian Muslims and Croats could seek refuge from Serb attacks.

rity Council, the presence of UNPROFOR[11] peacekeepers, and the might of NATO air power, would ensure their safety. Instead, the Serb forces ignored the Security Council, pushed aside the UNPROFOR troops, and assessed correctly that air power would not be used to stop them. They overran the safe area of Srebrenica with ease, and then proceeded to depopulate the territory within 48 hours. Their leaders then engaged in high-level negotiations with representatives of the international community while their forces on the ground executed and buried thousands of men and boys within a matter of days.

469. Questions must be answered, and foremost among these are the following: how can this have been allowed to happen? And how will the United Nations ensure that no future peacekeeping operation witnesses such a calamity on its watch? In this assessment, factors ranging from the most proximate to the more over-arching will be discussed, in order to provide the most comprehensive analysis possible of the preceding narrative.

A. *The role of UNPROFOR forces in Srebrenica*

470. In the effort to assign responsibility for the appalling events that took place in Srebrenica, many observers have been quick to point to the soldiers of the UNPROFOR Dutch battalion as the most immediate culprits. They blame them for not attempting to stop the Serb attack, and they blame them for not protecting the thousands of people who sought refuge in their compound.

471. As concerns the first criticism, the commander of the Dutch battalion believed that the Bosniacs could not defend Srebrenica by themselves and that his own forces could not be effective without substantial air support. Air support was, in his view, the most effective resource at his disposal to respond to the Serb attack. Accordingly, he requested air support on a number of occasions, even after many of his own troops had been taken hostage and faced potential Serb reprisal. These requests were unheeded by his superiors at various levels, and some of them may not have been received at all, illustrating the command-and-control problems from which UNPROFOR suffered throughout its history. However, having been told that the risk of confrontation with the Serbs was to be avoided, and that the execution of the mandate was secondary to the

[11] **UNPROFOR**: United Nations Protection Force, the multinational force sent by the United Nations to enforce the safe zones set up in 1993.

security of his personnel, the Dutch battalion withdrew from Observation Posts under direct attack.

472. It is true that the Dutch UNPROFOR troops in Srebrenica never fired at the attacking Serbs. They fired warning shots over the Serbs' heads and their mortars fired flares, but they never directly fired on any Serb units. Had they engaged the attacking Serbs directly it is possible that events would have unfolded differently. At the same time, it must be recognized that the 150 fighting men of the Dutch battalion were lightly armed and in indefensible positions, and were faced with 2,000 Serbs advancing with the support of armor and artillery.

473. As concerns the second criticism, it is easy to say with the benefit of hindsight and the knowledge of what followed that the Dutch battalion did not do enough to protect those who sought refuge in their compound. Perhaps they should have allowed everyone into the compound and then offered themselves as human shields to protect them. This may have slowed down the Serbs and bought time for higher level negotiations to take effect. At the same time, it is also possible that the Serb forces would then have shelled the compound, killing thousands in the process, as they had threatened to do. Ultimately, it is not possible to say with any certainty that stronger actions by the Dutch would have saved lives, and it is even possible that such efforts could have done more harm than good. Faced with this prospect and unaware that the Serbs would proceed to execute thousands of men and boys, the Dutch avoided armed confrontation and appealed in the process for support at the highest levels.

474. It is harder to explain why the Dutch battalion did not report more fully the scenes that were unfolding around them following the enclave's fall. Although they did not witness mass killing, they were aware of some sinister indications. It is possible that if the members of the Dutch battalion had immediately reported in detail those sinister indications to the United Nations chain of command, the international community may have been compelled to respond more robustly and more quickly, and that some lives might have been saved. This failure of intelligence-sharing was also not limited to the fall of Srebrenica, but an endemic weakness throughout the conflict, both within the peacekeeping mission, and between the mission and Member States.

B. The role of Bosniac forces on the ground

475. Criticisms have also been levelled at the Bosniacs in Srebrenica: among them that they did not fully demilitarize and that they did not

do enough to defend the enclave. To a degree, these criticisms appear to be contradictory. Concerning the first criticism, it is right to note that the Bosnian Government had entered into demilitarization agreements with the Serbs. They did this with the encouragement of the United Nations. And while it is true that the Bosniac fighters in Srebrenica did not fully demilitarize, they demilitarized enough for UNPROFOR to issue a press release, on 21 April 1993, saying that the process had been a success. Specific instructions from United Nations Headquarters in New York stated that UNPROFOR should not be too zealous in searching for Bosniac weapons and, later, that the Serbs should withdraw their heavy weapons before the Bosniacs gave up their weapons. The Serbs never did withdraw their heavy weapons.

476. Concerning the accusation that the Bosniacs did not do enough to defend Srebrenica, military experts consulted in connection with this report were largely in agreement that the Bosniacs could not have defended Srebrenica for long in the face of a concerted attack supported by armor and artillery. The defenders were an undisciplined, untrained, poorly armed, totally isolated force, lying prone in the crowded valley of Srebrenica. They were ill-equipped even to train themselves in the use of the few heavier weapons that had been smuggled to them by their authorities. After over three years of siege, the population was demoralized, afraid, and often hungry. The only leader of stature was absent when the attack occurred. Surrounding them, controlling all the high ground, handsomely equipped with the heavy weapons and logistical train of the Yugoslav army, were the Bosnian Serbs. There was no contest.

477. Despite the odds against them, the Bosniacs requested UNPROFOR to return to them the weapons they had surrendered under the demilitarization agreements of 1993. They requested those weapons at the beginning of the Serb offensive, but the request was rejected by UNPROFOR because, as one commander explained, "it was our responsibility to defend the enclave, not theirs." Given the limited number and poor quality of the Bosniac weapons held by UNPROFOR, it seems unlikely that releasing those weapons to the Bosniacs would have made a significant difference to the outcome of the battle; but the Bosniacs were under attack at that point, they wanted to resist with whatever means they could muster, and UNPROFOR denied them access to some of their own weapons. With the benefit of hindsight, this decision seems to have been particularly ill-advised, given UNPROFOR's own unwillingness consistently to advocate force as a means of deterring attacks on the enclave.

478. Many have accused the Bosniac forces of withdrawing from the enclave as the Serb forces advanced on the day of its fall. However, it must be remembered that on the eve of the final Serb assault the Dutch Commander urged the Bosniacs to withdraw from defensive positions south of Srebrenica town — the direction from which the Serbs were advancing. He did so because he believed that NATO aircraft would soon be launching widespread air strikes against the advancing Serbs.

479. There is also a third accusation levelled at the Bosniac defenders of Srebrenica, that they provoked the Serb offensive by attacking out of that safe area. Even though this accusation is often repeated by international sources, there is no credible evidence to support it. Dutchbat [Dutch battalion] personnel on the ground at the time assessed that the few "raids" the Bosniacs mounted out of Srebrenica were of little or no military significance. These raids were often organized in order to gather food, as the Serbs had refused access for humanitarian convoys into the enclave. Even Serb sources approached in the context of this report acknowledged that the Bosniac forces in Srebrenica posed no significant military threat to them. The biggest attack the Bosniacs launched out of Srebrenica during the over two years during which it was designated as a safe area appears to have been the raid on the village of Viûnjica, on 26 June 1995, in which several houses were burned, up to four Serbs were killed and approximately 100 sheep were stolen. In contrast, the Serbs overran the enclave two weeks later, driving tens of thousands from their homes, and summarily executing thousands of men and boys. The Serbs repeatedly exaggerated the extent of the "raids" out of Srebrenica as a pretext for the prosecution of a central war aim: to create a geographically contiguous and ethnically pure territory along the Drina, while freeing up their troops to fight in other parts of the country. The extent to which this pretext was accepted at face value by international actors and observers reflected the prism of amoral equivalency through which the conflict in Bosnia was viewed by too many for too long.

C. The role of air power

480. The next question that must be asked is this: Why was NATO air power not brought to bear upon the Serbs before they entered the town of Srebrenica? Even in the most restrictive interpretation of the mandate the use of close air support against attacking Serb targets was clearly warranted. The Serbs were firing directly at Dutch

Observation Posts with tank rounds as early as 5 days before the enclave fell.

481.   Some have alleged that NATO air power was not authorized earlier, despite repeated requests from the Dutchbat Commander, because the Force Commander or someone else had renounced its use against the Serbs in return for the release of United Nations personnel taken hostage in May–June 1995. Nothing found in the course of the preparation of this report supports such a view.

482.   What is clear is that my predecessor, his senior advisers (amongst whom I was included as Under-Secretary-General for Peacekeeping Operations), the SRSG and the Force Commander were all deeply reluctant to use air power against the Serbs for four main reasons. We believed that by using air power against the Serbs we would be perceived as having entered the war against them, something not authorized by the Security Council and potentially fatal for a peacekeeping operation. Second, we risked losing control over the process — once the "key" was turned "on" we did not know if we would be able to turn it "off," with grave consequences for the safety of the troops entrusted to us by Member States. Third, we believed that the use of air power would disrupt the primary mission of UNPROFOR as we then saw it: the creation of an environment in which the humanitarian aid could be delivered to the civilian population of the country. And fourth, we feared Serb reprisal against our peacekeepers. Member States had placed thousands of their troops under United Nations command. We, and many of the troop contributing nations, considered the security of these troops to be of fundamental importance in the implementation of the mandate. That there was merit in our concerns was evidenced by the hostage crisis of May–June 1995.

483.   At the same time, we were fully aware that the threat of NATO air power was all we had at our disposal to respond to an attack on the safe areas. The lightly armed forces in the enclaves would be no match for (and were not intended to resist) a Serb attack supported by infantry and armor. It was thus incumbent upon us, our concerns notwithstanding, to make full use of the air power deterrent, as we had done with some effect in response to Serb attacks upon Sarajevo and Gorazde in February and April 1994, respectively. For the reasons mentioned above, we did not use with full effectiveness this one instrument at our disposal to make the safe areas at least a little bit safer. We were, with hindsight, wrong to declare repeatedly and publicly that we did not want to use air power against the Serbs

except as a last resort, and to accept the shelling of the safe areas as a daily occurrence. We believed there was no choice under the Security Council resolutions but to deploy more and more peace-keepers into harm's way. The Serbs knew this, and they timed their attack on Srebrenica well. The UNPROFOR Commander in Sarajevo at the time noted that the reluctance of his superiors and of key troop contributors to "escalate the use of force" in the wake of the hostage crisis would create the conditions in which we would then always be "stared down by the Serbs."

D. Unanswered questions

484. The above assessment leaves unanswered a number of questions often asked about the fall of Srebrenica and the failure of the safe area regime. Two of these questions, in particular, are matters of public controversy and need to be addressed, even if no definitive answer can be provided.

485. The first question concerns the possibility that the Bosnian Government and the Bosnian Serb party, possibly with the knowledge of one or more Contact Group[12] states, had an understanding that Srebrenica would not be vigorously defended by the Bosniacs in return for an undertaking by the Serbs not to vigorously defend territory around Sarajevo.[13] However, the Bosniacs tried to break out of Sarajevo and were repulsed by the Serbs *before* the Serbs attacked Srebrenica. This would appear to remove any incentive the Bosniac authorities might have had to let the Serbs take Srebrenica. There is no doubt that the capture of Srebrenica and Zepa[14] by the Serbs made it easier for the Bosniacs and Serbs to agree on the territorial basis of a peace settlement: the Serbs, who felt that they needed to control the border with Serbia for strategic reasons, had the territory they wanted and would not trade it back; the Bosniacs, who felt that they needed to control Sarajevo and its approaches, were able to demand this in exchange for Srebrenica and Zepa. The fact that the result of the tragedy in Srebrenica contributed in some ways to the conclusion of a peace agreement — by galvanizing the will of the

---

[12] **Contact Group:** The United States, Great Britain, Italy, Germany, France, and Russia.

[13] **Sarajevo:** Serb forces laid siege to the Bosnian capital of Sarajevo between 1992 and 1996, launching artillery and sniper attacks but never storming the city itself.

[14] **Zepa:** Another of the enclaves, captured by the Serbs in summer 1995. There the Bosniac inhabitants were expelled rather than massacred.

international community, by distracting the Serbs from the coming Croatian attack, by reducing the vulnerability of UNPROFOR personnel to hostage-taking, and by making certain territorial questions easier for the parties to resolve — is not evidence of a conspiracy. It is a tragic irony. No evidence reviewed in the process of assembling this report suggests that any party, Bosnian or international, engineered or acquiesced in the fall of Srebrenica, other than those who ordered and carried out the attack on it. My personal belief is that human and institutional failing, at many levels, rather than wilful conspiracy, account for why the Serbs were not prevented from overrunning the safe area of Srebrenica.

486. A second question concerns the possibility that the United Nations, or one or more of its Member States, had intelligence indicating that a Serb attack on Srebrenica was being prepared. I can confirm that the United Nations, which relied on Member States for such intelligence, had no advance knowledge of the Serb offensive. Indeed, the absence of an intelligence-gathering capacity, coupled with the reluctance of Member States to share sensitive information with an organization as open, and from their perspective, as "insecure" as the United Nations, is one of the major operational constraints under which we labor in all our missions. As to whether any intelligence was available to Member States, I have no means of ascertaining this; in any case none was passed on to the United Nations by those Member States who might have been in a position to assist.

487. Had the United Nations been provided with intelligence that revealed the enormity of the Bosnian Serbs' goals, it is possible, though by no means certain, that the tragedy of Srebrenica might have been averted. But no such excuse can explain our failure in Zepa: before they began their advance into Zepa, the Serbs made a public announcement regarding their plans. Zepa was not overrun because of a lack of intelligence, but because the international community lacked the capacity to do anything other than to accept its fall as a *fait accompli* [a "fact realized," i.e., unpreventable].

E. The role of the security council and member states

488. With the benefit of hindsight, one can see that many of the errors the United Nations made flowed from a single and no-doubt well-intentioned effort: we tried to keep the peace and apply the rules of peacekeeping when there was no peace to keep. Knowing that any other course of action would jeopardize the lives of the troops, we

tried to create — or imagine — an environment in which the tenets of peacekeeping — agreement between the parties, deployment by consent, and impartiality — could be upheld. We tried to stabilize the situation on the ground through ceasefire agreements, which brought us close to the Serbs, who controlled the larger proportion of the land. We tried to eschew the use of force except in self-defense, which brought us into conflict with the defenders of the safe areas, whose safety depended on our use of force.

489. In spite of the untenability of its position, UNPROFOR was able to assist in the humanitarian process, and to mitigate some — but, as Srebrenica tragically underscored, by no means all — the suffering inflicted by the war. There are people alive in Bosnia today who would not be alive had UNPROFOR not been deployed. To this extent, it can be said that the 117 young men who lost their lives in the service of UNPROFOR's mission in Bosnia and Herzegovina did not die in vain. Their sacrifice and the good work of many others, however, cannot fully redeem a policy that was, at best, a half-measure.

490. The community of nations decided to respond to the war in Bosnia and Herzegovina with an arms embargo, with humanitarian aid and with the deployment of a peacekeeping force. It must be clearly stated that these measures were poor substitutes for more decisive and forceful action to prevent the unfolding horror. The arms embargo did little more than freeze in place the military balance within the former Yugoslavia. It left the Serbs in a position of overwhelming military dominance and effectively deprived the Republic of Bosnia and Herzegovina of its right, under the Charter of the United Nations, to self-defense. It was not necessarily a mistake to impose an arms embargo, which after all had been done when Bosnia-Herzegovina was not yet a Member State of the United Nations. But having done so, there must surely have been some attendant duty to protect Bosnia and Herzegovina, after it became a Member State, from the tragedy that then befell it. Even as the Serb attacks on and strangulation of the "safe areas"[15] continued in 1993 and 1994, all widely covered by the media and, presumably, by diplomatic and intelligence reports to their respective governments, the approach of the Members of the Security Council remained

---

[15] **safe areas**: U.N. Resolution 819 declared the areas around the cities of Sarajevo, Srebrenecia, Žepa, Goražde, Tuzla, and Bihać safe areas.

largely constant. The international community still could not find the political will to confront the menace defying it.

491. Nor was the provision of humanitarian aid a sufficient response to "ethnic cleansing" and to an attempted genocide. The provision of food and shelter to people who have neither is wholly admirable, and we must all recognize the extraordinary work done by UNHCR [the United Nations High Commission for Refugees] and its partners in circumstances of extreme adversity. But the provision of humanitarian assistance could never have been a solution to the problem in that country. The problem, which cried out for a political/ military solution, was that a Member State of the United Nations, left largely defenseless as a result of an arms embargo imposed upon it *by the United Nations*, was being dismembered by forces committed to its destruction. This was not a problem with a humanitarian solution.

492. Nor was the deployment of a peacekeeping force a coherent response to this problem. My predecessor openly told the Security Council that a United Nations peacekeeping force could not bring peace to Bosnia and Herzegovina. He said it often and he said it loudly, fearing that peacekeeping techniques inevitably would fail in a situation of war. None of the conditions for the deployment of peacekeepers had been met: there was no peace agreement — not even a functioning ceasefire — there was no clear will to peace and there was no clear consent by the belligerents. Nevertheless, *faute de mieux* ["for lack of anything better"], the Security Council decided that a United Nations peacekeeping force would be deployed. Lightly armed, highly visible in their white vehicles, scattered across the country in numerous indefensible observation posts, they were able to confirm the obvious: there was no peace to keep.

493. In so doing, the Council obviously expected that the "warring parties" on the ground would respect the authority of the United Nations and would not obstruct or attack its humanitarian operations. It soon became apparent that, with the end of the Cold War and the ascendancy of irregular forces — controlled or uncontrolled — the old rules of the game no longer held. Nor was it sufficiently appreciated that a systematic and ruthless campaign such as the one conducted by the Serbs would view a United Nations humanitarian operation, not as an obstacle, but as an instrument of its aims. In such an event, it is clear that the ability to adapt man-

dates to the reality on the ground is of critical importance to ensuring that the appropriate force under the appropriate structure is deployed. None of that flexibility was present in the management of UNPROFOR.

F. *The failure to fully comprehend the Serb war aims*

494. Even before the attack on Srebrenica began, it was clear to the Secretariat and Member States alike that the safe areas were not truly "safe." There was neither the will to use decisive air power against Serb attacks on the safe areas, nor the means on the ground to repulse them. In report after report the Secretariat accordingly and rightly pointed out these conceptual flaws in the safe area policy. We proposed changes: delineating the safe areas either by agreement between the parties or with a mandate from the Security Council; demilitarizing the safe areas; negotiating full freedom of movement. We also stressed the need to protect people rather than territory. In fact, however, these proposals were themselves inadequate. Two of the safe areas — Srebrenica and Zepa — were delineated from the beginning, and they were cited in our reports as relatively more successful examples of how the safe area concept could work. The same two safe areas were also demilitarized to a far greater extent than any of the others, though their demilitarization was by no means complete. In the end, however, the partial demilitarization of the enclaves did not enhance their security. To the contrary, it only made them easier targets for the Serbs. . . .

495. Nonetheless, the key issue — politically, strategically, and morally — underlying the security of the "safe areas" was the essential nature of "ethnic cleansing." As part of the larger ambition for a "Greater Serbia," the Serbs set out to occupy the territory of the enclaves; they wanted the territory for themselves. The civilian inhabitants of the enclaves were not the incidental victims of the attackers; their death or removal was the very purpose of the attacks upon them. The tactic of employing savage terror, primarily mass killings, rapes, and brutalization of civilians, to expel populations was used to the greatest extent in Bosnia and Herzegovina, where it acquired the now-infamous euphemism of "ethnic cleansing." The Bosnian Muslim civilian population thus became the principal victim of brutally aggressive military and para-military Serb operations to depopulate coveted territories in order to allow them to be repopulated by Serbs.

496. The failure to fully comprehend the extent of the Serb war aims may explain in part why the Secretariat and the Peacekeeping Mission did not react more quickly and decisively when the Serbs initiated their attack on Srebrenica. In fact, rather than attempting to mobilize the international community to support the enclave's defence we gave the Security Council the impression that the situation was under control, and many of us believed that to be the case. The day before Srebrenica fell we reported that the Serbs were not attacking when they were. We reported that the Bosniacs had fired on an UNPROFOR blocking position when it was the Serbs. We failed to mention urgent requests for air power. In some instances in which incomplete and inaccurate information was given to the Council, this can be attributed to problems with reporting from the field. In other instances, however, the reporting may have been illustrative of a more general tendency to assume that the parties were equally responsible for the transgressions that occurred. It is not clear in any event, that the provision of more fully accurate information to the Council — many of whose Members had independent sources of information on the ongoing events — would have led to appreciably different results.

497. In the end, these Bosnian Serb war aims were ultimately repulsed on the battlefield, and not at the negotiating table. Yet, the Secretariat had convinced itself early on that the broader use of force by the international community was beyond our mandate and anyway undesirable. A report of the Secretary-General to the Security Council spoke against a "culture of death," arguing that peace should be pursued only through non-military methods. And when, in June 1995, the international community provided UNPROFOR with a heavily armed Rapid Reaction Force, we argued against using it robustly to implement our mandate. When decisive action was finally taken by UNPROFOR in August and September 1995, it helped to bring the war to a conclusion.

G. Lessons for the future

498. The fall of Srebrenica is replete with lessons for this Organization and its Member States — lessons that must be learned if we are to expect the peoples of the world to place their faith in the United Nations. There are occasions when Member States cannot achieve consensus on a particular response to active military conflicts, or do not have the will to pursue what many might consider to be an

appropriate course of action. The first of the general lessons is that when peacekeeping operations are used as a substitute for such political consensus they will likely fail. There is a role for peace-keeping — a proud role in a world still riven by conflict — and there is even a role for protected zones and safe havens in certain situations. But peacekeeping and war fighting are distinct activities which should not be mixed. Peacekeepers must never again be deployed into an environment in which there is no ceasefire or peace agreement. Peacekeepers must never again be told that they must use their peacekeeping tools — lightly armed soldiers in scattered positions — to impose the ill-defined wishes of the international community on one or another of the belligerents by military means. If the necessary resources are not provided — and the necessary political, military, and moral judgments are not made — the job simply cannot be done.

499. Protected zones and safe areas can have a role in protecting civilians in armed conflict. But it is clear that they either must be demilitarized and established by the agreement of the belligerents, as with the "protected zones" and "safe havens" recognized by international humanitarian law, or they must be truly "safe areas," fully defended by a credible military deterrent. The two concepts are absolutely distinct and must not be confused. It is tempting for critics to blame the UNPROFOR units in Srebrenica for its fall, or to blame the United Nations hierarchy above those units. Certainly, errors of judgment were made — errors rooted in a philosophy of impartiality and non-violence wholly unsuited to the conflict in Bosnia — but this must not divert us from the more fundamental mistakes. The safe areas were established by the Security Council without the consent of the parties and without providing any credible military deterrent. They were neither protected areas nor "safe havens" in the sense of international humanitarian law, nor safe areas in any militarily meaningful sense. Several representatives on the Council, as well as the Secretariat, noted this problem at the time, warning that, in failing to provide a credible military deterrent, the safe area policy would be gravely damaging to the Council's reputation and, indeed, to the United Nations as a whole.

500. The approach by the United Nations Secretariat, the Security Council, the Contact Group and other involved Governments to the war in Bosnia and Herzegovina had certain consequences at both the political and the military level. At the political level, it

entailed continuing negotiations with the architects of the Serb policies, principally, Mr. Milošević[16] and Dr. Karadžić.[17] At the military level, it resulted in a process of negotiation with and reliance upon General Mladić,[18] whose implacable commitment to clear Eastern Bosnia — and Sarajevo if possible — of Bosniacs was plainly obvious and led inexorably to Srebrenica. At various points during the war, these negotiations amounted to appeasement.

501. The international community as a whole must accept its share of responsibility for allowing this tragic course of events by its prolonged refusal to use force in the early stages of the war. This responsibility is shared by the Security Council, the Contact Group, and other Governments which contributed to the delay in the use of force, as well as by the United Nations Secretariat and the Mission in the field. But clearly the primary and most direct responsibility lies with the architects and implementers of the attempted genocide in Bosnia. Radovan Karadžić and Ratko Mladić, along with their major collaborators, have been indicted by the International Criminal Tribunal for the Former Yugoslavia. To this day, they remain free men. They must be made to answer for the barbaric crimes with which they have been charged.

502. The cardinal lesson of Srebrenica is that a deliberate and systematic attempt to terrorize, expel, or murder an entire people must be met decisively with all necessary means, and with the political will to carry the policy through to its logical conclusion. In the Balkans, in this decade, this lesson has had to be learned not once, but twice. In both instances, in Bosnia and in Kosovo, the international community tried to reach a negotiated settlement with an unscrupulous and murderous regime. In both instances it required the use of force to bring a halt to the planned and systematic killing and expulsion of civilians.

---

[16] **Milošević**: Slobodan Milošević, the Serbian president, largely responsible for efforts to build a "greater Serbia" at the expense of the other members of the former Yugoslavia. He died while on trial for war crimes at the International Criminal Tribunal in The Hague in 2006.

[17] **Karadžić**: Radovan Karadžić, a psychiatrist and the leader of the Bosnian Serbs (Serbs outside of Milošević's government who wanted their land incorporated into greater Serbia). He was arrested in 2008 and is currently awaiting trial in The Hague.

[18] **Mladić**: General Ratko Mladić, chief of staff (highest-ranking officer) in Karadžić's government, the general most responsible for the military actions taken against the Bosnians. He is still at large.

503. The United Nations experience in Bosnia was one of the most difficult and painful in our history. It is with the deepest regret and
remorse that we have reviewed our own actions and decisions in the
face of the assault on Srebrenica. Through error, misjudgement,
and an inability to recognize the scope of the evil confronting us, we
failed to do our part to help save the people of Srebrenica from the
Serb campaign of mass murder. No one regrets more than we the
opportunities for achieving peace and justice that were missed. No
one laments more than we the failure of the international community to take decisive action to halt the suffering and end a war
that had produced so many victims. Srebrenica crystallized a truth
understood only too late by the United Nations and the world at
large: that Bosnia was as much a moral cause as a military conflict.
The tragedy of Srebrenica will haunt our history forever.

504. In the end, the only meaningful and lasting amends we can make to
the citizens of Bosnia and Herzegovina who put their faith in the
international community is to do our utmost not to allow such horrors to recur. When the international community makes a solemn
promise to safeguard and protect innocent civilians from massacre,
then it must be willing to back its promise with the necessary means.
Otherwise, it is surely better not to raise hopes and expectations in
the first place, and not to impede whatever capability they may be
able to muster in their own defense.

505. To ensure that we have fully learned the lessons of the tragic history
detailed in this report, I wish to encourage Member States to engage in a process of reflection and analysis, focused on the key challenges the narrative uncovers. The aim of this process would be to
clarify and to improve the capacity of the United Nations to respond
to various forms of conflict. I have in mind addressing such issues as
the gulf between mandate and means; the inadequacy of symbolic
deterrence in the face of a systematic campaign of violence; the per-
vasive ambivalence within the United Nations regarding the role of
force in the pursuit of peace; an institutional ideology of impartiality even when confronted with attempted genocide; and a range of
doctrinal and institutional issues that go to the heart of the United
Nations' ability to keep the peace and help protect civilian populations from armed conflict. The Secretariat is ready to join in such a
process.

506. The body of this report sets out in meticulous, systematic, exhaus-
tive, and ultimately harrowing detail the descent of Srebrenica into

a horror without parallel in the history of Europe since the Second World War. I urge all concerned to study this report carefully, and to let the facts speak for themselves. The men who have been charged with this crime against humanity reminded the world, and, in particular, the United Nations, that evil exists in the world. They taught us also that the United Nations' global commitment to ending conflict does not preclude moral judgments, but makes them necessary. It is in this spirit that I submit my report of the fall of Srebrenica to the General Assembly, and to the world.

READING AND DISCUSSION QUESTIONS

1. Based on this document, what were the negative consequences of the breakup of communist Yugoslavia for its citizens?

2. In what ways did the Serbian goals conflict with the ideology that motivated the United Nations?

3. What problems prevented the United Nations forces from responding effectively to Serbian attacks? Could these problems have been resolved without altering the nature of the United Nations?

4. For what does Annan accept responsibility on behalf of the United Nations?

DOCUMENT 31-4

AMARTYA SEN

A World Not Neatly Divided

November 23, 2001

The idea that the fall of the Soviet Union made the world a safer place died its final death on September 11, 2001. In the wake of the al-Qaeda terrorist attack on the Pentagon and World Trade Center towers, leaders and ordinary individuals alike cast about for an explanation of the horror they had witnessed. One argument hinged around the fact that all of the plane

The New York Times, November 23, 2001.

hijackers were Muslim, and many began to wonder if some fundamental trait of Islam could be blamed. Amayarta Sen, an Indian academic then at Cambridge University, argued six weeks after the attacks that such categorizations were inherently flawed in dealing with a diverse world.

When people talk about clashing civilizations, as so many politicians and academics do now, they can sometimes miss the central issue. The inadequacy of this thesis begins well before we get to the question of whether civilizations must clash. The basic weakness of the theory lies in its program of categorizing people of the world according to a unique, allegedly commanding system of classification. This is problematic because civilizational categories are crude and inconsistent and also because there are other ways of seeing people (linked to politics, language, literature, class, occupation or other affiliations).

The befuddling influence of a singular classification also traps those who dispute the thesis of a clash: To talk about "the Islamic world" or "the Western world" is already to adopt an impoverished vision of humanity as unalterably divided. In fact, civilizations are hard to partition in this way, given the diversities within each society as well as the linkages among different countries and cultures. For example, describing India as a "Hindu civilization" misses the fact that India has more Muslims than any other country except Indonesia and possibly Pakistan. It is futile to try to understand Indian art, literature, music, food or politics without seeing the extensive interactions across barriers of religious communities. These include Hindus and Muslims, Buddhists, Jains,[19] Sikhs,[20] Parsees,[21] Christians (who have been in India since at least the fourth century, well before England's conversion to Christianity [sixth century C.E.]), Jews (present since the fall of Jerusalem [70 C.E.]), and even atheists and agnostics. Sanskrit has a larger atheistic literature than exists in any other classical language. Speaking of India as a Hindu civilization may be comforting to the Hindu fundamentalist, but it is an odd reading of India.

---

[19] **Jains:** Followers of one of the oldest religions in India, which encompasses several ancient religions, who believe in the potential of each individual soul. Jains have many beliefs similar to Hindus.

[20] **Sikhs:** Followers of another Indian religion, founded in the fifteenth century but only becoming prominent in the seventeenth. Sikhs were once persecuted by both Hindus and Muslims.

[21] **Parsees:** Members of a branch of Zoroastrianism, the religion of the ancient Persians, believed to have been in India for at least a thousand years.

A similar coarseness can be seen in the other categories invoked, like "the Islamic world." Consider Akbar and Aurangzeb, two Muslim emperors of the Mogul[22] dynasty in India. Aurangzeb tried hard to convert Hindus into Muslims and instituted various policies in that direction, of which taxing the non-Muslims was only one example. In contrast, Akbar reveled in his multiethnic court and pluralist laws, and issued official proclamations insisting that no one "should be interfered with on account of religion" and that "anyone is to be allowed to go over to a religion that pleases him."

If a homogeneous view of Islam were to be taken, then only one of these emperors could count as a true Muslim. The Islamic fundamentalist would have no time for Akbar; Prime Minister Tony Blair, given his insistence that tolerance is a defining characteristic of Islam, would have to consider excommunicating Aurangzeb. I expect both Akbar and Aurangzeb would protest, and so would I. A similar crudity is present in the characterization of what is called "Western civilization." Tolerance and individual freedom have certainly been present in European history. But there is no dearth of diversity here, either. When Akbar was making his pronouncements on religious tolerance in Agra [in northern India, near Nepal], in the 1590's, the Inquisitions were still going on; in 1600, Giordano Bruno[23] was burned at the stake, for heresy, in Campo dei Fiori in Rome.

Dividing the world into discrete civilizations is not just crude. It propels us into the absurd belief that this partitioning is natural and necessary and must overwhelm all other ways of identifying people. That imperious view goes not only against the sentiment that "we human beings are all much the same," but also against the more plausible understanding that we are diversely different. For example, Bangladesh's split from Pakistan was not connected with religion, but with language and politics.

Each of us has many features in our self-conception. Our religion, important as it may be, cannot be an all-engulfing identity. Even a shared poverty can be a source of solidarity across the borders. The kind of division highlighted by, say, the so-called "antiglobalization" protesters — whose movement is, incidentally, one of the most globalized in the world — tries to unite the underdogs of the world economy and goes firmly against religious, national or "civilizational" lines of division.

---

[22] **Mogul:** The Moguls were descendants of the Mongols in central India who converted to Islam. Akbar ruled from 1556 to 1605, and Aurangzeb from 1658 to 1707.

[23] **Girodano Bruno:** An Italian who argued that the Earth went around the sun, though that was not precisely why he was burned in a Roman plaza.

The main hope of harmony lies not in any imagined uniformity, but in the plurality of our identities, which cut across each other and work against sharp divisions into impenetrable civilizational camps. Political leaders who think and act in terms of sectioning off humanity into various "worlds" stand to make the world more flammable — even when their intentions are very different. They also end up, in the case of civilizations defined by religion, lending authority to religious leaders seen as spokesmen for their "worlds." In the process, other voices are muffled and other concerns silenced. The robbing of our plural identities not only reduces us; it impoverishes the world.

READING AND DISCUSSION QUESTIONS

1. According to Sen, when are generalizations about the world possible? In what ways are they necessary in talking about a complex world?

2. Why might both the extremists behind the September attacks and the leaders of the governments who oppose them find this article disturbing?

3. Sen cites the diversity of Mogul culture approximately four hundred years ago as an example. Does Sen's analogy underestimate the complexity of the Western societies to which he compares the Moguls, and why or why not?

COMPARATIVE QUESTIONS

1. Where do the leaders of Solidarity and Mikhail Gorbachev seem to agree on the priorities of society? Where do they disagree?

2. Based on Amartya Sen's article and Solidarity's workers' rights demands, what overgeneralizations regarding solidarity might Gorbachev be making in his speech?

3. What are the important differences between the Serbian point of view Annan references in the UN report and Amartya Sen's vision of the world?